"Discipleship is a daunting task. In this book, Bill Wichterman takes the biblical dynamics of following Christ and explains not just what the Bible teaches but how to apply it. It's a moving personal testament and a profound theological reflection whose exhortations, if practiced, quite literally transform one's life."

Rob Schwarzwalder
Sr. VP, Family Research Council

"Originally written as a letter to his children in the aftermath of the attacks of September 11 on how to live joyfully and humbly, Bill Wichterman's *Dying to Live*, is a wise, reasoned, winsome, and passionate case for the spiritual disciplines, worship, and an orthodox understanding of reality as essential to living well. A seasoned veteran of Capitol Hill and the White House, Bill uses his own life struggles and joys as fascinating illustrations of the ways in which one man sought to live as a 'mere' Christian in the midst of conflict and challenge - and what he learned along the way. A wise book from a winsome pilgrim."

Cherie Harder
President, The Trinity Forum

"Bill Wichterman is gifted with a fluid pen. He has written an elegant, lithe, and powerful book. In the contest of ideas that power the contemporary world, Bill's contribution sets out a worldview that confirms any life worth living begins in the recognition that there exists an enduring moral order, and that there is a certain greatness in humility. Christ is the Center of this book because He is the Lord of Bill's life."

Timothy Goeglein
VP, External Relations, Focus on the Family

"In this heartfelt Christian manifesto, Bill Wichterman masterfully elucidates the scriptural paradox of dying to live. His work is both personal and practical, but best of all, it effectively inspires Christians to embrace an often neglected yet life-giving truth. This is a must-read for earnest believers interested in unlocking the mysteries of authentic biblical living."

Diane Palmer, Historian

"In a culture that proclaims human existence to be accidental and produces empty souls with lives revolving around pleasure seeking and instant gratification, this book is significant. It is not a mere call to self-denial proposed to produce feelings of gratification, but a triumphant announcement of fullness found in God. I've been a friend of Bill Wichterman's for more than three decades, and his character and integrity are second to none. His commitment to present a logical and accurate representation of fellowship with God is done only for the glory of God and the fullness of life of the reader; there is no other agenda. Read, meditate and allow God to speak on how a faithful, full life should be lived."

Joel Steindel, Entrepreneur

Dying to Live

Finding Joy
In Giving Yourself
to God

William B. Wichterman

Oakton, Virginia
www.oaktonfoundation.com

For Dana,
My Wife, My Best Friend and My Soulmate

And For Jenna, Justin, and Krista,
My Precious Children Whom I Love and Adore

CONTENTS

*"He is no fool who gives what he cannot keep
to gain that which he cannot lose."*

Jim Elliot, Martyr

INTRODUCTION

This book began as my last will and testament borne out of a tragedy that struck close to home.

On the morning of September 11, 2001, Ziad Jarrah and three of his fellow hijackers boarded United Airlines Flight 93 in Newark and began what was supposed to be their cross-country journey to San Francisco. Fifteen more hijackers were boarding three different planes, all with the same mission: to strike terror into the hearts of the American people in the name of Allah.

Minutes after takeoff, the first of the four hijacked planes was flown into one of the World Trade Center towers. I learned about the first plane while working in a building adjacent to the U.S. Capitol Building. A friend told me to turn on CNN, because a small plane had flown into one of the Twin Towers. We talked about it for less than a minute, and both concluded that it was an accident and we returned to our conversation. Fifteen minutes later, the second plane hit the other tower. As soon as I found out, I instantly knew it was a terrorist attack, and I knew the world had changed forever. I remained glued to the television.

Soon, I was on the phone with my boss, Congressman Joe Pitts, who was driving in to work. He told me he saw a huge plume of black smoke coming from the Pentagon. Within minutes we learned that a third hijacked plane was to blame, and there were reports that there might be additional hijacked planes still in the air. In fact, the fourth plane was headed towards Washington. Ziad Jarrah was at the helm, and intelligence indicates he was planning to fly into the U.S. Capitol or the White House. The former was much more likely given the difficulty of hitting the White House (a relatively small target from the air).

I was angry. I felt all of the "fight" instinct and none of the "flight." I wanted to lash out at the perpetrators. My staff was worried and wanted to leave the building, as other buildings in Washington were being evacuated. They all left, but I stayed at my desk. I refused to run away from the terrorists—something I now recognize as foolish. A Capitol police officer soon knocked on my door and told me that I was required to leave the building. Reluctantly and angrily, I left and made my way to the Metro Station to escape the city.

The passengers on Ziad's plane had learned about the fate of the other hijacked planes. They were determined to prevent their plane from hitting its intended target. Todd Beamer, who led the passengers, first recited the 23rd Psalm with the cell phone operator before asking his fellow passengers if they were ready, and then saying, "Okay, let's roll." Beamer then rushed the hijackers. In the ensuing battle for control of the plane, Ziad swerved left and right, up and down, trying to knock the passengers off their feet. When it was clear that the passenger revolt was succeeding and Ziad would not reach his target, he said "Allahu Akbar," meaning "God is great," and pointed the nose of the plane towards the ground. In less than a minute, the plane hit the ground at 563 miles per hour, killing all 44 people on board and creating a crater measuring 10 feet by 50 feet.

In the following days and years, I assumed that I would die in a terrorist attack on the U.S. Capitol. Today, that sounds melodramatic, but at the time it seemed anything but. In 2004, Senator Frist, for whom I was policy advisor, told me that intelligence reports indicated there would be a terrorist attack on the Capitol Building in the near future. My office was a few paces away from the Capitol Rotunda where Ziad likely had been heading three years before. I often imagined my death, wondering whether I would have any warning or see a bright light before the explosion blew me to bits. My wife and I even briefly considered whether we should leave politics and move out of the city so my children would not grow up fatherless. In the end, we both concluded that God had called me to work for justice on the national political scene and our lives were in his hands. So we stayed.

One thing I did, however, was write a long letter to my then young children, so they would know what their dad had believed and tried to live out. My letter eventually became this book. It remains principally for my children, but I hope it may be helpful to others as well.

A superficial reading of this book might suggest it is just about self-denial and humility and servanthood. Yet the Bible's hard teachings about giving up our lives are not ends in themselves but means to the end. Jesus said, "I have come that they may have life, and have it to the full" (John 10:10). That is what I want for myself, and it is, I hope, what you want for your life. I wish there were some shortcut to experiencing a full life, but there is not. Ultimately, the hard way leads to the green pastures; the easy path leads to death.

Years ago, my sister, a food photographer, flew into Washington, DC, for a photo shoot with one of her clients. I met her at the airport, helping lug heavy bags of equipment to the car rental pick-up, only to be told that we needed to take a shuttle to a different terminal. After the frustration of carrying so many bags to the next counter, we were told by a different agent that, in fact, we needed to return to the first place.

As we got back on the shuttle to retrace our journey, she looked at me in exasperation and said, "Don't they know it's all about me?" The absurdity of that one sentence made us laugh, and the tension of the day evaporated.

That facetious remark also made me think about how often I live as if life were all about me. I repeat that sentence to myself to mock my self-centered ways. How ridiculous to act as if I am the center of the universe!

Yet most of us live like that at least sometimes. We expect to have our careless words overlooked or contextualized, yet we resent others' careless words spoken to us, feeling deeply wronged. We expect to be treated kindly and gently when we come home frazzled from a long day at work, but quickly lose patience with others in the same boat. We want to be affirmed and appreciated, but we neglect to do that for others. We act like infants demanding to be fed, nurtured, and coddled.

Rick Warren's *The Purpose-Driven Life* captures the truth that we are loath to admit:

> It's not about you. The purpose of your life is far greater than your own personal fulfillment, your peace of mind,

> or even your happiness. It's far greater than your family,
> your career, or even your wildest dreams and ambitions.
> If you want to know why you were placed on this
> planet, you must begin with God. You were born by his
> purpose and for his purpose (17).

Exactly. We were made by God and for God. This truth
shocks our sensibilities in our self-exalting, comfort-seeking
society. We are bombarded with advertising telling us to "spoil
yourself," "obey your thirst," "make your own road," "have it
your way," "because you're worth it." Madison Avenue pushes
the messages we want to be true, justifying our own self-centeredness.

Yet, to say that "it's not about you" is not the same as
saying "you don't matter." In fact, you are of infinite worth
precisely because it is not principally about you. As created
beings, we are made to love, serve, and adore the Great I AM.
We derive our value from God. We have intrinsic worth, from
the lowliest street sweeper to the superstar athlete, precisely
because we are made in God's image. Without God, we would
be just dust in the wind.

Having eternal value is also completely at odds with the lie
that we should spoil ourselves because we only live once. "Let
us eat and drink, for tomorrow we die" propagates the fiction
that, careening toward the inevitable, facing down our own
death, we should indulge our every wish in the pursuit of personal happiness. I have heard divorcees explain to their grieving children, "I know you miss our family being together, but
you want me to be happy, don't you?" And we have all heard
(and perhaps said ourselves), "if it's not fun, why do it?" These
lies ruin many lives.

God does want us to be happy, but in that deep and satisfying way better characterized as joy. And when the thorns of
this fallen world are finally cleared away, joy will give way to
enduring happiness.

The impulse to center the universe around ourselves
causes us to struggle to get to the top of the ant heap. Like un-
ruly children vying to be first in line for a carnival, we primp
and preen to be better than our peers, to be the most beautiful

or the smartest or the most popular or the funniest. We care desperately what others think about us and relatively little about what God thinks of us.

Many people ignore the grim reality that we will die and be forgotten by our peers and those who come after us. Within just a few decades, we will be a distant memory to our progeny, and within 100 years, few of us will be remembered by anyone. In the end, our vain pursuits to look younger and healthier will fail, and the people about whose opinions we care so much will also die. Stroll through a cemetery to remember what happens to everyone.

Though our death is a certainty, we cloak this fact behind words designed to make death seem like the exception instead of the rule: asking whether a sick friend is going to die—as if we are not all terminal. The only question is *when* we will die. Operationally, we act immortal, minimally planning for the inevitable, shoving it out of our minds.

Even in this life, our big achievements fade fast. U.S. Senator Dick Stone represented Florida from 1974 to 1980. He later became ambassador-at-large to Central America and ambassador to Denmark. But less than two decades after his prominent service, his name has been virtually erased from public memory. I met him a few years ago and inwardly marveled that I had never even heard of him. That will be the same story for most of us. Our greatest temporal victories will vanish into the mist of history, almost totally forgotten by those we have sought to impress.

But we will never be forgotten by God.

One day, perhaps tomorrow, we will stand before the audience of One, our Creator and our Judge, being called to account for how we spent our time on Earth. It is around this moment that I seek to orient my life. I try to think about my death every day and to live accordingly. Of course, I often forget and live out of fear of others or fear of failure or just plain vanity. But I know that my chief end should be to "glorify God, and enjoy him forever" (Westminster Shorter Catechism).

Glorifying God in all things requires that we master self-denial. Contrary to conventional wisdom, real power lies in the ability to say no to oneself and say yes to God. Counter-intui-

tively, in denying ourselves we learn to live life to the full. It is
the hard work of self-mastery that leads to joy. The more we
deny ourselves, the more we have. The more we humble ourselves, the more we are exalted. The last shall be first. The losers will be the winners. The meek will inherit the earth. The
power in saying "no" to ourselves frees us to say "yes" to God
and find the life for which we were made.

The reason joy begins in self-denial is because we must be
freed from the sin in which we were born and which taints
every part of us and others. The world is not how it is supposed
to be. It is twisted, corrupted, and wrong.

This is not to say that nothing is good in the world. To the
contrary, much good remains since Adam and Eve's fateful
decision to rebel. We see God's beauty in a sunset, his genius
in fantastical deep-sea creatures, his love in a mother, his joy in
our friends. But these whispers of transcendence are set in the
context of the cruelty of an abusive parent, the inhumanity of
war, the insanity of the asylum, the destruction of a tornado,
the tragedy of melanoma. The evil of our world runs right
through our hearts, though we are often too blind to see our
own sin and can only recognize it in others.

Learning to say no begins with laying down our lives at
the cross and accepting God's forgiveness. In plunging ourselves into God's grace in the person of the God-Man Jesus, we
simultaneously say no to ourselves and yes to God. In this act,
God's mercy secures us as his own, imputing Christ's righteousness to us. We are sealed as God's own, his righteousness
covers our unrighteousness, and we are set free to serve our
Savior out of gratitude, rather than to try to earn our salvation
out of fear or pride.

This first act of saying no to ourselves is followed by
countless more acts of self-denial as we seek to be sanctified—
made more like God. Although followers of Christ have been
ransomed by God, we are still sinful and remain in a sinful
world. Denying our natural impulses to sin requires enormous
effort and moment-by-moment practice. It takes a lifetime—
and the grace of God—to seek to overcome the sin into which
we are born. We are called to strive for perfection, and it is

hard duty, indeed. Yet it is in the unceasing and wearying effort to reject rebellion that we find joy.

Unfortunately, we will never arrive at perfection this side of death. Our best efforts always fall short, which is why grace carries us from first to last. There is no room for boasting about our efforts, because they will never suffice. The power of salvation is not in our self-denial, but in the power of the cross. We do not preach ourselves, but Christ crucified.

Although this book focuses on our efforts to be faithful followers of Christ, our hope is fully in God's grace. It is not a cheap grace, and it will cost us everything to accept it, but neither can we earn it. When we stand before God, our sole response must be that we have thrown ourselves on the mercy of our Advocate, Jesus Christ the Righteous. Our most righteous acts are still as filthy rags before the Holy God. This does not mean we cannot please him. In fact, God is easily pleased, but he is impossible to satisfy.

To modern ears, lauding the power of self-negation sounds so negative. The world tells us to taste, touch, feel, do, and just be who we are. Of course, God wants us to do all those things, but he knows we will enjoy the sensual life most within boundaries. The Evil One lies that we will be happiest without limits. Take sex, a very good gift of God, intended for our pleasure and for bearing children. Outside of marriage, sex sows pain and destruction in our lives.

God does not call us to deny ourselves because he is grouchy and mean but because he loves us and wants us to be happy—his kind of happiness, which is deep and true and right. Like a key to a locked door leading to a wonderful room, self-denial is the means of restoring a measure of the life he originally intended for us before sin and death entered the world. We say no to ourselves to say yes to life. In heaven, sin will not be present and self-denial will no longer be necessary, because we will be free of selfishness. We will only want to do good, and the enervating resistance to sin will be no more.

Living like it is not about you, but all about God, turns the natural order of the world on its head. It unlocks the deep mysteries of the universe. The way up is the way down. The way to live is first to die. To become wise we must become fools. These counter-intuitive mysteries make sense when we understand who God is, how we were originally made, how we rebelled, how we can be redeemed, and God's plan for a new heaven and a new earth. The more we walk in reality, the more the "foolishness" of the cross—of life triumphing over death— shames the "wisdom" of the world.

God's ways are more invigorating than our ways. He leads us to live a more daring life. He is not safe, and he will challenge us to walk through minefields with our eyes closed. He wants us to walk by faith, not by sight. He wants to lead us, and he wants us to learn to hear his voice and to trust him.

Thankfully, he can see around corners, making all things work together for good for those who follow in faith. This is not to say we will never be blown up by one of the mines, figuratively or literally. We will all die, and before that we may lose our reputations, our homes, our families, our health, our comfort.

But like the apostles, ten of whom were martyred, God will also use our triumphs and our defeats to his glory and for our eternal good. In the words of the twentieth-century martyr Jim Elliot, "he is no fool who gives what he cannot keep to gain that which he cannot lose" (174).

God's ways are also more peaceful than ours. We can know peace because of our trust in who he is and what he intends for us. He loves us more deeply than anyone else, knows us better, and has a "good, pleasing, and perfect will" for all who follow (Rom. 12:2). As followers, the weight of the world is not on our shoulders, but on his. Our calling is to faithfulness, not success. This realization makes our challenges more manageable and less stressful. It is our responsibility to hear his voice and do his bidding. The results belong to him. Ours is the trying.

By participating in the work of the Most High God, we become partners with him in his exciting plans. When we are busy conquering the world for ourselves, we inevitably become dissatisfied. Our most ambitious plans cannot match the grandeur of his plans. Multi-millionaires grow discontent with their wealth, rock stars cannot drink enough fame, kings long for more lands to vanquish. In the end, what the world has to offer just is not enough.

When I worked for President George W. Bush in the White House, I had a full access pass enabling me to go anywhere in the West Wing—which is really the power center of the White House. In the beginning of my service, I experienced the thrill of walking through those storied passageways, remembering all of the historical figures who had trod there, from James Madison and Thomas Jefferson to Abraham Lincoln and Franklin Deleanor Roosevelt. Wars began and ended in those hallowed rooms. The place was brimming with the thrill of history.

But in time, the thrill waned for me. I well remember when the initial magic of the Rose Garden wore off. I was walking through the Garden just outside the Oval Office, typing on my mobile phone as I walked. I glanced up at the Rose Garden and then returned to my phone. Then it struck me: the Rose Garden had become just a garden.

We were made for so much more than worldly designs. Our grandest schemes are pale shadows of his far more thrilling plans. In learning to serve, we grow into the greatness he has in store for us. Only storming the Gates of Hell is an adventure worthy of the eternity he has sown in our hearts. In the words of the song, "Dare You to Move" by Switchfoot, God dares us "to move like today never happened before." [1]

God's work is not confined to just "winning souls." It includes that, but it is far more. He cares about every part of his world. He wants to straighten out twisted political systems, heal the sick, lift up the good, the true, and the beautiful, triumph over Evil, feed the hungry, empower the powerless, and set the captive free. His Great Commission complements his creation mandate to steward the Earth, building societies that reflect God's Kingdom.

Pietistic theologies that reduce God's concerns to just the spiritual realm distort the all-encompassing message of the Bible to bring everything under the Lordship of Christ. No square inch of the world is beyond God's concern. He cares

---

[1] Lead singer Jon Foreman's lyrics are profound and moving. I strongly recommend Switchfoot's body of work.

deeply about architecture, theater, philosophy, and math. Once we learn the comprehensive nature of the Kingdom, every part of our lives becomes God's workshop. Worship becomes singing *and* sewing. Mission becomes evangelism *and* energy exploration -- and everything else.

As all of life comes under the lordship of Christ, invigorating every moment, our longing for heaven grows stronger, not weaker. On the one hand, we find a contentment and joy in doing God's work in God's way. On the other hand, a deep and abiding satisfaction eludes us as we fight against the thorns of sin that infest our work. We are sinners to the core. Even at our best we are flawed and broken and not what we are supposed to be. We groan, along with all of creation, under the weight of sin and death. We ache to escape the shadowlands and to live full and unfettered lives. We long to see God face-to-face, and not just through a glass darkly. We want to feel the transcendent joy of whole and healthy relationships, of well and completely fit bodies, of life as it was made to be before humanity's rebellion. We do not want to live in the valley of the shadow of death, but in complete freedom and immortality. We long for our true home, a place we have never seen but yearn for nonetheless.

Ever since my childhood I have loved New England lakes. Their beauty captivates me. I am enchanted looking at the sun dance on the crystal clear water surrounded by stands of pine trees under a deep blue sky. On one vacation to Connecticut, I swam to the middle of a lake on a perfect summer day and floated on my back looking up at the sky. Even as I exulted in one of the things I most enjoy, I felt its deficiency. It just was not enough. Gaining what I dreamed about reminded me that the lake is not what I really want in my deepest part. What I truly want and need is God. Only he can satisfy my deepest longings. All of my desires point me back to the Creator who wants me to be completely his. Our full and final consolation lies in heaven.

The greatest joys in this world can only give us a glimpse of what we really want. Our fulfillment comes from walking with God imperfectly now, but perfectly in the future. Our longing to be with him keeps us going. It gives us strength to fight demons within and demons without. It draws us on when despair threatens to undo us. We yearn to receive a rich welcome into the Kingdom of Light, so we press on. Like a marathon runner tempted to quit, we keep our eyes fixed on the prize, "the author and perfecter of our faith" (Heb. 12:2). We do not want to be among those who are ashamed upon seeing him and shrink back, but among those whose hearts leap at the thought of being in his presence. We stumble again and again, but we keep going because of him who calls us. We run alongside others so we do not lose heart, urging one another on, remembering the saints who have gone before us who endured every conceivable hardship yet claimed the prize in the end.

It is not about you or me, but all about him.

Seek to save your life in self-gratification and you will lose yourself. But give yourself away in humble service, and you will find life, and much more, you will find him who made you and for whom you were made.

The book is divided into four sections. The first two chapters are about dying to self. Chapters 3 and 4 are about living in the shadow of our certain death. Chapters 5 and 6 are about living for God, and chapters 7 and 8 are about the importance of relationships.

I hope you will find nothing in these pages that you cannot find in other books. If you do, it is either because I have devised a novel error or you have not yet read enough. I do not pretend to be an original thinker. My wisdom, to the extent I have any, is all derived from the Bible and others who have gone before me. I have simply repackaged this ancient wisdom in my own unique way. If you find it helpful, I am glad. If not, please read better books.

William B. Wichterman
Oakton, Virginia
May 2014

Dead to Self and Alive in Christ

"For whoever wants to save their life will lose it,
but whoever loses their life for me will find it."
Jesus

As you read this chapter about dying to self, keep in mind that I am writing about the *path* to a joyful, full, and exciting life. And death to self is the only way to get to the life we really want.

Before becoming a Christian, T. S. Eliot wrote poems of despair. "The Hollow Men" (1925) outlined the contours of forlornness and desolation:

> We are the hollow men
> We are the stuffed men
> Leaning together
> Headpiece filled with straw. Alas!
> Our dried voices, when
> We whisper together
> Are quiet and meaningless
> As wind in dry grass
> Or rats' feet over broken glass
> In our dry cellar

Just two years later, Eliot became a follower of Christ, leaving behind his poems of despair and hopelessness for the eternal hope in Christ. That same year, he wrote a poem that portrayed the meaning he found in death. In "The Journey of the Magi" (1927)—a poem I love so much that I have memorized it—one of the wise men writes of the conflicting feelings he has about having found the Christ child:

> All this was a long time ago, I remember,
> And I would do it again, but set down

This set down
This: were we led all that way for
Birth or Death? There was a Birth, certainly,
We had evidence and no doubt. I have seen birth and
death,
But had thought they were different; this Birth was
Hard and bitter agony for us, like Death, our death.
We returned to our places, these Kingdoms,
But no longer at ease here, in the old dispensation,
With an alien people clutching their gods.
I should be glad of another death.

Eliot captured the implications of becoming a follower of Christ: the joy of the Incarnation has deadly implications for our dreams and aspirations. To live, you must first die. The cross comes before the resurrection. You cannot skip the first to get to the second.

The apostle Paul captured the same in Gal. 2:20: "I have been crucified with Christ and I no longer live, but Christ lives in me. The life I live in the body, I live by faith in the Son of God, who loved me and gave himself for me." The paradox at the heart of the Gospel is that we must die in order to live. Christ's death does not have its saving effect without our embracing death to self. To receive the forgiveness that is available to us by Jesus' sacrifice, we must give up ownership of ourselves, turning over our lives to God as "living sacrifices" (Rom. 12:1). This is not optional. Without repentance, there can be no forgiveness.

This hard truth of the gospel contradicts the easy Christianity peddled by many American churches. They gloss over the hard implications of the Gospel in the hopes of bringing more people into the Kingdom (or, more cynically, to have larger congregations). They bifurcate salvation from sanctification, saying that salvation comes to those who believe in Jesus and his work on the cross—a desire to turn from sin will come naturally later on, but it is not necessary for salvation. So they talk about the free gift of salvation without any mention of the total surrender that is part and parcel of accepting the gift. These Christian leaders rightly believe that the Gospel, which literally means "good news" in Greek, may not sound like such good news at first hearing. It actually sounds like a death sentence, which it is, but only en route to the incomparably excellent news of our eternal salvation.

When I was a Youth for Christ (YFC) leader, a high school student asked me whether he had to stop taking illicit drugs to be saved. He told me that he loved his sinful habit and, though he wanted to be saved, he was not willing to "pray the sinner's prayer" if it meant he had to give up his habit. I told him that he had to have the will to give it up, even if he failed along the way. But he could not *intend* to continue taking drugs and have any confidence that he would be saved, because that would indicate he wanted to follow Christ on his own terms.[2] The Bible is clear that to be a disciple requires laying down our lives. It is not just for the "super holy" but for every Christian. Jesus said, "If anyone would come after me, he must deny himself and take up his cross daily and follow me. For whoever wants to save his life will lose it, but whoever loses his life for me will save it" (Luke 9:23-24). No wonder T.S. Eliot would write that the birth of Jesus was "hard and bitter agony for us, like Death, our death."

A fellow YFC leader contested my interpretation of the Gospel. She said that Christ accepts us as we are, and that to require that we *intend* to turn from all of our sins is to require that we *work* for our salvation. Salvation, she said, is about believing in Christ and accepting his forgiveness, and nothing more. Repentance of sin is part of the sanctification process that can come later. The first step is simply to embrace his unconditional forgiveness "just as I am," in the words of the old hymn. She said that I was *adding* to the gospel, much as some false teachers were doing in Galatia when they said Gentile men must be circumcised if they wanted to be saved.

This notion may sound persuasive at first, especially since it is often presented from church pulpits as such, but it contradicts the sweep of Scripture. It is true that Jesus said in John 3:16 that "whoever *believes* in him shall not perish but have

---

[2] He decided, at least at the time, that he was not willing to give up illicit drug use and did not pray "the sinner's prayer" with me. I did not keep in touch with him and do not know whether he is now a Christian.

eternal life." Yet he also said that following him costs everything:

> Suppose one of you wants to build a tower. Will he not
> first sit down and estimate the cost to see if he has
> enough money to complete it? For if he lays the foun-
> dation and is not able to finish it, everyone who sees it
> will ridicule him, saying, "This fellow began to build
> and was not able to finish." Or suppose a king is about
> to go to war against another king. Will he not first sit
> down and consider whether he is able with ten thousand
> men to oppose the one coming against him with twenty
> thousand? If he is not able, he will send a delegation
> while the other is still a long way off and will ask for
> terms of peace. In the same way, any of you who does
> not give up everything he has cannot be my disciple
> (Luke 14:28-33).

In the Jewish mind, there was no contradiction between
knowing and doing, precisely because knowing implied doing.
In the post-modern era, "belief" is untethered from action,
based on our faulty assumption that truth is relative. Today one
can claim to believe in the gospel without *acting* as if it were
true. Thus, we tend to read John 3:16 with twenty-first-century
eyes instead of the way Jesus' hearers would have received the
admonition to *believe*.

What does it mean "to give up everything" and to die to
ourselves? It does not necessarily mean we must physically die,
though that is a possible implication of following Christ. It
does not mean ceasing to have desires, wishes, preferences, and
dreams. Disciples are not robots. We do not cease to be ourselves, nor does our identity vanish. In Buddhism, the individual is considered illusory, and the aim is to give up all individ-
uality and merge into the cosmic "one." Not so in Christianity,
in which we become our true selves.

Dying to ourselves means giving up our claims on our
lives and instead taking on God's plans. It means becoming
"living sacrifices" whose every act is intended to please God. It
means beginning each day with a prayer that we be God's man

or woman in everything we think, say, and do. It means that our hopes, desires, and dreams take second place to God's. "But seek first his kingdom and his righteousness, and all these things will be given to you as well" (Matt. 6:33).

I find it very hard to die to myself. It goes against everything inside of me. My natural self yearns to be served, obeyed, comforted, admired, and exalted. And I know I am not alone. We are born in sin. Anyone who has children knows that they come out little barbarians who must be civilized. Our natural inclinations are twisted and self-seeking. In contrast, French philosopher Jean Jacques Rousseau said that man is born good, but is slowly twisted by society. Rousseau wrote a book, *Emile,* in which he put forward the idea that the best education allows children to be themselves without forcing them to conform to others' wishes. (Yet Rousseau never really tested his own proposition since he abandoned his own children to an orphanage.)

Self-sacrifice requires work—hard work. There is no getting around it. Christ's death was more than just *substitutionary*. It was that, to be sure. We can now have eternal life with God in heaven thanks to the ransom he paid for us. But the crucifixion was also *exemplary*, teaching us how to live:

> Your attitude should be the same as that of Christ Jesus: Who, being in very nature God, did not consider equality with God something to be used to his own advantage; rather, he made himself nothing by taking the very nature of a servant, being made in human likeness. And being found in appearance as a man, he humbled himself by becoming obedient to death—even death on a cross! (Phil. 2:5-8)

If the God of the universe would debase himself to take on flesh and blood in a nasty world—even being a King in this world would be an infinite step down for him—and further humble himself to be a common worker in a disreputable province of a poor country, how can we do otherwise but surrender our lives to him? Our call is to serve, to wash the feet of our friends and enemies, whether we are a plumber or a prime minister.

My career has put me in the company of many famous and powerful people—movie stars, rock stars, celebrity preachers, billionaires, senators, renowned authors, and a sitting President. Some are vain and pompous and self-serving. (I knew of one member of Congress who required that one of his staff meet him at the airport gate with a folder of papers—the content of which was entirely irrelevant—and then have another staff member drive him to his car just 200 feet away so everyone around him would be impressed with his importance.) Others are humble servants. For example, when I called Senator Rick Santorum to congratulate him on the night of his Iowa Caucus victory in the 2012 Presidential race, he was keenly interested in how I was doing since my mother had died just days earlier. To be honest, the pompous ones disgust me and the humble ones impress me deeply.

It is important to remember that none of us is perfect. Christians are sometimes pompous -- just look at me in my darker moments. Some of our faults that are obvious to others are hidden from us. We cannot earn our salvation. We serve God out of love and gratitude, not merely duty. We must be on our guard against legalism. In our striving to please God, it is easy to become self-righteous when we succeed or despairing when we fail. Neither response is appropriate. "For it is by grace that you are saved . . . not by works" (Eph 2:8-9).

Life is the Goal, Death is the Means

The good news is that death to self is not the end, but the means to the end. Just as physical death precedes eternal life for those who are saved, so spiritual death to ourselves precedes the life we are meant to live in the here and now.

God is not cruel. He takes no joy in our struggle to die to ourselves anymore than he takes a morbid joy in physical death. (Jesus wept when Lazarus died. Death violates God's original design.) When I struggle to give up some sinful habit or even a good and wholesome dream that is not part of his plan for me, God does not delight in my emotional pain. He knows how hard it is. But he also knows the good plans he has for us if we will just release our clenched fist of willfulness to receive the better gift that awaits us.

In C. S. Lewis' *The Voyage of the Dawn Treader,* the self-centered Eustace has been turned into a dragon due to his avarice. Aslan the Lion, representing Christ, wants to free Eustace from his enchantment. Eustace tries scratching off his dragon scales himself, but is unsuccessful. Eustace describes his experience this way:

> Then the lion said—but I do not know if it spoke— "You will have to let me undress you." I was afraid of his claws, I can tell you, but I was pretty nearly desperate now. So I just lay flat down on my back to let him do it.

> The very first tear was so deep that I thought it had gone right into my heart. And when he began pulling the skin off, it hurt worse than anything I've ever felt. The only thing that made me able to bear it was just the pleasure of feeling the stuff peel off (115-116).

The process of dying to self is miserable. The sense of loss, sadness, and grief is painful. It feels like death. Thankfully, it is only temporary.

I well remember my own conversion as a sixteen-year-old boy. I believed the gospel and wanted to follow Christ, but I did not want to give up everything, especially my girlfriend. I knew our relationship was not pleasing to God, and I knew I had to break up as my act of repentance. This specter of self-denial was made more daunting by the prospect of what other hardships might lay ahead. If God would call me to give up my girlfriend, he might demand even harder things of me (and he has). But all I knew in 1980 was that I was being called to die to myself, for then and for the rest of my life.

For weeks I wrestled with the choice that lay before me, desperately looking for a way that did not require dying to myself. I was terrified to lay down my life, but I was also terrified to die and face God in my unrepentant state. One day during a tenth grade biology class, I remember having an overwhelming fear of death and feeling the blood drain from my face when I thought about meeting God. I was sure I would go to hell if I died then. Another time, I had a vivid dream that I was with my church youth group at a picnic when Christ returned, and the other kids were taken in the rapture, but I was left behind. I also remember listening to a song by Resurrection Band with the line "and to those of our friends who know the king is your king keep shining until we meet again." I knew Jesus was not my king, and I was petrified at the thought of dying.

As a teenager, I craved for the experience of being high. Psychedelic drugs like LSD were very attractive to me, and I longed for the transcendent feeling of experiencing something outside of my body. A friend encouraged me to try cocaine as a first step, and I agreed. I had no doubt it was against God's will, but I did not care. I made plans to have my first drug experience after a high school dance, and I was very excited. At the dance, a childhood friend of mine was very drunk and needed help getting to the bathroom. When I told him what I planned to do that night, he implored me not to take drugs. He said that very night his father had kicked him out of his house because of his drug use and that drugs had messed up his life. He said he had always respected me for staying clean. His unwelcome drunken sermon pricked my conscience enough to make me reluctantly decide not to go through with my plans. As I walked back to my car in the darkness to drive home, I said aloud to God, "Why don't you just leave me alone!" I felt pursued by the "hound of heaven"[3] who had a claim on my life, though I did not want to bend my knee to this ravenous God who would devour me and my dreams. At least not until I had drunk more deeply from the forbidden cup.

Eventually, in the fall of 1980, both my fear of hell and my desire to be right with God drove me to repentance. The first step was awful, similar to what it must feel like to jump out of an airplane without a parachute. The break-up with my girlfriend was painful. She did not understand why I had to break up with her when I still liked her. But the pain of the breakup

---

[3] From a poem by the same name by Francis Thompson (1893).

and all of the loss of self that it represented was soon replaced with an inexpressible joy in knowing that I now belonged to God, I had embraced my salvation in Christ, and I would now be "married" to God. For the following two years, I was "in love" with Jesus in a fresh and special way, much like newly-weds who cannot bear to be apart.[4]

With thirty-four years of following Christ behind me, I still do not like the feeling of giving up what I love. I hear God daily calling me to put aside my natural inclinations, my hopes and dreams, and taking on his. Sometimes he calls me to take an intern to lunch, meet with a job seeker, or set aside my weekend plans to follow my wife's agenda. I have been called to prolonged fasting, to give up a job I loved for the sake of my family, to sell my most prized possession—my stereo—in college and give the money to the poor, and even give up my plans to marry (only to have marriage given back to me). Whether big or small, God is a demanding and "jealous God" (Exod. 20:4-5). His demands are incessant.

And yet the ongoing hardship of "giving up" and "giving away" does not begin to compare with the joy of embracing Christ. All of my God-imposed acts of self-denial pale in comparison with what I experience here and now in my walk with God, much less with the "glory that will be revealed in us" when we see God face to face (Rom. 8:18). My friends and family will tell you that I am not a dour ascetic weighed down by the burdens of self-denial, but a joyful and happy person overwhelmed with the temporal blessings I have received. One friend even labels me "annoyingly happy." I am content with my life—not with every aspect of my life, of course, but with the totality of my life. In fact, the joy I know is a byproduct of death to self.

Take fasting. I often get a headache when I fast, and it makes me cranky. I am told some people get greater spiritual

---

[4] I still love Christ deeply and passionately, but, much like my maturing love for my wife, it is no longer the intense euphoria of those early years. This change in my emotions is not sinful or due to a lack of zeal. Some people mistake feelings for commitment. But it is our will that counts. I am glad not to have all of the emotional undulations—for my God or my wife—of my adolescence.

clarity and a sense of lightness from it, but not I. I dread it in advance and do not enjoy the experience. Yet I do so love the fruits of fasting. I love walking in the confidence that I have again cleared away the brambles of my heart and that I am assured that my first desire is to do God's will. Fasting gives me confidence that I have done my best to seek God's will in some particular matter, and it puts me at peace with whatever decision I have made as a result of my fasting.

The Bible teaches that fasting mysteriously unleashes power "in the heavenly realms." I cannot claim to entirely understand why or how this happens, but I believe it. Most of the time I have fasted I have not been privileged to see any discernible difference in the world, but on occasion it has produced a dramatic change. One time I was led to pray and fast all day for one of my children whom I sensed was being held back from giving her life to the Lord by demonic forces. I told no one about my fasting other than my wife, Dana. That night my daughter told me she wanted to talk to us just when she was supposed to be going to bed. At first I assumed she was playing the "stall-queen" as she had done so many other times. When she told me that she did not believe she had truly given her life to the Lord and asked to pray the sinner's prayer with us, I was floored. She then proceeded to pray a genuine and moving prayer for forgiveness and repentance, convincing me that my fasting played an important role in my daughter's life.

Self-denial leads us to the life God wants us to have—and the life we truly want once we experience it. C. S. Lewis said it best:

> Give up yourself, and you will find your real self. Lose your life and you will save it. Submit to death, death of your ambitions and favorite wishes every day and death of your whole body in the end: submit with every fiber of your being, and you will find eternal life. Keep back nothing. Nothing that you have not given away will be really yours. Nothing in you that has not died will ever be raised from the dead. Look for yourself, and you will find in the long run only hatred, loneliness, despair, rage, ruin, and decay. But look for Christ and you will

find Him, and with Him everything else thrown in
(*Mere Christianity, 190).*

Abraham was prepared to slay his only son, Isaac, the son
for whom he had waited for decades and by which God had
promised to bless him with descendents too numerous to count.
Daniel laid down his life by praying to God in contravention of
the king's edict. The apostles defied a direct governmental order not to preach the gospel. Yet each of these heroes found
consolation—both in this life and, we trust, in the life to
come—in their sacrifice. Death is the means to the end, not the
end in itself. Knowing God and being in right relationship with
him is the end. And once we know him, we find the sacrifice is
totally worth it. In "The Bargain," the 1970s rock band The
Who accurately captured how well death to self nets out posi-
tively on the ledger. Although lyricist Peter Townshend was
influenced by Indian mystic Meher Baba's Eastern religious
thought in writing the song, his words accurately capture the
Christian idea of dying to self.

> I'd gladly lose me to find you
> I'd gladly give up all I had
> To find you I'd suffer anything and be glad
>
> I'd pay any price just to get you
> I'd work all my life and I will
> To win you I'd stand naked, stoned and stabbed
>
> I'd call that a bargain
> The best I ever had
> The best I ever had
>
> I'd gladly lose me to find you
> I'd gladly give up all I got
> To catch you I'm gonna run and never stop
>
> I'd pay any price just to win you
> Surrender my good life for bad
> To find you I'm gonna drown an unsung man

I'd call that a bargain
The best I ever had
The best I ever had

I sit looking 'round
I look at my face in the mirror
I know I'm worth nothing without you
In life one and one don't make two
One and one make one
And I'm looking for that free ride to me
I'm looking for you

C.S. Lewis put it similarly in *The Weight of Glory*:

> . . . it is not so much of our time and so much of our attention that God demands; it is not even all our time and all our attention; it is ourselves. For each of us the Baptist's words are true: "He must increase and I decrease." He will be infinitely merciful to our repeated failures; I know no promise that He will accept a deliberate compromise. For He has, in the last resort, nothing to give us but Himself; and He can give that only insofar as our self-affirming will retires and makes room for Him in our souls. Let us make up our minds to it; there will be nothing "of our own" left over to live on, no "ordinary" life. I do not mean that each of us will necessarily be called to be a martyr or even an ascetic. That's as may be. For some (nobody knows which) the Christian life will include much leisure, many occupations we naturally like. But these will be received from God's hands. In a perfect Christian they would be as much part of his "religion," his "service," as his hardest duties, and his feasts would be as Christian as his fasts. What cannot be admitted—what must exist only as an undefeated but daily resisted enemy—is the idea of something that is "our own," some area in which we are to be "out of school," on which God has no claim.

For He claims all, because He is love and must bless. He cannot bless us unless He has us. When we try to keep within us an area that is our own, we try to keep an area of death. Therefore, in love, He claims all. There's no bargaining with Him (140-141).

Dying To Self Is Hard . . . And Easy

Taking up my cross daily takes practice and trust. I am never pleased to sense God's call to give up something I cherish, big or small. But with practice, I have found that the terror I first experienced when I was sixteen is mostly gone. Time and time again I have seen God's work in my life, redeeming loss, bringing hope out of despair, and opening new doors when others were shut. I have definitely gotten better at dying to myself, but it is still not easy. And even as I write this, I wonder how I will respond the next time I hear God's still small voice bidding me "come and die" (Bonhoeffer, *Discipleship,* 44). I do not know what lies ahead, and I have no room to boast in my self-dying skills. Each challenge is another fork in the road: will I submit to God's direction and grow in godliness and faith, or will I insist on being "my own man" and wither?

I remember wrestling with God early in my Christian life, trying to talk him out of some new and difficult step I was being called to do. In time, I have learned to do that less and less. I know he would not call me unless he had some good purpose in it, and I know that resistance is futile. I am regularly called to do plenty of things I do not like.

I am always amused when non-Christians refer to Christianity as a crutch. To me, it sometimes feels like a bed of nails. Flannery O'Connor wrote, "What people don't realize is how much religion costs. They think faith is a big electric blanket, when of course it is the cross" (229). I agree. God challenges me every day. My daily devotions are filled with reminders of things I am called to do contrary to my natural desires. In fact, I have made a practice of asking the Lord what he wants me to do today, and then I pause to listen. So often what I "hear" is the same challenge to live in purity and humility and integrity, ordering my life according to first principles. Sometimes I hear a very specific admonition to reach out to an unemployed friend, to do the house project my wife has been asking me to do, to set aside time to spend quality time with one of my children, or to do some task at work that I was avoiding.

Just as I know there is emotional turmoil in resisting God, I also know that there is tremendous reward in obeying. I have often experienced the joyful fruit of obedience, fruit I would not have tasted but for my obedience in laying down my life. That experience has built up my trust in God, knowing that he wants what is best for me and has hidden plans to bless me if I will obey.

Following God *is* hard, like exercise is hard. I do not like getting up early, the panting, the burning muscles, the tiredness. But I love the exhilaration, the sense of physical well-being, and the ease of daily activities that all come with my exercise regimen. So is it easier or harder to be in good shape? Both, of course. But who would believe that the obese couch potato who pants on his way to the refrigerator is better off than the agile and well-toned athlete?

Jesus said that we are to carry our own cross daily. Jesus essentially told us to carry our own instrument of torture—the cross—to the place where it will be used against us. It is amazing how we adorn ourselves with pretty little crosses, rarely thinking what they represent. We are wearing amulets and jewelry that are the equivalent of the electric chair or the noose, though far less humane.

But he also called the weary and burdened to rest in him, for he is gentle and humble in heart. He is described as the Good Shepherd who rescues his little lambs. He is the Great Physician, the Comforter, the one who leads us beside still waters. So is it hard or easy to be a Christian? It is both. To experience the rest he intends for us, we need to carry our cross. To embrace life, we must first embrace death. The way down is the way up. The last shall be first. The humble will be exalted. The meek shall inherit the earth. This is the paradox of Christian faith.

We must learn to trust that God is good, loving, and all-powerful. The longer we follow, the better we get to know God's character. If we doubted God's goodness, then self-sacrifice would be much more difficult. But when we know that "in all things God works for the good of those who love him, who have been called according to his purpose" (Rom. 8:28), our dying to self becomes more rational and definitely easier. Although our daily walk with God can sometimes feel like it is about dying, it is really about living.

God loves life. The Garden was without death, and so is heaven. That is his ultimate plan. He does not ask us to walk a tightrope across a chasm because he wants us to experience terror, but because he wants us to experience the joy of the other side where he is. He has a "good, pleasing, and perfect" will for us (Rom. 12:2). He bids us to die to self only because it leads to life and away from death. He is like the firefighter pleading with us to jump out of the burning house with the assurance that he will catch us. He knows we will eternally weep and gnash our teeth if we do not and we will miss out on the excellent plans he has for us, so he pleads and cajoles us to do the terrifying thing.

Feeling the terror of dying to ourselves is not sinful. Jesus himself experienced it in the Garden of Gethsemane when he sweat blood contemplating his own crucifixion. He begged the Father to let "this cup be taken from me." We are not called to be Stoics or Buddhists, both of whom strive not to grieve personal loss. Grieving for death and loss is normal. And it is hard. The writer of Hebrews says, "No discipline seems pleasant at the time, but painful. Later on, however, it produces a harvest of righteousness and peace for those who have been trained by it" (Heb. 12:11). Discipline, understood in this scriptural passage as any trial that comes our way, is difficult.

Nietzsche said that, "What does not kill me, makes me stronger" (33). Nietzsche was wrong. Suffering can make us bitter, not better, if we do not submit to God's purposes in the suffering. Only if we humble ourselves can humiliation, defeat, disease, and poverty strengthen us. The choice is ours.

Not Yet What We Really Are

Lest we feel discouraged about how we are *supposed* to act as disciples of Christ and how much we struggle and fall short, it is important to remember our death to self is a spiritual reality to which we aspire in the here-and-now but will not be fully realized until we are in heaven. The spiritual reality is that we are dead to self and alive in Christ.

Col. 3:1-3 says, "Since, then, you have been raised with Christ, set your hearts on things above, where Christ is seated at the right hand of God. Set your minds on things above, not on earthly things. For you died, and your life is now hidden with Christ in God. When Christ, who is your life, appears, then you also will appear with him in glory." Until we are with him in heaven, we *strive* to match up our present lives with whom we already are in the spiritual realm—righteous by the blood of the Lamb and united with him. This tension between the spiritual reality and our "not yet" temporal reality is reduced (though never eliminated) as we walk in the Spirit. We have been called to be dead to ourselves, and in Christ that is already true. Jesus already died for us on the cross, and that reality guarantees our salvation.

Yet our daily experience reminds us how often we fall short. We commit ourselves to live only for Christ, then we complain when we are slighted or shown disrespect by a store clerk. We worry about what others think about us. We fret over our next job. We sin and we sin and we sin and we sin. Often, we act profoundly un-dead, as if it were all about us and our desires. We find comfort to read the Apostle Paul's similar struggles in Rom. 7:

> We know that the law is spiritual; but I am unspiritual, sold as a slave to sin. I do not understand what I do. For what I want to do I do not do, but what I hate I do. And if I do what I do not want to do, I agree that the law is good. As it is, it is no longer I myself who do it, but it is sin living in me. I know that nothing good lives in me, that is, in my sinful nature. For I have the desire to do what is good, but I cannot carry it out. For what I do is not the good I want to do; no, the evil I do not want to do—this I keep on doing. Now if I do what I do not want to do, it is no longer I who do it, but it is sin living in me that does it.

So I find this law at work: When I want to do good, evil is right there with me. For in my inner being I delight in God's law; but I see another law at work in the members of my body, waging war against the law of my mind and making me a prisoner of the law of sin at work within my members. What a wretched man I am! Who will rescue me from this body of death? Thanks be to God—through Jesus Christ our Lord! (vv. 14-25a)[5]

Or again in Phil. 3:12-14, Paul writes about how far short he has fallen from living the life he wants to live:

Not that I have already obtained all this, or have already been made perfect, but I press on to take hold of that for which Christ Jesus took hold of me. Brothers, I do not consider myself yet to have taken hold of it. But one thing I do: Forgetting what is behind and straining toward what is ahead, I press on toward the goal to win the prize for which God has called me heavenward in Christ Jesus.

The key is striving. We may sin seventy times seven each day, but if we are trying not to sin, God is quick to forgive. He knows our sinful state. He knows we are made of dust. But his anger is aroused if we stop trying. He was tough on the Israelites when they gave themselves over to their idolatry, but ever merciful in their repentance. He is gracious with us sinners when we seek his will and his ways, but hard when we shake our fist at him and tell him we know better.

This is a vital point. We are saved by grace, and we cannot work our way into heaven. But if we do not even desire and strive to turn from sin, then it calls into question whether we

---

[5] Some commentators believe that this passage refers to Paul's state before he was saved. The passage so clearly comports with my experience as a sinner that I believe it refers to our state as Christians. Regardless, this experience of struggle with sin is endemic to the most godly people I have known. We have turned from sin and hate it, but we still have not completely conquered it until our nature is perfected in heaven.

have really repented. Forgiveness presupposes repentance. Without a repentant spirit, we stand in grave peril.

One of my kids asked me whether she had to stop a particular sin in order to go to heaven. I explained that she at least had to *want* to stop sinning to have the assurance of salvation. It was clear she did not want to stop, and she asked me whether she would still go to heaven. I told her that I did not know what would happen since God is the judge, but I could not provide her with any false security that she would be okay. Motivated by fear, she repented.[6]

In one way, the Good News is really bad news for us. It is like major surgery followed by chemotherapy and then radiation. It is painful, sad, and debilitating to what the Bible calls "the old man." But if we have terminal cancer, it is very good news. And the cure rate is one hundred percent. But we have to choose to undergo the treatment.[7] And the treatments go on daily until we die and find ourselves in heaven, fully healed, free of pain, sin, and sorrow.

Michael Card's song, "Livin' We Die," captures well the paradox of dying to find life:

> Saved by His death, healed by His pain
> Raised to new life to never die again
> Before you can have the hope of the call
> You've got to give it all

---

[6] Many Christians deride fear as a motivator to do the right thing. But Jesus employed the fearfully vivid imagery of eternal fire and weeping and gnashing of teeth to motivate his hearers to follow him. The desire to please God is a superior motivation, but fear is also legitimate and too quickly dismissed. God uses many negative emotions to drive us to do right. Fear, shame, and pain are useful tools God employs to good effect.

[7] This analogy is imperfect because, unlike radiation and chemotherapy that do heal us, our "treatment" of dying to self does not save us. It sanctifies us, making us more like Christ, but the salvation is Christ's work on the cross. Yet if we do not make a practice of dying to self, it calls into question whether we have been saved. Jesus said a tree is known by its fruit, and without the fruit of dying to self we have reason to worry whether we are truly Christ's.

It sounds too good to be true
That the Son of God should die for you
That it could give you the key
To open up your life and set you free
But that's not all of the story
There's something that He gave you
That you got to pay
No matter what that good time gospel tells you
The battle is uphill all the way

Livin' we die, dying we live
Givin' it all is what you've got to give
Just look to the Lord and all that He gave
When He died to save you
Saved by His death, healed by His pain
Raised to new life to never die again
Before you can have the hope of the call
You've got to give it all

Humility and Service:
The Implications of Dying to Self

"Whoever wants to become great among you must be your servant, and whoever wants to be first must be your slave—just as the Son of Man did not come to be served, but to serve, and to give his life as a ransom for many."
Jesus

"Pride makes us artificial and humility makes us real."
Thomas Merton

Dying to ourselves is the first step. Living for God in humble service is the second.

I have long struggled with pride. But who better knows the power of alcohol than an alcoholic who has fought liquor for a long time? And who knows the power of pride but a pompous fool who has struggled to right his heart? Pride is my daily struggle. If you, like my wife, do not wrestle with pride because you are truly humble, feel free to skip this chapter. But for the rest of you, read on.

What Is Humility?

In the Latin, humility means "low-lying" and to humble means "to make low." Humility is the opposite of pride. Pride is exaltation above one's actual position.

Pride was the fundamental sin of the Garden of Eden. Adam and Eve believed the Serpent's lie that they knew better than God. God had warned them not to eat the forbidden fruit lest they die, but by their actions Adam and Eve insisted that God was wrong and they were right. At its core, their sin was placing themselves in the position of God, the ultimate arbiter of right and wrong. Pride is the father of all other sins. It is fundamentally rebellion against God and his ways. It twists and distorts and lies.

In contrast, humility reflects the way things really are. To make ourselves low before God reflects the right and true order of the universe. As creatures made from dust, we are contingent beings. Our first cause is God himself who willed us into existence and on whom we depend for our every breath. We do not truly possess any good thing. Every good thing we have is ultimately derived from God. Wealth, health, intelligence, beauty, personality—all comes from the Great I Am, the Creator of all that is. Therefore, humility is right because it reflects the true order of the universe.

No God = No Humility

If there were no God, humility would be meaningless. If there is no First Cause that brought all things into being, and if matter is eternal and humans are random accidents, then we owe nothing to anyone. To suppose otherwise would be a lie. We could then truly be proud. Atheist philosopher Ayn Rand's books on the virtue of selfishness testify to that. Rand believed humankind was the center of the universe. She saw selflessness as weak and wrong, because it denies humanity's nobility:

> Discard the protective rags of that vice which you call a virtue: humility—learn to value yourself, which means: to fight for your happiness—and when you learn that *pride* is the sum of all virtues, you will learn to live like a man (179).

To Rand, humility denies the truth of our existence. And if there is no God, Rand is right. Why pretend to be servants when we are masters? The fifth-century-B.C. philosopher Protagoras said, "Man is the measure of all things: of things which are, that they are, and of things which are not, that they are not." The French Enlightenment celebrated this humanistic creed, rejecting transcendent truth as illusory. Friedrich Nietzsche, who famously declared God dead, inveighed against humility as an agent for the weak to suppress the strong. It is logical for those who disbelieve in God to reject humility. Indeed, if there is no God, man is the greatest sentient being in all the world and humility a lie. Self-worship makes sense.

Like all powerful lies, there is truth mixed in. We are noble creatures. We were made to be bold and independent and courageous, facing life's challenges with gusto and vision. Rand's heroes in her novels stand against the prevailing group-think that makes too many people timid, risk-averse, and conformists. They are willing to challenge conventional wisdom and pursue their plans against long odds. They have the courage to eschew the praise of the crowd for the satisfaction that comes from pursuing a dream. I love Rand's heroes for these admirable traits.

Yet humility is entirely consistent with the bold life lived unto God. Indeed, if there is an omniscient, omnipotent, all-loving and all-good Deity, then humility is logical. "Every good and perfect gift is from above, coming down from the Father of the heavenly lights . . ." (Jas. 1:17). God is the source of all goodness. To the extent that humanity is good, it is a reflection of the author of virtue and creator of all things. There is no room for human boasting.

Every human achievement is traceable to God. The excellent violinist received her innate abilities from her Maker. Her cultivated talent that came from hours of self-sacrifice and practice were due in part to her parents who taught her deferred gratification, who were in turn products of others who instructed them, who are ultimately derived from God. The violin itself was wrought from centuries of invention at the hands of master craftsmen. The violinist is a pygmy standing on the shoulder of giants who came before her. As the Giver of Life, every good thing is ultimately traced back to him. No man is an island. The human propensity to "own" our achievements is as natural as sin itself. And as deceptive.

I am very organized and self-disciplined. These traits have been enormously beneficial in my personal life and in my career. In fact, I would trace many of my achievements to these traits. I remember being awed by the intellect of one of my classmates in graduate school who clearly had far more brain power than I. Yet he stayed up too late, rose late in the morning, pursued more leisure, and consequently, received worse grades than I did. He was the proverbial hare and I the tortoise. My diligence overtook his slothful intellect. But my organization and self-discipline are traits partially born from my genetic predisposition to routine, traits I witnessed in my parents, traits I was encouraged to cultivate in my childhood and for which I was rewarded through my academic studies and in my various jobs. When I inwardly admire myself and wrongly "own" my accomplishments, I am denying that I have inherited gifts for which the proper response is gratitude, not pride.

We have no room to boast in anything—not even in the good things we do. Our righteous acts are themselves God's working in us. Isaiah writes about our righteousness, which is no better than "filthy rags" (Isa. 64:6). Jesus derided the Pharisees for their self-righteousness—a self-righteousness that was illusory and prevented them from entering the Kingdom of God. If we think we possess whatever goodness we exhibit, then we cannot become truly good. It is only as Christ imputes his righteousness to us—a true righteousness that can cover our sinfulness only through his atoning work on the cross—that we can enter the presence of a holy God who cannot tolerate sin. Paul writes in Gal. 6:14, "May I never boast except in the cross of our Lord Jesus Christ, through which the world has been crucified to me, and I to the world."

That we *should* be humble is not surprising given that we are created beings who are saved by grace and yet who continue to sin. But that the God of all creation is humble is both surprising and perplexing. He who rightly deserves our constant devotion deigned to become a man. His Incarnation is alone shocking. But that he would become a carpenter, instead of an earthly king, is still more incredible. And to play the part of a servant to his servants, the Apostles, in washing their feet at the Last Supper is beyond amazing. Finally, to suffer an ignoble and unjust death to pay the price for our rebellion against *him* conclusively demonstrates that Jesus is "gentle and humble in heart" (Matt. 11:30).

But does not God seek people who will bring him glory? Is not that in a way . . . proud? Why does God want our praise and constant devotion? Why is he a jealous God who forbids the worship of any other god (Exod. 34:14)? Would not a humble God be content to let his creatures give their devotion to others? And if Satan is wrong to desire our worship, why is it okay for God?

In fact, God wills that his creatures bring him glory precisely because he deserves it and it is best *for us*. Acknowledging and praising the source of all goodness brings us into the full light of truth. We come to understand and live in the world as it is, not as we may wish it to be in our rebellion. God is worthy of all praise because of who he is. He loves truth, and he knows that when we love and live in truth, we thrive. When we deny truth, in word or deed, we wither. So his desiring our praise is out of his love for us, not from self-love. God does not need our praise. In fact, he does not *need* anything. He is self-sufficient. He wants our praise principally for our benefit.

I want my children to love, respect, and honor me. Unlike God, my motives are not pure, and some of my sinful self desires love, respect and honor for my own sake. But most of me wants these things from my kids for their sake, because I know they are more likely to lead a good life if they honor their parents. So when I chide them for their disrespectful comments with the parental refrain "Just who do you think you are talking to?" I am loving them and seeking their best.

Humility Entails Service

Once we understand who we are and who God is, humility is the necessary corollary. With humility comes service to God and to our fellow humans.

Paul writes that "in view of God's mercy" we are to be "living sacrifices" (Rom. 12:1). In 1 Cor. 6:20, he writes, "you are not your own; you were bought at a price. Therefore, honor God with your bodies." Our job is to devote our every breath to God and his purposes. One of my favorite verses is "So whether you eat or drink or whatever you do, do it all for the glory of God" (1 Cor. 10:31). Our every action should be holy, i.e. set apart for God. Nothing remains for us to own. All becomes his.

But what does it mean practically to spend ourselves in service to God and our fellow humans? Does it mean we are barred from worldly positions of power? Should we seek the lowest earthly positions—the teacher's aide instead of the teacher, the orderly instead of the doctor, the White House usher instead of the President? Not necessarily. What it does mean is that in whatever position we find ourselves, we should emulate Christ by serving God and others.

I work in politics, and I love it because I love justice, and politics at its best is the handmaiden of justice. Unfortunately, politics can also be about self-serving power and pomposity. In fact, that is the way many people view politics and politicians. I have often heard it said that anyone who seeks elective office must be motivated principally by ego. I think this is wrong. To be sure, there is no shortage of self-serving politicians. But I have also known many politicians—of the Left and the Right— who are motivated to do justice.

Politics has some perks, but it has far fewer than many people realize. Most members of Congress have to endure weekly travel to-and-from their congressional districts, lower salaries and longer hours than they would have in the private sector, the expense of maintaining two houses, and a steady stream of disparaging comments from the media and their political opponents. What keeps many politicians in the arena is the desire to restrain evil and promote the good. (We do not all share the same understanding of what is good and what is evil, but that is different than supposing that one side seeks justice and the other consciously seeks to do what is wrong.)

I served as a staffer in the House of Representatives, the United States Senate, and the White House for almost twenty years, not counting my ongoing work on presidential campaigns and for various political causes (pro-life, pro-marriage, pro-abstinence education, anti-pornography, and so on.). The pace of work on Capitol Hill is grueling. I typically worked sixty hours per week or more, and at a very fast pace, receiving about four hundred emails per day. My salary was substantially less than my counterparts in the private sector. My work space was often inferior, the fringe benefits were modest. My time, even outside of the office, was always available to the member of Congress whom I served. I well remember trying to hush my young children as I advised my senator about a particularly pressing policy matter while I sat on a bag of wood chips in the garden department at Home Depot on a Saturday morning, and then doing the same an hour later while shoe shopping.

The weightiness of my job often trumped family matters. I remember leaving my wife—with her permission—sitting alone in a restaurant booth while I stepped outside to talk to Judge Ken Starr about a judicial nomination battle. I felt like a foot soldier fighting on the front lines of a fierce battle for the heart and soul of our nation. My work was a calling. In fact, when I left my job as policy advisor to U.S. Senate Majority Leader Bill Frist in 2005, I felt like I was abandoning my fellow soldiers. I chaffed at the misperception that I was "selling out" to earn more money in the private sector. My wife and I had decided that my career in politics would have to be put on hold so I could be a more attentive husband and father. No more late night calls from the empty Rotunda of the U.S. Capitol, which stood just outside my office, saying goodnight to my children. No more handing off my children's bedtime rituals to my wife so I could handle another political "emergency." It was time for me to be the kind of father to my children that my father had been to me.

I hope that I am no less a servant now, working in the private sector on government relations for corporate clients, than I was working in Capitol Hill's vortex of power. At least my desire to serve is no less. But the point is that politics requires sacrifice, and the reflexively cynical attitude towards those working in the political realm is often unfair. Our nation has many good and godly men and women who are laying down their lives to create a just political order. Many of these servant leaders live out humble lives of service.

Service is an inward disposition of love and concern for others. It is centered in the motivation for our actions. The custodian cleaning the Oval Office may be serving himself, whereas the President may be serving others. Humble service is not immediately apparent based on our social rank or stature. Whether we are genuinely serving others is only fully known by God, and as we come to grow in holiness, more clearly known by us. As we spend more time in prayer and Bible study and serving, we come to see our shortcomings better. Conversely, being less aware of God's requirements provides us with a false sense of righteousness. Who knows better the power of the river's current than the fish striving to swim upstream?

Cancer Surgery

I wish that I could say that I have always sought to be a servant in my political career. I have not.

I came to Washington, D.C., in 1987 with the mixture of a yearning for justice and the young man's disease of an overarching ambition. The first time I heard the term "Potomac Fever" was during a trip to Washington in 1986, when I was the student government president at Houghton College. As soon as I heard the term, I knew I had it. Everything about the place was alluring to me: the stately Roman columns, the marble halls, the "speechifying," the media attention, and the roiling debate. Politics does hold a special attraction for people who care about justice *and* wrestle with pride. It may be that pride tends to drive people to politics or that politics tends to fan the flames of our pride. Whichever it is, a yearning for justice and personal power can go hand-in-hand.

I am not saying that I had completely given myself over to pride. To the contrary, from my first day in Washington as an entry-level staff assistant in the office of a congressman, I have been aware of my pride and fought mightily against it. I regularly prayed to be humble. Outwardly, I did well, at least according to my friends. I was not known as pompous or self-seeking. But God knew my heart. I remember being at a political function when a student was waiting to talk to me. As my eyes scanned the room to find the strategic people to advance my career, I brushed past the student to make my way to a prominent man on the other side of the room. I knew my sin, even later that day as the Holy Spirit showed me how I had wronged the student, but I did a poor job in successfully fighting my self-seeking ambition. Intellectually, I trusted that

God had a good plan for my life, but I could not stop helping his plan along with some self-promotion of my own.

It took a humiliating event to get me to make progress in my quest for humility. In one job, I was forced to resign—resign or be fired. I had done nothing wrong, and the stated reason for my dismissal was unwarranted and inexplicable. I was counseled by my circle of godly brothers not to widely share the back-story, both because the story did not sound plausible and being at odds with my former employer would only hurt my future job prospects. So I kept the story to myself. As I looked for a new job, speculation swirled about what I might have done to merit my abrupt departure. Had I had an affair? Had I misused taxpayer funds? Was I delinquent in my responsibilities? Newspaper accounts theorized false and unflattering stories about me. I have always prided myself on my conscientious work, and not responding to the rumor mill was very difficult.

One morning, as I ascended from the Washington subway en route to a job interview, I felt the pain of my situation like a knife between my ribs, and I felt despair about my future. I silently raised my hands, palms upwards, offering to God my reputation. I concluded then that God could use me with a good reputation or a bad one, providing that I humbly submitted to him each day.

So I let my career be God's problem. I repeatedly recited Col. 3:1-4, telling myself over and over again that Bill Wichterman was a dead man—and I almost felt that way, seeing my promising career slip away. I imagined that my next job would be dull and unfulfilling. But I concluded that my life was now "hidden with Christ." The trial I was enduring was not my problem. I had been treated unjustly, but God still had good plans for me, both during my job transition and eventually in a new job. I knew that God's will for me would not be thwarted by any injustice. I alone could stop God's will from being accomplished in me. I knew that if God could take the worst thing in the world (the unjust crucifixion of Jesus at the hands of evil men) and turn it into the best thing in the world (the salvation of the world), then I knew his plans for me would not be thwarted by anyone other than me.

However, I did not know this all at once. It was a daily struggle to die to myself, to internalize the outward humiliation so I could be inwardly humbled. It hurt more than anything else I had ever experienced. But I now see that God was doing his cancer surgery on me, removing the malignant tumor of pride so I could be healed. He was answering my fervent prayers to become more humble. Through humiliation, I was learning humility.

Within just a couple of years, I was able to look back on that painful period as the best thing to have happened in my spiritual life since I had become a Christian. It was a turning point. I learned with my heart what I had already known in my head: I am a servant. My life is not about seeing how high I can climb on the professional ladder before I die. It is about how I can live every moment with a desire to serve God and serve others. That is how we please God.

I came to experience the unfettered joy that comes from being fettered to Christ. He is a good, kind, and loving master. Even as he gives us specific jobs to do, he is ever mindful of our needs and our wants. At my better moments when my trust in him is at its highest, I find comfort in hardships that come my way, knowing that he has a good plan for me. With James, I have sometimes been able to confidently say, "Consider it pure joy, my brothers, whenever you face trials of many kinds, because you know that the testing of your faith develops perseverance. Perseverance must finish its work so that you may be mature and complete, not lacking anything" (1:2-4). I wish I could maintain this confidence all the time, but I often forget and am prone to curse hardship, forgetting the God who is there with me, waiting to redeem it for my good . . . if I will let him. Hardship can just stink unless we allow God to use it for our eternal benefit. The choice is entirely ours.

I also learned that God can take any experience and turn it for good. We know he will always do that spiritually, but he often does it for our temporal good as well. In my case, my career was propelled forward, eventually leading me to the White House. Like Joseph, who was sold into slavery by his brothers, what others had intended to harm me "God intended it for good" (Gen. 50:20). God does not always prosper us here and now. Although Shadrach, Meshach and Abednego were saved from the fiery furnace for their fidelity in not bowing down to the golden statute of King Nebuchadnezzar, they knew that God could have let them be burned up and he would still be God. Contrary to the health-and-wealth gospel falsely preached in some churches, fidelity to God does not necessarily lead to our earthly benefit, but I have been amazed at how often it has in my life.

"Look Down, Not Up"

One practical way to emulate Christ is to serve within your current sphere of influence. You have people in your life who look up to you because of your job, your age, your looks, your car, your grade point average, or whatever, good reason or bad. Begin by serving those people. Jesus washed the feet of his biggest admirers, his disciples. Imagine the impact you can have on those who already esteem you.

In God's economy, there are no people who are loved less by God. He loves us all as much as an all-loving God can love us, which is infinitely. But the world's valuation system puts some people higher and some lower. This "power pyramid" has a pernicious way of tempting us to focus on those "above" us on the social ladder. Many people would like to serve the President or an American Idol winner or a Hollywood celebrity or the Super Bowl quarterback, but few people aspire to serve the interns in their office. Yet those interns—or the equivalent people of low position in your world—would go home with a smile if you remembered their names, took an interest in them, or went to lunch with them. I remember feeling like a million bucks when a chief of staff to a member of Congress remembered my name when I was a staff assistant. In my world, he was a rock star, and I was thrilled that he noticed me.

And you are a rock star to someone "below you" on the worldly pyramid. This is where the otherwise twisted pattern of power relationships can be used to good advantage for Kingdom purposes. Serve everyone alike, powerful and powerless, but pay special attention to the outsized influence you can have on "lowly people" by serving them. Paul wrote that we should not be proud but "be willing to associate with people of low position" (Rom. 12:16). Sadly, by spending so much energy trying to maneuver ourselves into position to influence people of high position, we neglect the areas where we can have the greatest influence today. It is not wrong to seek to influence people at the top of the pyramid. When you have the opportunity, take it. And some people are specifically called to minister to those in leadership. But service to "the least of these" is readily available to all of us, and we are foolish to neglect the opportunities we have already been given, preferring to fight for those we have not been given.

Dr. Dick Halverson is an example of one who knew well the power pyramid but chose to ignore it. Dr. Halverson served as the chaplain to the United States Senate from 1981 to 1994. He ministered to some of the most powerful men and women on the planet, but he also knew the names of the elevator operators, the shoeshine men, and the mailroom clerks and loved them as if they were all senators. For him, there were no unimportant people, just people made in God's image whom he was called to love. For his vivid imitation of Jesus, he was loved, admired, and respected by the powerful and the powerless.

In short, we are wise to "look down on people," not to think less of them but to pay special attention to them through our service. In God's economy, everyone is of equal rank—a person made in the image of God with eternity in his heart. Begin serving where your influence will be powerful and effective.

Bloom Where You Are Planted

Jesus said, "Whoever can be trusted with very little can also be trusted with much, and whoever is dishonest with very little will also be dishonest with much" (Luke 16:10). You may not be where you want to be. Perhaps you are in prison, in a menial job, or a homemaker who sacrificially left behind the excitement of the professional world. Do not miss the opportunity to serve God in these "little things." In truth, there are no little things if God has called you to do them. We are foolish to plan for how we can serve God tomorrow in some big and flashy way if we neglect the things he wants us to do today.

God has a plan for the world that includes you, where you are today. Every day that we humbly submit to God and seek to serve him, he uses us. Of that we can be certain. He is not too busy to notice the corner of the earth where we are, and he is not indifferent to our little world. The nineteenth-century Dutch Prime Minister and theologian Abraham Kuyper said, "There is not a square inch in the whole domain of our human existence over which Christ, who is Sovereign over all, does not cry: 'Mine!'" (488)

At points in my career, I have been blessed with considerable worldly influence. I have known the heady rush of making split-second decisions that could have enormous implications. I have felt hundreds of pairs of eyes turn to me when I walked on stage to make an announcement or deliver a speech. And I have labored on small and seemingly insignificant matters that matter to almost no one and had an imperceptible impact on the world.

God cares about both. Assuming you are supposed to be working on those "small things," do it with the full assurance that your service is important to God. The inmate whose job is cleaning the toilets should remember that God has a will for him in that job, and he displeases him if he does not do it well and to God's glory. We must learn to "fix our eyes not on what is seen, but on what is unseen. For what is seen is temporary, but what is unseen is eternal" (2 Cor. 4:18). Cultivating eyes for the invisible things will help us to serve in things big and small.

Sometimes we are so focused on our future that we see everything we are doing as preparation for that time. But who knows the future? That time may never come. You may be struck by lightning today, and all of your carefully laid plans will evaporate. God calls us both to live in the present but prepare for the future. Like other aspects of the Christian life, these things are held in tension. You should plan for what might be next even as you thrive in the present. Planning for tomorrow is today's responsibility, and it is in itself something God calls us to do. The job *search* is as important as the next job, the planning as important as the doing, the transition as important as the next step. Every moment and every deed matters to God.

Once, while Francis of Assisi was hoeing his garden, he was asked, "What would you do if you suddenly learned that you were to die at sunset today?" He replied, "I would finish hoeing my garden." God is as interested in today's mundane task as in tomorrow's spectacular potential. This is not to say that we should eschew opportunities to gain greater worldly influence. God may be calling you to become the superintendent of schools, the head coach, or the CEO. But you should be no less a servant at the top of the pyramid than at the bottom. Moreover, you will be better prepared to serve at the top if you have first learned to serve at the bottom.

When I worked for President George W. Bush in the White House, I was deeply impressed by his attitude of humble service. Behind closed doors, the President displayed a concern for heads of state and busboys. I heard it again and again, and I saw it. When my family met with the President in the Oval Office, my then-twelve-year-old daughter thanked the President for caring more about what God thinks than what the polls say, and he replied with a twinkle in his eye, "There you go!" He was a servant in the highest position in the world. He had the trappings of great power, but his heart was humble. High or low, our call is to serve where we find ourselves today, blooming where we are planted.

No More Personal Kingdom Building

As servants of the King of Kings, we have no right to build our own kingdoms. Our careers, our reputations, our relationships, our aspirations—all fall under his rule. He is a consuming fire and a jealous God.

But what does this mean? Does it mean that your lifelong desire to be an astronaut or a stay-at-home mom or an attorney or a train engineer is ungodly? Does it mean you should pretend not to want what you want? Or that you should ignore your longings? Does it mean you should no longer care whether you get to eat your favorite food, cheer for your favorite team, or pursue your favorite hobbies? Does it mean that you become hollowed out of all that is distinctively "you" and become a Jesus-robot?

Jesus said, "If anyone comes to me and does not hate his father, mother, wife, children, brothers, and sisters, as well as his own life, he cannot be my disciple" (Luke 14:26). That sounds harsh, and contrary to biblical admonitions to honor and care for our parents. Jesus was speaking polemically, saying that our love and devotion to God should be so strong that our natural and right affections for our parents should seem like hate in comparison. In the same way, our desire to do God's will should be so strong that our natural desires should seem insignificant and unimportant in comparison to building God's kingdom.

We will still have desires that are appropriate to pursue: watching football, playing golf, sailing, swimming, and so on. Following Christ is not necessarily a call to asceticism. We do not deny ourselves as an end in itself but as a means to saying yes to Jesus and his Kingdom. When God's commands and his particular call on our lives conflict with our natural desires, God is supposed to win.

The good news is that very often it is God himself who has placed longings inside us. They often point us to the very things that God is calling us to do. For instance, your desire for adventure may be just the thing God has planted in you to compel you to go wherever he calls. Your desire to lead may be an indication of his call. We should take seriously our natural desires and carefully evaluate how God may be leading us to serve him based on how we are wired.

Even our desires for certain pleasures—ice cream, coffee, skiing—can be reflections of God. First Tim. 6:17 says that God "richly provides us with everything for our enjoyment." God placed man in the Garden of Eden and filled it with good things, and he is preparing a beautiful place for us in heaven because he loves us. Many of our desires are planted inside us to be fulfilled.

But not always. Sometimes we are wired wrong, since we are born in sin. The boy, whose natural inclination is towards aggression against weaker playmates or towards vengeance, is experiencing the effects of the fall. He will have to learn to suppress his natural inclinations. Sometimes our wiring will lead us to experience frustration and self-denial. Or, God may give us good desires that will not be fulfilled on this side of heaven. I think of my friend, Prof. Jerry Herbert, who has longed to serve as a Congressman, but has instead devoted himself to teaching politics to college students. He feels keenly his unfulfilled longing, even while he knows he has done his master's bidding in being an outstanding and inspiring teacher to thousands of students.

In contrast, Jonah was called to go to Nineveh but he followed his natural inclinations first, fleeing from Nineveh. Only after the God got his attention in the belly of a fish did he ultimately submit his own desires to the Lord's directions. Even then, Jonah's heart still was not right, even after obeying. God wants more than our outward obedience at the tip of a sword -- he wants our willing inward submission.

Our chief aim should be to bring God glory. This means we should busy ourselves with his Kingdom. As such, fulfilling our natural desires should be a distant second to his. When those desires conflict with his, they should be suppressed. When our natural desires are consonant with his, the question then becomes whether we should seek to fulfill them, given the other duties we have been given. Admittedly, these are murky waters, and discernment is required to help us sort out God's will.

For years I wanted a new house. Was my longing sinful? Mostly, no. I recognized the temptation to have a house that would impress others, and I resisted it. More important than living in a nice house is that I honor God with my money and that I practice contentment with my current circumstances. I am commanded to remember the world's poor and care for them. I am commanded not to presume on tomorrow's finances. I am commanded to save for future needs. I want to have the flexibility to take a lower paying job without having to worry that I cannot meet my mortgage.

Thankfully, I was eventually blessed with a house that satisfied my longing and did not entail debt. Now my challenge is to hold it loosely, not "owning" it, but remembering that God is my landlord, and I am just his tenant. When he wants me to move on, then move I must.

I have found it useful to precede each transition in my life with a day of prayer and fasting at a local retreat center. The focus of the day is not to figure out what I should do next in my life, but to examine whether my first desire is to do God's will, come what may. I use the time to meditate on Scripture, sing songs of praise to God, to write in my journal, and to pray. The days are not boring, and they are always fruitful for my spiritual clarity. I encourage others to do the same, because I have found these days to be excellent times of clearing away the brambles of sin and desire that can so easily crowd out the good plants I want to be growing in my heart.

Humility entails giving up our rights to build our personal kingdoms. Laying down our rights would be foolish if God were not personally interested in us, just, merciful, and committed to what is best for us. Imagine humbling yourself under a cruel or capricious god who took pleasure in tormenting us! Then, humility would be suicidal. Thankfully, God's character makes our sacrifice worthwhile.

It is Not About You

In *The Great Divorce*, C. S. Lewis presented hell as a choice we make in putting ourselves above God, rather than a punishment cruelly thrust upon us. If we say, "my will be done," it is done, with all of its hellacious implications. Exalting ourselves, presuming to be what we are not, reaps destruction in our lives. Our little kingdoms will evaporate in time. Fighting to be on the top of the ant heap may get us that for which we aimed, but at a terrible price. Exalting ourselves is the business of hell, and we should want no part of it.

In one vignette in *The Great Divorce,* a man who has taken the bus ride from hell to heaven is angry to find that a former colleague, who had murdered someone on Earth is in heaven, while the man (now a ghost) is in hell. He is incensed at the seeming inequity of it.

Ghost: "I gone straight all my life. I don't say I was a religious man and I don't say I had no fault, far from it. But I done my best all my life, see? I done my best by everyone, that's the sort of chap I was. . . . I'm asking for nothing but my rights. . . . But I got to have my rights same as you, see?"

Murderer: "Oh no. It's not so bad as that. I haven't got my rights, or I should not be here. You will not get yours either. You'll get something far better. Never fear." . . .

Ghost: "That's just what I say. I haven't got my rights. I always done my best and I never done nothing wrong. And what I don't see is why I should be put below a bloody murderer like you. . . . I'd rather be damned than go along with you. I came here to get my rights, see? Not to go sniveling along on charity tied onto your apron-strings. If they're too fine to have me without you, I'll go home" (33-34).

The Ghost storms off to return to hell, letting his will triumph over submitting to God's plan. Later, one of the redeemed men of heaven explains about those in hell:

For a damned soul is nearly nothing: it is shrunk, shut up in itself. Good beats upon the damned incessantly as sound waves beat on the ears of the deaf, but they cannot receive it. Their fists are clenched, their teeth are clenched, their eyes fast shut. First they will not, in the end they cannot, open their hands for gifts, or their mouths for food, or their eyes to see (123).

Fighting to "own" ourselves will make us shrink. We were made to grow in God's likeness. Insisting that we "do it my way," as Frank Sinatra sang, brings death.[8] Adam and Eve decided they knew better than God what would make them happy, and they lost the perfection of the Garden. They ended up with thorns, sadness, grief, and death. He who denies the Gospel "stands condemned already" (John 3:18), though the full measure of his condemnation will not be revealed until after his death. "Everyone who does evil hates the light, and will not come into the light for fear that his deeds will be exposed" (John 3:20).

If the spiritual reality is that we are dead to self and alive in Christ, then what happens to you is no longer principally your problem, but God's. When you are passed over for a promotion, it is God's problem. When you are insulted by a co-worker, it is God's problem. When your reputation is unjustly sullied by jealous gossip, it is God's problem. When your desire to run for political office is thwarted by an unscrupulous political opponent, it is God's problem. When someone else takes credit you deserve, it is God's problem.

If you are a dead man, then all that matters is God and his Kingdom. This is not to say that slights, insults, and disrespect are not painful. They are. But we can bear up under the suffering when we remember that our business is doing God's business. He can use us when we are vilified or glorified, when passed over or promoted, when denied our due or given more than we deserve. Every day that we humbly submit to God and his purposes and seek to serve him, he will use us for his glory. His eternal purposes in our lives cannot be thwarted by others, but only by us when we rebel against him and his ways.

---

[8] Apparently, even the song itself can bring death. According to *The New York Times* ("Sinatra Song Often Strikes Deadly Chord," February 6, 2010), over the last decade in the Philippines, at least six people have been murdered due to karaoke performances of Frank Sinatra's song "My Way." Bar owners who have banned the song report that audiences would often object to the poor singing of the song and the arrogant way in which it was sung. I suspect the hubris of the song—insisting that life be lived "my way"—has been reflected in both the karaoke singer and the audience, resulting in a little piece of hell in the here and now. In any case, this is a bizarre story.

God does care about the ignominies we suffer. But he will redeem them for our good only if we let him. He can use unjust suffering to make us patient, though the Evil One may have intended to make us bitter. He can use insults to teach us perseverance, though the Evil One may have intended to make us despair. God is the master chess player who can turn any bad move to good in our lives . . . if we let him. The choice is ours.

So there is good news in bad news. He refines us like silver through hardship. He is the trustee of our reputation, our salary, our stature, our position. He can take us to the penthouse or solitary confinement—or at least *allow* us to be taken there—and use us in either place just as effectively, but only if our heart is in the right place.

Trusting God's Provision

Can anyone really be indifferent to one's own suffering? No, and that is not wrong. Indifference is not our charge. We are not passionless Stoics. It is not sinful to feel pain over sinful behavior towards us. The truly humble man or woman of God will feel the pain and offer it to the Lord for his use.

And since we have a God who loves us deeply and personally, we can trust him to be our career manager, our financial planner, our insurance broker. Everything belongs in his hands. We can then afford to take the humblest seat at the table with full confidence that we are where we belong. If God chooses to exalt us to the head of the table, that is his business. Wherever we sit, God will use us for his glory *if we humbly submit to him and his purposes.* God never wastes our talents. He gave them to us to be used, not to lie fallow. And he will use them in his way and in his time.

Maybe you are the person seemingly on the outer rim of the action. You may be there because that is where God needs you. God is as interested in the outer rim as the inner circle. Maybe you have gifts that are not being expressed. You may be an excellent manager, but you are riveting fenders on an assembly line. Not all of your gifts may be used right now, but you might find yourself as a manager in heaven.

The key is to commit yourself to God's provision. You may miss out on some opportunities by not seeking to exalt yourself. That is God's "problem" (of course, it is no problem at all!). He can put you anywhere he wishes if you faithfully follow him. His arm is never too short. But he may call you to be the PTA president instead of the United States President, or the homeroom mom instead of the university dean. He has a magnificent plan for every minute of your life, and he intends to use you to accomplish it—if you will let him. But if you resist his will and insist on puffing yourself up and going to the best seat at the table, if that is not where he has called you, you will miss out on his plan. You may get that for which you aimed, but not that for which you were made. And you will be the loser.

This is not to say that we should be indifferent to how others perceive us. Paul sought to be "a Greek to the Greeks and a Roman to the Romans" for the sake of the Gospel. He knew that cultural and personality issues can be distracting to others, so he sought to minimize them so that God's purposes would be accomplished. We should care about our reputations only inasmuch as they impact what other people think of God. We are God's ambassadors, and our concern should be how our behavior reflects on God.

In my world, wearing a business suit is obligatory. I could wear a cheap suit and an old tie and still meet the minimum requirement. However, my attire would be a distraction. So as to focus on the things that I am called to do, i.e. advocating for the voiceless and the defenseless in the public square, I wear a dark suit and a power tie. Yes, my vanity sometimes asserts itself, and I relish what someone may think of my clothing, but I try to quickly repent of my selfishness. I do not want my clothing to distract from my call, so I seek to be a Washingtonian to the Washingtonians.

Slaves And Partners

As slaves of Christ, we should busy ourselves with our Master's business. He cares about bringing people into a right relationship with him, promoting justice, thwarting evil, extending mercy, exalting beauty, and so on. Being outside of time, he is the Grand Strategist who can see around corners. To serve him requires that we spend time with him, listening to his Word and reflecting on its implications for our lives. The Holy Spirit is eager to walk with us through each day's challenges and guide us.

King Hezekiah was a godly ruler of Judah. When the powerful Assyrian King Sennacherib camped outside Jerusalem in preparation for battle, the city appeared doomed. Sennacherib personally insulted Israel's God as weak and ineffectual. Hezekiah responded by seeking the Lord in prayer. The Lord revealed through the prophet Isaiah that Hezekiah should not capitulate and promised that Sennacherib and his army would be repelled. Overnight, 185,000 of the Assyrian soldiers died, and Sennacherib retreated (2 Kings 19). Hezekiah could not see in advance what God would do, but he chose to trust him and follow his lead. Hezekiah acted as a humble vassal, obeying the Lord in his as yet unseen plans.

I have often seen God work the same way in my life, acting in ways beyond my reckoning or imagining to accomplish his purposes. My sole responsibility was to wait and trust. He plays the role of the master strategist, and I play the role of the weak and trusting servant.

When I was in a senior policy role in the U.S. Senate, I experienced something that was somewhat unusual in my career: I sensed God speaking to me very clearly throughout my day, in especially directive ways concerning the smallest details of my job. I was regularly prompted by the Spirit to call someone in another Senate office, or go to a particular meeting at a given time, or call a strategy meeting, and when I obeyed, I would see amazing results. I was often moved to call someone about a particular matter, and the hard-to-reach person answered the phone and gave me just the information I needed. I felt as if I were a pawn in God's hands, and he was the one actually doing my job. During that season of my life, he was the electricity and I was the extension cord. This happened for about two-and-a-half years, until I moved to another job. I have not experienced God's direction so regularly in the same way since that job.

While it is true that we are his slaves, we are also his partners. Jesus said, "I no longer call you servants, because a servant does not know his master's business. Instead, I have called
you friends, for everything that I learned from my Father I have
made known to you" (John 15:15). We are made in God's image, meaning that while we are not the same as God, we are
much like him in many respects. God is a creator, planner, and
strategist. So are we. He invites us to partner with him in King-
dom-building. Paul said that we are "God's fellow workers" (1
Cor. 3:9). We are more than just hapless pawns who channel
his Spirit. He has made us to think freely and independently, to
dream and scheme about the future. God allows himself to be
influenced by our actions. He is present in our scheming, but
he does not dictate our every thought. We are free creatures
with independent thoughts. Of course, finite beings can never
out-think an omniscient and all-powerful God. Still, he inter-
acts with us and reacts to us.

This interplay of servants and partners with Christ was
evident in my experience in the launching of an investment
group dedicated to facilitating the creation of mainstream arts
and entertainment that lifts up the good, the true, and the beautiful. While I worked in the U.S. Congress, my friend and colleague Mark Rodgers and I began reaching out to leaders in the
entertainment industry. We did this out of our conviction that
the culture is upstream from politics—meaning that politics is
primarily reflective of the soul of a nation, whereas the arts are
primarily influential in our civilizational destiny.[9] It has been
said, "Give me the songs of a nation and it matters not who
writes its laws."[10] We realized that we knew none of the cul-
ture-shapers, so we decided to begin strategic relationships
with as many as possible. We began inviting entertainers to

---

[9] I am indebted to Don Eberly for his coining the phrase "culture is upstream from politics" in an unpublished essay that was influential in shaping
my own writing in political theory. Don Eberly is a far-sighted strategist
and thinker who has a gift for thinking big and acting big. As the founder of
the National Fatherhood Initiative, two policy organizations, and the author
of many books, he is the rare combination of theoretician and builder.
[10] Whether this quote comes from Damon of Athens or the eighteenth-cen-
tury Scottish politician Andrew Fletcher is unclear. Either way, the wisdom
of the saying is clear.

have lunch with us in the Senators' dining room. We focused on the artists who either evidenced an active Christian faith or whose work reflected a love of truth, beauty, and goodness. We soon found ourselves in relationship with hundreds of media-types. At the time, we did not have specific plans for our outreach.

One thing we heard again and again from the artists was that most investors in the arts are seeking to advance a libertine social agenda. The artists were frustrated not to be able to produce more of the art that would help to renew the culture because funding for such projects was absent. We knew many people who were concerned about our nation's moral drift and who contributed to political candidates in an effort to restore ethical norms, but they overlooked the arts. Therefore, after about six years of concerted relationship-building with artists, we began the Wedgwood Circle, an angel investment network[11] that connected the artists whom we had met with the financial contributors. Our goal was to help facilitate the creation of commercially viable, mainstream arts and entertainment that lifts up the good, the true, and the beautiful and tells the truth about the world.

God was both the unseen chess master and the partner with us in the creation of the Wedgwood Circle. In one way, the Wedgwood Circle had been planned for years and years, but not by us. It was the Spirit who had been putting all the pieces in place for its creation. Yet the idea seemed to be ours. It was our idea to initiate the artist outreach, and our idea to launch the Wedgwood Circle (*www.wedgwoodcircle.com*). The exact interplay between human freedom and divine providence is mysterious. Scripture teaches both.[12] It seems that God was both silently guiding us *and* partnering with us in our efforts.

---

[11] "Angel investing" has nothing to do with God or angels, per se, but is derived from the British word for investors in theatrical productions. It is currently used to denote the investors who fund start-up businesses.

[12] The ancient controversy continues between those who believe that God ordains everything and those who believe that humans have freedom to choose. Scripture teaches both that God is active in orchestrating events in time and space and that humans have the freedom to choose to do right and wrong, moved by their own will. I believe that both are true. This is a mys-

Humility Leads To Effectiveness

"Blessed are the meek, for they will inherit the earth" (Matt. 5:5). When will this inheritance occur? Now, or when the New Earth comes at the end of the world?

I think the answer is both. Acting humbly results in effectiveness, even when our work is obscure. We make a huge impact on the world when we seek to humbly serve God and man. Ronald Reagan liked the saying, "There is no limit to what you can accomplish if you do not care who gets the credit." When we fix our eyes on the unseen and the eternal and cease worrying about ourselves and getting "our due," we accomplish so much more to eternal effect. Conversely, when we worry and fret about ourselves, we are hampered in our effectiveness.

When I was a chief of staff to a member of Congress, I resisted the attempts of a committee chairman with greater seniority than my boss to "steal" a legislative bill that our staff had developed. It was called "Dollars to the Classroom," and it entailed statutorily limiting how much money could be spent on school administration so more money could be spent for teachers and students. I was furious that this committee chairman thought he could simply take our well-crafted policy proposal without giving proper credit to my boss. After a pitched battle in which I appealed to the staff for the Speaker of the House to intervene, the committee chairman relented and did not adopt the bill as his own. Consequently, the bill did not move through Congress and died, like so many other good ideas. In my effort to protect the reputation of my Congressman boss, I thwarted the good that could have occurred. My pride stood in the way of effectiveness.

It is often said that being too heavenly-minded makes us no earthly good. Not so. Being heavenly-minded makes us more effective on the earth. The more we focus on how fleeting is our life and that our reward lies beyond the grave, the more likely we are to shape our world for good in the here and now. Jesus' call is for us to be fully *in* the world, but not *of* the world. That means we should be actively engaged in straight-

---

tery to us who are finite. God is outside time and space and yet acts within both. This is beyond our understanding.

ening out that which is twisted and wrong. In *Total Truth*, author Nancy Pearcey writes,

> In Genesis, God gives what we might call the first job description: "Be fruitful and multiply and fill the earth and subdue it." The first phrase, "be fruitful and multiply" means to develop the social world: build families, churches, schools, cities, governments, laws. The second phrase, "subdue the earth," means to harness the natural world: plant crops, build bridges, design computers, compose music. This passage is sometimes called the Cultural Mandate because it tells us that our original purpose was to create cultures, build civilizations—nothing less (47).[13]

God cares not just about saving souls, though he certainly cares about that. He also wants us to care for the poor and the powerless, the orphan and the widow. We do so not just so they will be saved, but because it is right to do. Our job is to do what he has called us to do.

For several years, I volunteered at a soup kitchen serving the homeless. I have no idea if anyone came to Christ because of my service. But if I could have known in advance that no one would come to faith, it was still right and good for me to serve there.

Jesus accomplished his most important task, the crucifixion—the task for which he principally became incarnate—through humility. Paul writes in Col. 2:15, "And having disarmed the powers and authorities, he made a public spectacle of them, triumphing over them by the cross." Jesus' enemies, and especially the Enemy[14], thought they were making a public

---

[13] Pearcey is a brilliant author and thinker—one of the smartest people I know. I have learned so much from her important writing.

[14] I suspect Satan did not realize what Jesus was accomplishing through the cross. He moved his minions to crucify Christ because he thought it was a victory for him. There are some people who believe, with some scriptural foundation, that Satan did not want Jesus to be crucified. Jesus rebuked Satan when Peter was trying to persuade Jesus not to go to Jerusalem and to be killed. Yet the crowd calling for his crucifixion seemed to be moved by evil spirits, not merely human spirits. Not being omniscient, perhaps Satan was

spectacle *of him* by crucifying him. Yet it was through this act of public humiliation that Jesus robbed Evil of its power. I love the thought that in the demonic chanting of the mob, "Crucify him! Crucify him!" God's plan of salvation was unfolding. What appeared to the human eye as the ultimate defeat was actually the ultimate triumph. Through the pain, humiliation, and death at the cross, death lost its power and life was victorious.

God's ways are upside down from our natural inclinations. With God, the way up is the way down. The way to be strong is to be weak in our natural selves. Paul writes of his own frailties, presumably a physical limitation that he called his "thorn in the flesh, a messenger of Satan, to torment" that God used for Paul's benefit. Despite his pleas to have it taken away, the Lord replied, "My grace is sufficient for you, for my power is made perfect in weakness." Paul goes on to write, "Therefore I will boast all the more gladly about my weaknesses, so that Christ's power may rest on me. That is why, for Christ's sake, I delight in weaknesses, in insults, in hardships, in persecutions, in difficulties. For when I am weak, then I am strong" (2 Cor. 12:9-10). The very thing that seems to be a burden can be a conduit through which God brings glory to himself and improves us. Still, this is so only when we submit to God and his ways. If we "kick against the goads" and curse our lot in life, we may miss the opportunity to let God refine us and use whatever Satan dishes us to glorify God. In "making peace with reality"[15] and letting God have his way in the midst of adversity, we unlock the power of God to thwart evil and turn it to good. Satan can never checkmate God.

My wife, Dana, is chronically ill. Three months after our wedding, her health spiraled downward. At first we thought it was just a back problem, but after visiting scores of doctors over three years, we finally received the diagnosis of fibromyalgia, a sometimes debilitating muscle condition that has kept her in continual and often excruciating pain and fatigue for

---

divided, both wanting Jesus to be crucified and yet fearing that the crucifixion would defeat him.

[15] A phrase given to us by Virginia Watson, a godly woman who mentors my wife.

more than twenty-four years. Her life's dreams were to use her prodigious intellect and strong ambition to empower the poor in developing countries, write books, get a Ph.D., and travel. Instead, her ambitions have been thwarted by the need to be in bed most of the day. Initially, she struggled with God's purpose in her illness and questioned his goodness. But she soon realized that she was called to trust God, though she could not and still cannot see God's plan for her illness. We have had to make many sacrifices to accommodate her illness, including hiring a full-time in-home nanny to care for our children.

Last year, she gave this testimony at our church:

> I was asked to share some of my personal spiritual journey with you as a testimony to God's mercy and grace. My main point is best stated through Rom. 8:28: "And we know that in all things God works for the good of those who love him, who have been called according to his purpose."

> For the past twenty-three years, I have suffered from fibromyalgia (a chronic and incurable neurological disease that results in pain, fatigue, and weakness). I don't have "good" days and "bad" days—I have bad days and worse days. I haven't had one pain-free day in twenty-three years. I spend much of my day in bed. I am blessed with an extremely loving, helpful, and compassionate husband, as well as with a full-time nanny who functions as my "arms and legs" to manage a family of five.

> Prior to my illness, I was an A-type, active, highly motivated, and optimistic person with a strong sense of purpose, meaning, and faith in God. At the onset of my illness, the impact of daily pain, loss of my physical abilities, and shattering of dreams of "what could have been" all translated into a spiritual crisis. God became distant, untouchable, and disinterested in my life. When I approached Scriptures, the passages about God's wrath, anger and judgment seemed very real to me. I

couldn't relate to Scriptures and sermons dealing with God's tender care of his children. The illness impacted every aspect of my life. It shattered hopes and dreams I have as a mother and wife, as a professional in the work world, and severely limited my ability to do even the most basic tasks of daily living. So I turned to questioning who God really is.

I asked if God exists: I rejected atheism as utterly incompatible with all I see in the world. As far as I am concerned, all of nature cries out "God is our maker."

Then I asked if God was all-powerful and just. And, yes, I again concluded he is.

So I questioned whether God is good. This took me a bit longer to resolve. But, I realized this question was really just my way of "shaking my fist" at God and telling him I didn't trust him. So, yes, I can affirm that God is good and that his gift of life on this earth is good.

I then struggled with reasons for my illness: Was it punishment for my past sins, God's lack of concern for me, my lack of faith? Admittedly, my response to chronic illness has not always been admirable, and it exposed the depth of my spiritual poverty. But as far as I know, I have confessed all known sin and received His full forgiveness. So again, I came to the conclusion that God loves and has a purpose for each and every one of us. Phil. 2:13 says, "for it is God who works in you to will and to act in order to fulfill his good purpose." Eph. 2:10 says, "For we are God's handiwork, created in Christ Jesus to do good works, which God prepared in advance for us to do." What I had to learn was that I was created to do His good works and to fulfill His good purpose. God used my illness to shatter my agenda for my life and the good works I thought I was meant to do, and instead replaced it with His agenda.

Over time, God has used this experience to mature my faith, expose my utter dependence on Him, and guide me to a less self-oriented worldview. I now accept my illness as something God allows in my life, my daily "cross to bear," as a means of refining and perfecting my faith. I don't doubt He could heal me in an instant. But thus far, He has chosen not to. Hence, as a servant of God and daughter of the King, my role is to trust and obey, to wait on Him for strength, and to reaffirm His goodness and power.

Heb. 12:11 says "No discipline seems pleasant at the time, but painful. Later on, however, it produces a harvest of righteousness and peace for those who have been trained by it." God doesn't delight in our suffering and pain, but because of the Fall, disease, pain, suffering, and loss came into the world. God can and will use it for our good, IF we let him.

I urge you to let God use your pain—your daily cross, whatever it is—as a means of burning off your warped and wrong actions and attitudes, and replacing them with a humble and sincere faith that is utterly dependent on him. And I finish by reaffirming this hope: Rom. 8:18 says, "our present sufferings are not worth comparing with the glory that will be revealed in us."

Amen. I am married to an amazing woman. The bottom line is that when we do what we have been called to do, in things big and small, God uses us and prospers our work, even when we cannot see his purposes. We become like the good seed in Jesus' parable, producing "a crop, yielding a hundred, sixty or thirty times what was sown" (Matt. 13:23). God is the Master Strategist. He will use us powerfully when we humbly submit to him and his ways. The earth will be vastly different because of us, and we will, in a sense, inherit the earth on this side of heaven by the effectiveness of our service.

Seeing The Unseen

Having the faith to do the things God has called us to do is made more plausible by training our eyes to see the eternal, though still invisible, things. We thus become more interested in harvesting eternal consequences in the temporal world.

Jesus said, "Do not store up for yourselves treasures on earth, where moth and rust destroy, and where thieves break in and steal. But store up for yourselves treasures in heaven, where moth and rust do not destroy, and where thieves do not break in and steal. For where your treasure is, there your heart will be also" (Matt. 6:19-21). How else can you store up heavenly treasure than by correctly spending your earthly treasure? Eternal rewards require temporal actions. A greater focus on heaven entails more purposeful and effective action on earth. When we neglect our temporal responsibilities, we risk harvesting eternal consequences. Falsely religious people are out of touch with this world's problems. They would do well to read Jesus' parable of the sheep and the goats and tremble as they hear God's awful words of eternal damnation for those who neglect others' needs on earth.

Fixing our eyes on the unseen as Paul commands us to do requires effort. The visible seems so real, as if that is all that is. In C. S. Lewis' *The Screwtape Letters,* the demon Screwtape writes to his nephew, a junior demon, about one of his achievements in coaxing humans to deny the eternal implications of the visible. Of humankind, he writes:

> Remember, he is not, like you, a pure spirit. Never having been a human (Oh that abominable advantage of the Enemy's!) you do not realize how enslaved they are to the pressure of the ordinary. I once had a patient, a sound atheist, who used to read in the British Museum. One day, as he sat reading, I saw a train of thought in his mind beginning to go the wrong way. The Enemy, of course, was at his elbow in a moment. Before I knew

where I was I saw my twenty years' work beginning to totter. If I had lost my head and begun to attempt a defense by argument I should have been undone. But I was not such a fool. I struck instantly at the part of the man which I had best under my control and suggested that it was just about time he had some lunch. The Enemy presumably made the counter-suggestion (you know how one can never *quite* overhear what He says to them?) that this was more important than lunch. At least I think that must have been His line for when I said "Quite. In fact much *too* important to tackle it the end of a morning," the patient brightened up considerably; and by the time I had added "Much better come back after lunch and go into it with a fresh mind," he was already half way to the door. Once he was in the street the battle was won. I showed him a newsboy shouting the midday paper, and a No. 73 bus going past, and before he reached the bottom of the steps I had got into him an unalterable conviction that, whatever odd ideas might come into a man's head when he was shut up alone with his books, a healthy dose of "real life" (by which he meant the bus and the newsboy) was enough to show him that all "that sort of thing" just couldn't be true. He knew he'd had a narrow escape and in later years was fond of talking about "that inarticulate sense for actuality which is our ultimate safeguard against the aberrations of mere logic." He is now safe in Our Father's house. (22-23)

Seeing the invisible requires sustained attention to the eternal. I know of no other way to do this than regularly reading the Bible and praying. For me, daily devotions (or quiet time, or a walk with God, or whatever you call it) are indispensable to seeing the eternal in the temporal. Bible memorization is another great tool.[16] It is not just for kids. Committing to

---

[16] See the appendix for a compendium of verses I have memorized, enrich my thought life, and act as a "lamp to my feet." You may find other verses more meaningful, but these verses speak loudly to my sinful tendencies,

memory scriptural passages helps us hear God in the daily press of life. Another helpful tool is meditating on Scripture. We benefit when we spend a prolonged period of time thinking deeply about a few verses, pondering the author's word choices, the context of the verse, and the implications for our lives. Meditation forces us to actively engage the Word and makes it "living and active" (Heb. 4:13) instead of a dead letter.

Being a committed member of a local church is also essential. In the Church, we have fellowship with other sinners who are striving for righteousness. We can sharpen one another as iron sharpens iron, reminding one another of the "really real things," things that the world sees as foolish fairytales. It is as we see real faith—warts and all—lived out among our brothers and sisters that seeing the invisible becomes more sensible. In the lyrics of the Christian musician Steve Taylor (harkening back to Flannery O'Connor and Augustine), "it is harder to believe than not to." It requires constant vigilance to believe that this world is not the end of the story. The Church, as expressed in the fallen men and women who make up the local congregation, is indispensable in that fight to remember that the No. 73 bus is not all there is.

Expressions Of Pride

Pride can be hidden. Since pride is a disposition, acts that seem proud may be done by a humble person, and acts that seem humble may be done by a proud person. God sees the heart and knows the motivation. Pride is all about our motivation.

I have sometimes left a social event reflecting back on my behavior, wondering whether I had *appeared* proud, only to be brought up short by the Holy Spirit who showed me that I had been seeking to exalt myself while trying to conceal my pride. So whether I *appeared* proud was of minor significance. My concern about how I appeared was also a symptom of my pride. We should care about appearances only to the extent it reflects on our witness. The problem was that I had been proud,

---

challenge me to die to self, and comfort me in the hope of salvation beyond the grave.

seeking to puff myself up, albeit sometimes artfully. God opposes "those who are proud in their inmost thoughts" (Luke 1:51). He wants a deep and genuine humility, not one that is skin-deep.

I am skilled at making smooth transitions to topics which will likely lead to some apparently casual mention of my accomplishments. Or I have often asked questions that would inevitably lead to counter questions that would reveal my accomplishments. I have asked about others' professions so they would ask me about mine, giving me an opportunity to boast about my position. It looks so innocent, but it is so self-serving. I am quite good at disguising my pride. In fact, few people identify pride as my chief sin. But I know better, and so does God. Many proud people are adept at concealing their true motivations and may be known for their humility.

Only the Holy Spirit can reveal the thoughts and attitudes of our hearts. On the one hand, over-analyzing the complexity of our motives can drive us crazy. On the other hand, careful self-examination of our motivations is integral to discipleship. Introspection should be done in the context of the grace that covers all of our sins. Yet it should be done. Plato said the unexamined life is not worth living. For the follower of Christ, self-examination is a necessary part of our sanctification.

Self-Righteousness

Perhaps the most insidious expression of pride is self-righteousness. Ironically, people who strive to do the right thing are often the most prone to self-righteousness. Some forms of pride may be only skin-deep, e.g. boasting and bravado, which may be sorry attempts to mask deep feelings of inadequacy. Self-righteousness is the worst expression of pride, because its roots are planted deep in the soul. It is hideous to admire ourselves, overlooking our sins and weaknesses, and ignoring how many of our righteous acts are due to the good example of others.

In Luke 18, Jesus tells a story about the insidious nature of pride in those who strive for righteousness:

To some who were confident of their own right-eousness and looked down on everybody else, Jesus told this parable: "Two men went up to the temple to pray, one a Pharisee and the other a tax collector. The Pharisee stood up and prayed about himself: 'God, I thank you that I am not like other men—robbers, evil-doers, adulterers—or even like this tax collector. I fast twice a week and give a tenth of all I get.'

"But the tax collector stood at a distance. He would not even look up to heaven, but beat his breast and said, 'God, have mercy on me, a sinner.'

"I tell you that this man, rather than the other, went home justified before God. For everyone who exalts himself will be humbled, and he who humbles himself will be exalted" (vv. 9-14).

Boasting

The French philosopher and mathematician Blaise Pascal wrote, "Vanity is so deeply rooted in a man's heart, that a sol-dier, a criminal, a cook, or a porter will boast and expect to have admirers. Even philosophers want them. Those who write against such will themselves want to enjoy the prestige of having so written. . . ."(60).[17] Pride, like an onion, has many layers.

With the help of my truly humble wife, I have learned to identify variants of pride. Boasting is one obvious example as we seek to inflate our accomplishments and downplay God's role and the roles of others. But when is it appropriate to share our accomplishments? In job interviews, certainly. With family. With potential clients. One handy rule of thumb is the same as that for sharing classified information: do other people *need to know* or will they benefit by knowing about our accom-plishments? I want my surgeon to tell me if she is board-certi-fied and has successfully performed similar surgeries. I want my children to tell me about the accolades they receive from their teachers. I want my best friend to share with me the good

---

[17] To my chagrin, as I write this chapter on humility I recognize my same vain hope to be admired. I repent of my pride again and again.

performance review he received from his boss. In contrast, my neighbors do not need to know what bonus I received or what my college GPA was.

One added benefit of sharing our triumphs on a need-to-know basis is that when favorable information about us becomes known *without* our boasting, it inspires less jealousy in others and more genuine admiration. I know how I react to people who boast about their admirable achievements: with a mixture of admiration and disrespect—admiration for what they have accomplished, but disapproval of their boasting. In contrast, when I learn that an acquaintance speaks four languages and graduated from Harvard, and that she had many opportunities to share this information with me but did not, I am doubly impressed.

My friend David McIntosh is a former member of Congress who ran for governor of Indiana and who founded a very successful national legal organization. His accomplishments are impressive. Yet what most impresses me about him is that he never speaks of his accomplishments unless specifically asked about them, and even then he does so without a hint of boasting. He volunteers as a playground monitor at his children's school once a week, and few of the teachers and students know anything about his biography. I am inspired by his humility more than by his accomplishments, because he has ample reasons to boast yet he does not. I look to him as a role model. Given the strong human propensity to jealousy, my friend is protected by his humility, because he is less likely to become a target for destruction by those who might otherwise want to take him down a notch.

Sometimes whether or not we should share our accomplishments with someone else is a close call. What constitutes boasting is not always obvious. In those situations, it is best to err on the side of not sharing the information. "God opposes the proud but gives grace to the humble" (1 Pet. 5:5). God can lift you up in his own time, if that is his will. But you do not want him to oppose you. It is better to let potential opportunities pass you by than to fall into sin.

False Humility

A second expression of pride is false humility. Sometimes we deny our accomplishments with the specific aim of soliciting praise. False humility is pride in disguise, because its aim is just as pernicious as boasting.

When the singer with a beautiful voice who knows she has a good voice is praised for her singing and she responds, "Oh no, my voice is not good at all!" she has just denied the truth. Genuine humility is never about denying truth, but living in truth. Jesus said, "But whoever lives by the truth comes into the light, so that it may be seen plainly that what he has done *has been done through God*" (John 3:21, emphasis added). Our accomplishments are "done through God." The singer would have been more honest to have said, "Thank you so much for your encouraging words," and perhaps adding, "I am grateful for what God has given me"—at very least in her heart, if not in her words. Likewise, when the computer programmer is praised for the software he wrote, he may rightly and humbly say, "I am so glad you find it helpful." Such responses are true, and God loves truth. We are called to be humble because it reflects the right and true order of the universe. Denying our talents is not true.

Focusing On What Others Think of Us

Another sign of pride is focusing on what other people think of us. We do not belong to other people, but to God. Author Os Guinness says that we should play to "an audience of one," not to the crowd. Whether we are happy or unhappy about what others think of us is beside the point. Our chief aim should be to please God in all things. In Gal. 1:10, Paul writes, "Am I now trying to win the approval of men, or of God? Or am I trying to please men? If I were still trying to please men, I would not be a servant of Christ."

It is hard not to think about what others think of us. It comes to mind all day long. When you wear an especially attractive piece of clothing that complements your eyes, when you play your musical instrument well, when you freeze up during a public speech, when you tell a joke that bombs—our thoughts come back again and again to what others think of us, good or bad. Most of us are wired that way. The question is what we do with those thoughts? Do we nurture them, relishing the admiration or hating the opprobrium we are receiving? The more we dwell on such thoughts, the more we care about whether we win the approval of men. It takes self-discipline and practice not to dwell on such thoughts, quickly turning our thoughts to what God thinks of our behavior and whether we are serving our neighbors.

C. S. Lewis wrote in *Mere Christianity*, "True humility is not thinking less of yourself, but thinking of yourself less." I do not believe that is entirely correct. Thinking about ourselves and our responsibilities is what we should do. The question is whether our self-analysis rightly focuses on what we are made to be and do.

Humility Is Not Low Self-Esteem

Some people may genuinely not recognize the gifts God has given to them. They esteem themselves and their talents less than are warranted. Here again, denying the truth about what God has done for us may be a form of rebellion against God. God made humans in his image and endowed us with gifts and talents. If we are ignorant of this truth, our poor self-esteem is rooted in ignorance. It may also be that we are aware of what God says about us and our gifts, but we have trouble accepting this truth. People with low self-esteem should *choose* to believe what God and others say about their talents, accepting both their innate human dignity and the particular gifts they possess, giving thanks to God for what they have been given. We do not please the Lord if we deny our gifts.

Pride is deadly and hard to shake in whatever form it takes. Dana Gioia's poem the "The Seven Deadly Sins" aptly captures the tenacity of pride that is the hardest sin to shake:

> Forget about the other six, says Pride.
> They're only using you.
> Admittedly, Lust is a looker,

but you can do better.

And why do they keep bringing us
to this cheesy dive?
The food's so bad that even Gluttony
can't finish his meal.

Notice how Avarice
keeps refilling his glass
whenever he thinks we're not looking,
while Envy eyes your plate.

Hell, we're not even done, and Anger
is already arguing about the bill.
I'm the only one who
ever leaves a decent tip.

Let them all go, the losers!
It's a relief to see Sloth's
fat ass go out the door.
But stick around. I have a story

that not everyone appreciates –
about the special satisfaction
of staying on board as the last
grubby lifeboat pushes away.

The Joy Of Making Ourselves Nothing

Perhaps the most surprising thing about humbling ourselves is
the joy that it produces in us. As we anticipate being humbled,
we are terrified. No one enjoys self-mortification. Dying to
ourselves goes against our instincts.

Yet as we give it all over to the Lord and resolve to serve
him and others, we find that we get ourselves back again, and
we find a deep joy. The joy comes because our Master is so
good, so kind, and so loving. He calls us to carry our cross so
we can make it to the resurrection. Our death is the necessary
predicate to living the life God has designed for us. Humbling

ourselves eventually lifts us up. "Humble yourselves, therefore, under God's mighty hand that he may lift you up *in due time*" (1 Pet. 5:6, emphasis added).

We were made to serve God and one another. Service is not just for those with the "gift of service." It was for Jesus, and it is for us. The joy that comes from service is incomparable—and far greater than the fleeting pleasure that comes from being served. By serving, we change the world, and we find significance. Being served grows stale.

In *The Gorgias*, Socrates makes the case that it is better to be unjustly tortured than to torture unjustly. He understood that a right ordered soul is happiest, and cruelty to others damages our essential being. In contrast, being tortured does not necessarily diminish our joy. Betsy Ten Boom (sister of author Corrie Ten Boom) was more joyful as a concentration camp prisoner than her guards who tormented her. The same equation is true of service. As created beings even before sin entered the world, we were given the mandate to tend the garden, thereby serving God and his creation.

Our self-indulgent culture tells us to "obey our thirst" (this awful and deceptive slogan was coined in Sprite commercials). It sounds tempting, but it is a death trap—like drinking salt water on a life raft at sea. We quickly grow weary of feeding our insatiable desires. When we deny our thirst and seek to please God by satisfying others' thirst, our thirst is sated. We become part of something bigger than ourselves in serving God. We were not made to be the center of the universe, no matter how much we may think that sounds good. Lucifer was jealous of God receiving all of the glory in heaven. He preferred to be served. His insatiable desire to be served doomed him. Likewise, we are created beings made to serve the Creator. We find our true joy in glorifying God, which necessarily entails service. That is where we will find our "sweet spot."

But is it wrong to find joy in being served? After all, we are called to serve one another, and Jesus himself came to serve us. Being served out of love is affirming and gratifying. It builds us up and makes us feel valued and loved. In a world without sin, we would all continually think of ways to serve others, so we would be both servant and served, finding joy in both. I expect heaven will be like that. It also requires a measure of humility to allow ourselves to be served by others, receiving that service gracefully and joyfully. Some people are too proud to be served by others, like those who refuse to ask for or accept help during an illness or crisis because their pride tells them to go it alone. I have seen this mentality at a soup kitchen in some homeless people acting demanding and ungrateful, trying to recover a sense of dignity they feel is lost in being served. Sometimes humbling ourselves requires that we seek and accept the service of others.

When service is our aim, we will find joy. It is like seeking happiness: seek it first, and it will prove elusive. Seek to be righteous, and happiness will be present in far greater measure. I have found this to be true in my life. When I give my time to serving others' needs, I feel satisfied. We were made to work, create, and build. In this, we are made in the image of God, who is busy creating. We rest so we can work, rather than work so we can rest. The lyrics of the old song, "Everybody's working for the weekend," point us in the wrong direction. To the extent that we see work as an obstacle to recreation, we will miss the good that God intends for us. Work is not a result of sin, but part of God's original creation. Work became toilsome and "thorny" as a consequence of the fall. In heaven, our work will be free from sin and wholly fulfilling.

Summary

Humility brings health to our souls because it brings us into the light of truth and reality. Pride leads to deception, illusion, and ultimately death. The proud man will not humble himself before God to say "thy will be done," but insists that "my will be done." God freely allows us to choose not to follow him, but we reap what we have sown to our eternal damnation. Humility runs counter to our naturally sinful instincts. It requires wisdom and courage to lay down our self-centered lives and become servants to God and our fellow man. But the rewards we reap far outstrip the costs.

In *Rediscovering Holiness,* J.I. Packer captures the essence of following Jesus:

> We grow up in Christ by growing *down* into lowliness... off-loading our fantasies of omnicompetence, we start trying to be trustful, obedient, dependent, patient and willing in our relationship to God. We give up our dreams of being greatly admired for doing wonderfully well. We begin teaching ourselves unemotionally and matter-of-factly to recognize that we are not likely ever to appear, or actually to be, much of a success by the world's standards. We bow to events that rub our noses in the reality of our own weaknesses, and we look to God for strength quietly to cope. . . . It is impossible at the same time to give the impression both that I am a great Christian and that Jesus Christ is a great Master. So the Christian will practice curling up small, as it were, so that in and through him or her the savior may show himself great. That is what I mean by growing downward (120-121).

My father is a humble man. He genuinely thinks he is not humble, but that is only because he fights his own pride and is quick to acknowledge it. When I was a boy, my father had a placard fixed to the wall in front of his desk, which read, "The true test of a servant is whether I can act like one when I am being treated like one." A good measure, that.

3

Living in Light of Your Death

*"As for man, his days are like grass, he flourishes like a
flower of the field; the wind blows over it and it is gone,
and its place remembers it no more."*
Psalm 103:15-16

*"In this world nothing can be said to be certain,
except death and taxes."*
Benjamin Franklin

Y ou are going to die. Your loved ones will die. Your
enemies will die. Of this, we can be sure.
The satirical newspaper *The Onion* ran a story under-
scoring this grim reality:

> World Health Organization officials expressed dis-
> appointment Monday at the group's finding that, despite
> the enormous efforts of doctors, rescue workers and
> other medical professionals worldwide, the global death
> rate remains constant at 100 percent.
>
> Death, a metabolic affliction causing total shut-
> down of all life functions, has long been considered
> humanity's number one health concern. Responsible for
> 100 percent of all recorded fatalities worldwide, the
> condition has no cure.
>
> "I was really hoping, what with all those new radi-
> ology treatments, rescue helicopters, aerobics TV
> shows and what have you, that we might at least make a
> dent in it this year," WHO Director General Dr. Gernst
> Bladt said.

"Unfortunately, it would appear that the death rate remains constant and total, as it has inviolably since the dawn of time."

Many are suggesting that the high mortality rate represents a massive failure on the part of the planet's health care workers.

The story is funny, but its humor stems partly from the fact that our society tries to hide the reality that we will all die, sooner or later. We ask whether a sick person "is going to die?" when we really mean "is he going to die *soon?*" We talk about friends who have "departed," "left," "passed on," "have been lost," but we rarely use the d-word. In a way, these words are truer than "death," because every human will continue to exist in eternity, either in heaven or hell. But they tend to conceal as much as they reveal, hiding the fact that our earthly life is over. Even many Christians who have the hope of eternal life avoid using the word. Somehow, speaking of death seems too stark and a bit impolite.

It is not just our language that avoids death, but our actions, too. Most people will have a funeral some day, but how many people plan for their own? What about their burial wishes? Life insurance for those they leave behind? A will? A letter to loved ones? We plan for a host of things that may never happen like car accidents, floods, and fires, but we often fail to plan for the one thing that is certain.[18] We prefer to avoid the inevitable and focus on the contingent.

In debates surrounding health care policy, we discuss the cost-savings that come from preventive health care as if people who do not get intermediate illnesses will not eventually get a terminal illness. In fact, the longer we live, the more we will utilize health care, potentially facing more chronic illnesses like Alzheimer's and dementia. We rightly celebrate cancer

---

[18] We will die, assuming the rapture does not take us first. But no one knows when that will happen. Though some people are confident that Christ's return is imminent, Christians throughout the ages have thought the same thing. Christ may not return for thousands of years. Since this is in God's keeping, we should plan for our own deaths.

survivors, but do we remember they will eventually die of something else? Even Lazarus eventually died after Jesus had raised him from the dead. We cannot cheat death.

Many of us are like children who think we can be safe by hiding under the covers. Death will come, and we are foolish not to actively prepare for it.

Fear of Death

Why do we tend to hide from our death? What do we gain from concealing it? Is it a sign of an unhealthy interest in morbidity to openly talk about death? Or does it bring to light a harsh reality that should help to rightly frame our lives?

There are many reasons we may avoid talking about death. One is the aversion to pain that so often accompanies death. Seeking to avoid pain is a healthy and natural impulse implanted in us by God. God has not created us to seek pain for its own sake. Dying is often complicated and messy. It involves tubes, needles, respirators, blood, and difficult medical decisions. Who wants to contemplate the final moments of a fatal car accident, stroke, aneurysm, heart attack, or asphyxiation? We would prefer to peacefully die in our sleep, free of pain and anxiety. Unfortunately, few of us are so fortunate.

Many people fear not just the process of dying, but death itself. They do not share the security that Christ brought to "free those who all their lives were held in slavery by their fear of death" (Heb. 2:15). This fear stems from different causes.

For some people who do not believe in an afterlife, their reluctance to openly talk about death stems from their fear of annihilation. Although they believe death involves non-being devoid of any emotions, death's approach and the impending extinguishment of all thought, movement, and sensation goes against our instinct to live. It is normal to cling to life. Those who willingly commit suicide often instinctively seek to save themselves once they have made the final decision. I know an atheist who hates to talk about his death. Far from it being a neutral or natural phenomenon, the thought of ceasing to exist terrifies him. "He has also set eternity in the hearts of men" (Eccles. 3:11). We are made eternal beings with longings for the eternal. Being content with annihilation denies our deepest longings. For those who believe nothing awaits them after death, fear is a rational response.

For others, fear of the unknown hangs over one's death. They do not know if they will be annihilated, go to heaven, hell, or purgatory, be absorbed into a universal soul, or be reincarnated. The uncertainty is frightening. Think of the fear of awaiting a grade on a test that will decide whether we graduate or not, then multiply it to encompass our entire lives. Not knowing is scary.

There is also the fear of loss. Loss was not part of the original creation but came from the fall. Losing good things is difficult. The first part of our lives is usually about accumulating diplomas, credentials, friends, a spouse, children, homes, cars, sailboats, stature, and reputation. The last part of a typical lifespan is usually about losing all of these things, making old age a steady battle with loss.

My parents once lived in a comfortable home with a decent-sized yard and two cars. As they aged, they steadily downsized, eventually renting a two-bedroom condominium and owning just one car. Their friends began dying off one-by-one, leading my mother to believe that cancer had become an epidemic. Then my mother died, leaving my dad alone. Some day, he too will die, and I will be the "older generation."

In fact, our happiness is closely associated with *not* losing things. Think of two men living next door to one another in one-bedroom shacks. One man is very happy with his home because he had grown up as a homeless orphan, and by hard work and thrift, he managed to scrape together enough money to buy the shack to keep him warm and dry. The other man is depressed and angry. He had been a wealthy businessman who lost his health and his ability to work, was deserted by his wife and friends, and was forced to leave his mansion to live in relative poverty. Each man shares the same lot in life, but one has gained much and the other has lost much—making all the difference in their respective emotional states.

Jesus wept when he lost his friend Lazarus. Though Jesus knew with certainty he would see his friend again very soon and that his friend was in heaven without suffering or sin, Jesus still grieved. He knew the pain of losing a friend here and now, and he knew that this loss was contrary to his original creation. Whereas Jesus was sad without being fearful, we who are sinful often combine fear with our sadness.[19]

My mother died on New Year's Eve day in 2011. She had collapsed in my arms with a sudden heart attack the night before and died with my father, my sister, and me at her side sixteen hours later in the hospital. I wept when Mom died, not because we had left anything unsaid, but because death feels so wrong. I cried many more times in the ensuing days, not with hopeless sorrow, but with sorrow nonetheless, and a deep understanding that death is not the way it is supposed to be.

We may fear for the loved ones whom we would leave behind, perhaps young children, elderly parents, or a needy spouse. Our death may bring hardship to others. Paul said he preferred to remain alive for the sake of those who had not yet heard the gospel, though he preferred to die for his personal gain of being with Christ and free from the effects of the fall (Phil. 1). Our fear may be less about our personal well-being during and after death than about the temporal consequences of our death for those who remain. This fear is perhaps the most laudable, though it still betrays a lack of trust in God, who cares more for our loved ones than we ever could.

Some people fear the hell to which they are headed. Although few in number (just six percent of Americans think they are going to hell[20]), these people are right to fear hell. Hell is the absence of God, and we were made to live *with* God. Jesus often warned his hearers of hell's torments, describing it as a place of extreme pain and suffering. In our psycho-therapeutic society, we tend to eschew the fear of hell as a reason to become a follower of Christ, preferring instead to attract people by the benefits of discipleship. We think that fear is an invalid motivator and avoid talking about hell lest people follow God

---

[19] Yet we are commanded not to fear—not because we can know that fearsome things may not befall us, but because our ultimate confidence should be in God from whose love we will never be separated.

[20] Gallup poll, 2004. Seventy percent of Americans believe in hell, and eighty-one percent believe in heaven.

for less than noble reasons. Yet fear can be a very healthy incentive to set us on the right path.

Some mainline denominations have abandoned the doctrine of hell, believing it to be inconsistent with a loving God. Many hold to universalism, the belief that everyone will go to heaven. Those churches are steadily losing members year by year, since it can be much more fun to belong to a country club if church attendance is just about seeking fellowship and not about learning how to make it to heaven. With so little at stake, these churches will someday be tossed on the ash heap of history.

During my adolescent rebellion, I was terrified of dying. My fear was a healthy spur to eventually move me to repentance. A fear of fire, tornados, avalanches, wild predators, violent crime, and a host of other things can produce very healthy responses in our lives. Nor should we look askance at the fear of hell.

Then there is the fear of heaven—or at least the anticipated tedium of heaven. Many people expect heaven to be a dull place of endless praise choruses and little activity. The adventure of this life, some believe, will be replaced by an eternity of boredom. This perspective is true not just for non-Christians whose views of heaven are shaped by Hollywood, but by many Christians. Many of us share cartoonist Gary Larson's view of heaven when he sketched a bored man clothed in white and sitting on a cloud, saying, "Wish I'd brought a magazine."

Author and preacher George MacDonald wrote,

> Children fear heaven, because of the dismal notions the unchildlike give them of it, who, without imagination, receive unquestioning what others, as void of imagination as themselves, represent concerning it. . . . But would that none presumed to teach the little ones what they know nothing of themselves! . . . What boy, however fain to be a disciple of Christ and a child of God, would prefer a sermon to his glorious kite, that divinest of toys, with God himself for his playmate, in the blue wind that tossed it hither and thither in the golden void! He might be ready to part with kite and wind and sun,

and go down to the grave for his brothers—but surely not that they might be admitted to an everlasting prayer-meeting! For my own part, I rejoice to think that there will be neither church nor chapel in the high countries; yea, that there will be nothing there called religion, and no law but the perfect law of liberty. For how should there be law or religion where every throb of the heart says God! where every song-throat is eager with thanksgiving! where such a tumult of glad waters is for ever bursting from beneath the throne of God, the tears of the gladness of the universe! Religion? Where will be the room for it, when the essence of every thought must be God? Law? What room will there be for law, when everything upon which law could lay a "shalt not" will be too loathsome to think of? What room for honesty, where love fills full the law to over-flowing—where a man would rather drop sheer into the abyss, than wrong his neighbor one hair's-breadth? (409-410)

Randy Alcorn, author of the book *Heaven*, has found that this negative view of heaven leaves many Christians unexcited about what truly awaits us, secretly thinking what we have now is better. Some Christians are sad when other Christians have died before getting married, or graduating, or seeing the Grand Canyon or their children marry—as if heaven does not hold incomparably greater joys for them. It makes sense to be sad for ourselves when loved ones die. But to see death as bad for the Christian who dies flies in the face of the Bible's promises. "Precious in the sight of the LORD is the death of his saints" (Ps. 116:15). Death is sad for those who remain, but not for the Christian whose prize has been won.

I long to be with God, and I look forward to my own death (though not the pain that will likely accompany it). Maybe I will feel differently when I am actually facing my imminent death, but since I gave my life to the Lord in 1980, I have often muttered to myself the words, "I can't wait until I'm done." Life is difficult, and I am so sinful. I weary of struggling with my sin, I worry about ways I could mess up my life, and I do hate seeing sin ravage others. At this writing, I am fifty years old, and the likelihood that I am now closer to heaven than to my birth thrills me.

I am not a morose person. In fact, I suspect I am one of the happiest people alive, whether because I am blessed with good genes or an abundance of rich blessings. I think it would be difficult to be happier than I am. So my longing for death is not because I am depressed. It is because I yearn to be with Jesus face-to-face. I have often imagined that I will fall at his feet in worship upon seeing him, and then he will lift up my face and embrace me. However it happens, I want to finish well the race marked out for me, and I long to hear the words, "Well done, good and faithful servant! You have been faithful with a few things; I will put you in charge of many things. Come and share your master's happiness!" (Matt. 25:21).

To Die is Gain

To have a right view of death, the first thing to straighten out is that Christians will be infinitely happier after we die, no matter how good our lives are now. Fearing an eternity of boredom would be understandable if that is what awaits us. We were made to live full lives here in the shadowlands of sin and sickness, but perfectly full and far more vibrant lives in heaven. Paul said, "For to me, to live is Christ and to die is gain" (Phil. 1:21). The best is yet to come.

Earth holds many joys for us, but it is still not the way it is supposed to be. Sin infects and twists everything, at least in part. Even the best relationship, the most beautiful vista, or the best food is tainted by sin. Sometimes the effects of the fall are readily apparent, as in a drug-infested ghetto, in a cancer ward, or in a divorce court. The sense that things are not right can be overwhelming. Other times the effects are invisible or barely perceptible, like on a romantic evening or on a picturesque cruise. Yet the effects of the fall are never far below the surface. The more we walk with God and internalize the truths of his Word, the more we see how sin discolors the world. The thorns and thistles inflicted on Adam and Eve, as Isaac Watts wrote in his hymn, "Joy to the World," extend "far as the curse is found."

Yet a proper understanding of heaven transforms us to imagine what is ahead for Jesus' disciples. Sometimes we opt out of all such musings, saying that it is "better than we can imagine." While that is partially true, that should not stop us from daydreaming about what lies ahead. We already think ahead to vacations, new homes, new children, new jobs, so why not do the same for heaven? We have many hints about what heaven will be like. God created the world and called it good and called humans "very good." The fall has distorted its original purpose, but not beyond recognition.

For one thing, we will have joyful and fulfilling work. Work is not a consequence of sin—only the thorns are from the curse. The tending of the Garden was God's original plan for us. Before the eating of the forbidden fruit, "The LORD God took the man and put him in the Garden of Eden to work it and take care of it" (Gen. 2:15). Leisure was also part of God's original plan, but only one day out of seven was dedicated to rest. The boredom of the slothful, whether rich or poor, old or young, is stultifying precisely because they have neglected that for which they were made.

This is not to say that we must forever be doing *paid* work. Retiring from our formal careers can be good and healthy, providing we continue to seek new ways to serve others. But work is our original purpose, our continued purpose, and our future purpose. Mothers (or sometimes fathers) who leave their paid employment to care for their children, as my wife has done, lay down their lives for the sake of others—a most noble calling, and often more demanding work than that of the marketplace.[21] Regardless, we were made to work. This may sound terrible for people stuck in a tedious or arduous job, but that is not the kind of work God will have for us. Think of the most fulfilling task you have ever undertaken, and then you will begin to get a sense of what heaven will be like.

---

[21] I have long believed that stay-at-home moms have a far more taxing job than those of us in the workplace, where accolades are more frequent and petty fighting less present.

Heaven will also be a grand adventure. God made the earth beautiful for our enjoyment. He made the universe big for our exploration and discovery. God revels in humans' joy of discovery just as parents enjoy watching their children hunt for Easter eggs or delight in a trip to the zoo. Heaven will not be the cessation of discovery. Though we will be free from sin, we will not be the same as God. Whereas God is all-knowing, we will not be, even in heaven. We will continue to learn, grow, and discover in eternity. I expect we will eternally explore God's domain, sharing in the joy of our discoveries with friends.

We all look forward to being free of pain, suffering and death in heaven, but we will not be free of our bodies. We are flesh and blood, and our brother Christ is also a man (though he is also God). We will forever be corporeal beings, though our bodies will be perfect and "glorified" in heaven—better than the best bodies on earth. For people who are chronically ill, the limiting and fallen nature of their bodies is more obvious than for Olympic athletes in their prime. But the Bible teaches the resurrection of the dead will be bodily. Just as Jesus' resurrection was bodily, so will ours be (Rom. 8:9-11, 1 Cor. 15, 1 Thess. 4:17). Moses and Elijah had bodies when they met with the transfigured Jesus on the mountain with Peter, James, and John (Matt. 17). The New Testament is consonant with the Old Testament's view of the body and material as good. In contrast, Greco-Roman thought held that the body was evil, encasing a good spirit. This essentially Gnostic[22] view of the body is an ongoing distortion of the biblical view of the body.

Heaven will be relational. Unlike the solitude of hell, Scripture teaches that we will be together with many other people. Although we will not be married, we will have deep and rich relationships, both those begun in heaven and those begun on earth. Just as the Trinity is relational, we were made to live in community. Even the best communities on earth are imperfect, tarnished by sin and selfishness and misunderstandings. Community in heaven will be perfect. Think of your best

---

[22] See chapter 4 on Gnosticism.

friends on earth, and then imagine what those relationships would be like without sin. Jesus spoke of heaven as a wedding feast with all of the joy and celebration that goes with it. Best of all, we will have perfect fellowship with the Lord. He will be our greatest joy.

Denying Death Is Unhealthy

Goth subculture's fascination with death is twisted because of its fixation on the act of dying and the state of the body after death. The grim images of corpses, bloodless faces, and black clothing glorify the loss of life. Death is not part of God's original plan and it will not be part of his eternal plan. It is a result of the fall, and it will disappear when Evil is finally destroyed.

Yet denying death is no more healthy than glorifying it. Death is real and certain, and we do ourselves no favors to conceal that fact. Concealing death requires mental, emotional, and linguistic effort. The problem is not in the use of cloaking words but in the way we are slow to prepare for our eventual death. For the infinitely more important question of what will happen to us after our deaths, our fear of death is yet more dysfunctional.

The writer of Hebrews warns us to get ready for our deaths while we can: "Today, if you hear his voice, do not harden your hearts" (Heb. 4:7). We should long to hear warm words greeting us in heaven. If we are afraid to die, it may be with good reason. We may be in rebellion against God in some area of our lives that has left us uncertain whether we are going to heaven. Or it may be from misunderstanding Christ's substitutionary death, thinking that we must work our way into God's favor to earn our salvation. While we work to "make our calling and election sure" (2 Pet. 1:10), we cannot work our way into heaven. The work is confirmation of our salvation, not our earning it.

Daily Remembering Our Death

On September 11, 2012, I was walking from the Washington subway to my office when I came upon a woman administering CPR to a suited and ashen-faced man lying on the sidewalk. I walked past, not wanting to be voyeuristic and seeing that other pedestrians were handling the situation.

But then I turned back to ask why the woman was not also administering mouth-to-mouth resuscitation. I was told by another passerby that the 911 operator had instructed her that was no longer deemed necessary. Just then, the woman performing the CPR asked for someone to relieve her since she was tired. Having undergone CPR training many times during my years as a lifeguard, I quickly took over. As I pumped on the man's chest, I prayed again and again that he would live or that he would be ready to face God.

Once the paramedics arrived, I left the scene. In the ensuing days I tried to find out who the man was and what had happened to him, but privacy laws blocked me. I resigned myself to never knowing what had happened.

Two months later, the heart attack victim managed to track me down through a notebook I had inadvertently left at the scene. He told me that he had been quite healthy prior to his attack and was stricken with a "widow maker" heart attack that few survive, and those that do wish they had not. He had been unconscious for a week after the attack and hospitalized for two additional weeks. Amazingly, he was making a full recovery and was back at work part-time. I shared with him my testimony in a letter, the Bible, and *Mere Christianity,* which he promised to read.

Healthy one day, and (almost) dead the next. The same could happen to any one of us. Death can come fast and unexpectedly.

It is good to remind ourselves everyday that we will die, not to be morose, but to frame the scope and meaning of our lives. Meditating on our death makes our present struggles both more *and* less important. We are likely to use our time more wisely when we realize that what we do now will have eternal consequences. Our temporal preoccupation with prestige, power, and position is dethroned when we realize how little they matter in the long run. The satirical bumper sticker, "he who has the most toys when he dies, wins" aptly reveals the ludicrous pursuit of things.

Alexander the Great's father, Philip of Macedon, told a servant to daily remind him, "Philip, you will die." When a victorious Roman general entered Rome in a parade of tribute, a slave would ride with him in the chariot whispering in his ear, "Remember, you are mortal."

Life is short and most of us are quickly forgotten. Few people remember Spiro Agnew, Vice President of the United States (1969 to 1973), House Speaker Carl Albert (1971-1977), pop singer Edwin Starr (whose song "War" topped the charts in 1970), or Cameron Hawley (whose book *The Hurricane Years* spent six weeks at number one on the *New York Times Best Seller* list in 1968). Within a generation, most Americans would be hard-pressed to recognize any of these one-time super-stars. I cannot string together more than a couple of sentences about my great grandparents. Even within our own family lines we will be forgotten. And for those lucky few whose legacies are remembered, what good does it do them after they are dead and gone? They hold no satisfaction to be remembered and are ignorant of their posthumous fame.

The first-century-B.C. Roman philosopher and politician Cicero wrote of the fleeting nature of fame in his dialogue *De Republica*:

> Of what value, pray, is your human glory, which can barely last for a tiny part of a single year? If you wish to look higher . . . you will not put yourself at the mercy of the masses' gossip nor measure your long-term destiny by the rewards you get from men. Goodness herself must draw you on by her own enticements to true glory. . . . In no case does a person's reputation last forever; it fades with the death of the speakers, and vanishes as posterity forgets.

Likewise, in Ps. 103, we are told, "As for man, his days are like grass, he flourishes like a flower of the field; the wind blows over it and it is gone, and its place remembers it no more" (vv. 15-16). Yet many people live as if all that mattered was "their good name" and reputation—the cotton candy of this world—while neglecting the praise of God, which lasts eternally. The temporal things so highly praised by the world— what we wear, whom we marry, where we work, what we drive—matter only inasmuch as they matter to God. "Am I now trying to win the approval of men, or of God? Or am I trying to please men? If I were still trying to please men, I would not be a servant of Christ" (Gal. 1:10). It is seeking the praise of people that drives us to waste our time—time that is lost to eternity. The one thing we cannot replace is our time devoted to worthless pursuits.

When we remember that we will die and be forgotten by everyone except by God—the audience of One, who will re-member our actions forever—we are reoriented to eternity. Enduring slights, insults, and disrespect becomes easier when we remember that God's approval is all that matters. Our earthly actions are imbued with a sense of meaning and pur-pose that extends beyond the grave and beyond the praise of others. We recognize that we are creatures made for eternity. "For God will bring every deed into judgment, including every hidden thing, whether it is good or evil" (Eccles. 12:14). This world's vainglories or petty slights will matter in eternity only to the extent that we let them re-shape us into God's likeness and bring glory to him. That makes our temporal actions both more and less important—more important because they are eternally significant, but less important because what others think of us now will not matter beyond the grave.

Living in light of our earthly death also helps us to be grateful for our moments with loved ones. We have the oppor-tunity to love people into the Kingdom of God on this side of death, not on the other side. Whether or not we treat others as creatures made in the image of God, including those who are the least lovable, will have an impact on their view of God. We are Christ's ambassadors, acting as God's hands, feet, and voice in our sphere of influence. When we consider that we can affect another person's eternal destiny by how we respond to the surly waitress, the unpleasant neighbor, or an overbearing boss, we are better able to bear temporal sufferings for the sake of eternal results.[23]

Knowing that we are living in light of eternity also helps us recognize that our dissatisfaction with the best the world has to offer is only temporary. One day, we will be in a place where our longings are fulfilled, where the best is good enough, unmarred by sin. Living on this side of the Fall, nothing is perfect, and we feel that imperfection, sometimes more acutely than others. The long-planned vacation that includes mediocre food and disappointing sights, the love-of-our-life who nags us, the church that is filled with sinners who grate on our nerves—nothing is exactly how it is supposed to be. Or, when we do get exactly what we want, we soon become discontented. The new house becomes old. The longed-for sailboat becomes commonplace. The higher salary becomes the baseline. Eventually, we yearn for new things.

Nothing is really enough, except for God. Yet, even our relationship with God is imperfect, since we see through a glass darkly. Just when we are in step with God and at perfect peace, we lose our close communion through sin or inattention or inexplicable dryness. In short, even the best is a shadow of what we experience in heaven. We are aliens and strangers in the world, not at home, but longing for a better home. "The world and its desires pass away, but whoever does the will of God lives forever" (1 John 2:17).

Ps. 39:4-7 teaches us that life is short and that our earthly ventures not done for God's glory are fleeting:

> Show me, O LORD, my life's end
> and the number of my days;
> let me know how fleeting is my life.
>
> You have made my days a mere handbreadth;
> the span of my years is as nothing before you.
> Each man's life is but a breath.

---

[23] My mother was excellent at this. She responded in tender kindness when maltreated by service people, turning their hostility to kindness by empathizing with their harried jobs. My tendency is often just the opposite.

Man is a mere phantom as he goes to and fro:
He bustles about, but only in vain;
he heaps up wealth, not knowing who will get it.

But now, Lord, what do I look for?
My hope is in you.

Nothing lasts. You will lose everything you have and love on this earth. Holding on to God amidst life's torrents is the only thing that will last. Of course, if the Lord is the center of our lives, then heaven will restore and make new the tired and worn and incomplete longings of this world. Living each day with the awareness that our temporal lives are coming to an end will frame our present lives to count for eternity. The 1832 hymn by Edward Mote, "On Christ the Solid Rock," lauds the one sure foundation on which to rest our lives:

My hope is built on nothing less
Than Jesus' blood and righteousness
I dare not trust the sweetest frame
But wholly lean on Jesus' Name

When darkness seems to hide His face
I rest on His unchanging grace
In every high and stormy gale
My anchor holds within the veil

His oath, His covenant, His blood
Support me in the whelming flood
When all around my soul gives way
He then is all my Hope and Stay

When He shall come with trumpet sound
Oh may I then in Him be found
Dressed in His righteousness alone
Faultless to stand before the throne

On Christ the solid Rock I stand
All other ground is sinking sand
All other ground is sinking sand

4

It's God's Problem:
Faithfulness, Not Success

"I do not pray for success, I ask for faithfulness."
Mother Teresa

*"But it does require the supernatural grace of God to live
twenty-four hours in every day as a saint, to go through
drudgery as a disciple, to live an ordinary, unobserved,
ignored existence as a disciple of Jesus. It is inbred in us that
we have to do exceptional things for God; but we have not. We
have to be exceptional in the ordinary things, to be holy in
mean streets, among mean people, and this is not learned in
five minutes."*
Oswald Chambers, My Utmost for His Highest

*"The growing good of the world is partly dependent on
unhistorical acts; and that things are not so ill with you and me
as they might have been, is half owing to the number who lived
faithfully a hidden life, and rest in unvisited tombs."*
George Eliot

Our job is to be faithful. It is up to God to bring the results. If we have done all that we are supposed to do,
then it becomes God's problem whether our efforts are
successful. Our righteous efforts already count in our favor
before God, no matter what happens.

Getting straight what is our responsibility and what is
God's makes a huge impact in how we live and whether we
experience God's peace. We are to "own" our actions, but
"disown" the results. We should not be indifferent to our plans'
success or failure, but after we have done everything we should
do, we do not have the primary responsibility for the *impact* of
our plans.

This does not mean we should shirk our responsibilities. In our culture of victimization, we are prone to readily assign fault to others. Harry Truman had a sign on his White House desk that said, "The buck stops here." He knew that it was chiefly his responsibility for what his Administration did right or wrong. Truman did not resort to ugly blame-shifting. Still, trusting God with the results of our good actions is not the same thing as blaming others when things go awry.

I once worked in a highly dysfunctional office. Every day I wondered whether I would be fired—not because my performance was poor, but because my boss was erratic and hot-tempered. He was known to fire staff on a whim. I coped with this work environment by seeking to do my job well. I tried to shun the back-biting and blame-shifting going on around me and do all I should do—but no more. I could not fix the office because that was beyond my authority. I aimed to "keep my yard clean"—performing my job well and above reproach—amidst the chaos. While the work environment was still difficult, things were more tolerable when I did not own responsibilities that were not mine.

However, we must not turn a blind eye to things we can and should fix. We should not be like the Priest and the Levite who passed the wounded Jewish mugging victim. Our model is the Samaritan who made his neighbor's problem his own.

God calls us "to act justly, to love mercy, and to walk humbly" with him (Mic. 6:8). These are things we should *own*—things for which we are responsible. We have complete control over whether or not we do these things. No one can take away our ability to obey God, even if by doing them we suffer martyrdom. But whether we are *successful* in straightening out our little corner of a twisted world, whether our mercy is well-received, and whether others follow us in following God is not ultimately our problem. It is God's problem.

Taking on responsibilities that belong to God alone leads to stress, guilt, worry, and sin. Our job is less complicated and less stressful when we focus on our own responsibilities.

When I committed my life to the Lord as a high school junior, I was eager to see one of my best friends give her life to the Lord. I talked to her for hours about her need for salvation, thinking that I could talk her into the Kingdom. She patiently listened but was clearly unpersuaded. I was not wrong to share the gospel with her, but in retrospect, I realize that I should have been less insistent. I have similarly worried about how effective I was in sharing with other friends, or, if I brought a friend to church, whether the service communicated the right things in the right way. All these things are beyond my control. Whether or not my friends decide to follow the Lord is not up to me. It is God's responsibility to save.

Of course, this is easier said than done. In my legislative work on Capitol Hill and in the White House, I would often be distressed when unjust policies advanced, yet the Holy Spirit was quick to remind me that he cares more about just policies than I do. I am his foot soldier, and he is the General. My job is simply to seek justice and righteousness. It takes a lifetime of practice to be faithful. My wife and I constantly remind one another that "it's God's problem" when we sense our spirits are tending towards owning the results. Getting our head in the right place about what is our job and what is God's is essential.

Fear God Alone

A crucial first step in ordering our priorities is deciding whom to fear. If we die to ourselves and seek to serve humbly, then we live to God and we are involved in his work. In laying down our lives for Christ, we do not become apathetic drones indifferent to the world, but servants in God's redemptive work. That is the key: it is God's business. He created the world, he set out a plan, he redeemed it after man's rebellion, and he is actively working to "fix" it. We follow behind him in his work, doing his bidding.

Unlike God, we are finite. That means we can only do so much to accomplish our mission. We cannot will into existence a rightly ordered world.[24] In trying to live out God's purposes, we will sometimes be opposed by others. Peter wrote to the persecuted church, "Who is going to harm you if you are eager

---

[24] God chooses to limit his sovereign will by allowing humankind to sin and rebel. He ordained freedom, which means that his will for a perfectly or-dered universe will not be fulfilled until sin is obliterated at the end of time.

to do good? But even if you should suffer for what is right, you are blessed. 'Do not fear what they fear; do not be frightened.' But in your hearts set apart Christ as Lord" (1 Pet. 3:13-15). What is it that "they" (meaning those who do not follow the Lord) fear? The disapproval of men, poverty, death, and all the things that occupy the worldly mind. In contrast, we are to fear God alone. The fear of God crowds out all other fears. Jesus said, ". . . do not be afraid of those who kill the body and after that can do no more. But I will show you whom you should fear: Fear him who, after the killing of the body, has power to throw you into hell" (Luke 12:4-5).

Holy fear is not like the fear we feel of being mugged in a sketchy part of town. Fear of God is more like what we feel toward a just police officer: respect, honor, submission, and a desire to obey. "Since, then, we know what it is to fear the Lord, we try to persuade others" (2 Cor. 5:11). Fearing God's wrath for our sinful rebellion compels us to accept God's forgiveness and to persuade our neighbors to do the same. We experience the darker side of biblical fear when our sin takes over. When we are in rebellion against God, being afraid to die is appropriate. Likewise, driving over the speed limit stimulates a fear of getting a ticket—the same kind of fear we should have towards God when we disobey.

Fearing God above everything else simplifies our lives. Once God becomes our top priority, what remains for us to fear? Ps. 27:1-3 is clear:

> The LORD is my light and my salvation—
>   whom shall I fear?
> The LORD is the stronghold of my life—
>   of whom shall I be afraid?
>
> When evil men advance against me
>   to devour my flesh,
>   when my enemies and my foes attack me,
>   they will stumble and fall.
>
> Though an army besiege me,
>   my heart will not fear;

> though war break out against me,
> even then will I be confident.

In fact, we are commanded not to fear. "Peace I leave with you; my peace I give you. I do not give to you as the world gives. *Do not let your hearts be troubled and do not be afraid*" (John 14:27, emphasis added). Worry demonstrates our lack of trust in a loving and all-powerful God who knows our every need. When we are fully dead to ourselves and alive to Christ, worry disappears.

But is it possible not to fear certain things, like an oncoming truck when our brakes fail, physical pain, or when we begin to fall down stairs? Such fear is innate and prudent and leads to self-preservation. It was ordained by God to help protect us. This is healthy. It also transcends physical matters; for example, a fearful wariness can keep us from entering into bad business deals with untrustworthy people.

In contrast, ungodly fear is when we let legitimate concerns lead to worry and anxiety. The single mother dying of cancer can trust the loving sovereignty of God without worrying or fretting. Of course, she should make every provision she can for her children, but she can also know that God has a good and perfect will even in extreme tragedy.

If our fear for God is preeminent, then our fear of a coming trial will be constrained by our confidence in him. Jesus sweat blood in the Garden of Gethsemane knowing what lay ahead of him. He pleaded with his Father to change his will if it were possible. When it was clear that the Father wanted him to proceed, he did so without flinching. His greater fear of the Father was the controlling determination. Operationally, he acted unafraid of death, though he did feel distress about the physical torture that lay before him and "becoming sin" for us, thus being judged by and separated from the Father for a time.

Serving God In All Things

God put us on this planet with a plan. In Gen. 1:28, the Creator God instructs Adam to "be fruitful and increase in number; fill the earth and subdue it. Rule over the fish of the sea and the

birds of the air and over every living creature that moves on the
ground." As image-bearers of God, we are to imitate our Creator in ruling the creation just as he rules over us. We can discern what it means to be just because God is just. We can learn
to rule well because God rules perfectly. We can learn to be
fruitful because God is fruitful. Paul writes that "we are God's
workmanship, created in Christ Jesus to do good works, which
God prepared in advance for us to do" (Eph. 2:10). God was on
the scene before we arrived, and he cares more deeply about
our mission because he is perfect and we are flawed.

The creation mandate extends to every part of our
world. There is no part of our day about which God is indifferent. Even in our seemingly mundane daily chores, we should
be serving God. "So whether you eat or drink or whatever you
do, do it all for the glory of God" (1 Cor. 10:31). Eating pizza
to the glory of God? Drinking a beer to the glory of God? That
is our call. And if it cannot be done to the glory of God, it
should not be done at all. Again in Colossians, Paul writes,
"Whatever you do, work at it with all your heart, as working
for the Lord, not for men, since you know that you will receive
an inheritance from the Lord as a reward. It is the Lord Christ
you are serving" (3:23-24). We are supposed to serve Christ in
everything we do—from cleaning bathrooms to changing diapers to partying with friends to singing in the church choir.
Nothing good is excluded if it is done to the glory of God.

But bad things are excluded. Pimping and drug-pushing
and purveying porn—and a host of other things—are outside of
his will. We cannot rightly ask for his blessing on our sin. Yet,
I suspect that even our wrong-doing may be credited to us as
righteousness when we think we are doing right.[25] Our motivation matters to God. I imagine that some people who defend an
unlimited right to abortion do so with a clear conscience,
thinking they are empowering women—just as I once did prior
to a friend helping me seen the consequences of my faulty rea-
soning. Even though they are contributing to the deaths of in-

---

[25] I am not suggesting that discreet actions that please God can justify us
unto salvation. I only mean that an individual action may please God. He
delights in our righteous acts, even as we are sinners. Yet only Jesus can
atone for our sins and make us worthy of heaven.

nocent children, they may not realize it. Thankfully, a perfectly just and good God is the ultimate judge and will make a fair rendering of all such matters.

One thing I dislike is attributing the worst motives to people holding opposing points of view. President Obama is hated by many conservatives who believe he wakes up each morning desiring to destroy the country. Nonsense. President Obama and most of my liberal friends earnestly believe they are furthering justice, just as my conservative friends do. I have heard from both liberals and conservatives that "the other side will say and do anything, because for them the ends justify the means." Yes, there are people of every political stripe who play fast and loose with the truth. I remember sitting in a meeting of conservative activists when one man said he did not care whether or not his charges against the policies of the other side were true, because they would be effective. At the time, I bit my tongue and said nothing, but I wish I had had the courage and wisdom to speak up to rebut that foolishness.

Right actions done for wrong reasons are not to our credit. Jesus condemned the religious classes of his day for their showy acts of righteousness:

> So when you give to the needy, do not announce it with trumpets, as the hypocrites do in the synagogues and on the streets, to be honored by men. I tell you the truth, they have received their reward in full. But when you give to the needy, do not let your left hand know what your right hand is doing, so that your giving may be in secret. Then your Father, who sees what is done in secret, will reward you (Matt. 6:2-4).

Likewise, whether someone thinks he or she is doing right matters to God. In Romans, Paul cautions against causing others to sin by doing permissible things that they think are wrong, because "if anyone regards something as unclean, then for him it is unclean" (14:14). If they, in turn, follow our actions, but with a guilty conscience, they have sinned. The action might have a good or neutral earthly consequence, but its eternal effect on them personally will not be good if they believe it to be wrong.

God cares about everything we do *and* why we do it. He is infinitely creative and intimately concerned about restoring the creation. Although the final restoration will not take place until the end of the world, our business should be furthering the Kingdom of God. His Kingdom extends to the creation of a just society, which excludes nothing. God cares about highways, labor standards, the rainforest, educational curricula, patents, bridge design, cleaning supplies, wildlife, architecture, cooking, photography, and accounting.[26] What he thinks about each of those things may be opaque to us, but that is different than his *not* caring. Part of the joy of the journey is seeking and discovering God's purposes.

If it is God's business in which we are involved, then God cares more about it than we do. And if he cares about it more than we, then our responsibility is finite compared to his. Once we have done our part, we can hand the problem over to him. Like the grandparents who enjoy the grandchildren but hand them back to the parents for discipline and diapers, we are limited in our responsibilities. We are stewards of God's work, not owners. Ownership lies with God.

Doing All We Should, But Nothing More

Sometimes duty requires extreme sacrifice, perhaps even our lives. The firefighter, the soldier, the police officer, the Chinese home church pastor, the missionary, the sea captain—all of them may be required to die to save others. Lesser sacrifices may also be required of us, giving up our savings, our security, our comfort, our personal time.

---

[26] This is not to say that God cares about all things equally. Some things, like salvation and the taking of innocent human life, are more important than monetary policy or pro football rules. Unfortunately, many people are today unable to differentiate between greater and lesser things. I know people who are prolife but support pro-choice legislators' elections because of some less important issue. This fallacy of moral equivalence is a growing problem rooted in an inadequate understanding of God's priorities.

"Doing all we should" may require that we refrain from doing or cease doing—a hard lesson for control-freaks. We may need to leave work early to see our children's ballgame or to help relieve our spouse after a long day with the kids. Since God cares about all of our responsibilities, and not just our professional ones, we may need to do less work for our employer in order to please God. And we may have to bear the consequences of disappointing our boss.

In my chosen career, politics, it is not unusual to work sixty to seventy hours per week. There is typically more work to do than time allows. Given the A-type people who are drawn to politics, many politicians and their aides prioritize their jobs over their families. For twenty years, I have struggled to know when my responsibilities at home take precedence over my job. Being faithful to God has usually meant that I leave work before my colleagues. This has often inspired tremendous guilt feelings in me, whether or not my colleagues thought ill of me. I hate to be the first one to leave the office, and given my druthers, I would be among the last to leave. Yet I want to be around to watch my kids grow up. Quality time with children is important, but quantity is just as important. It is often said that children spell "love" "T-I-M-E." If it is God whom we principally serve, then achieving less in the workplace and not going as far as we otherwise would in our career may be a part of our service to God.

Sabbath observance is one of the Ten Commandants that requires our obedience. Unfortunately, few Christians today treat the Sabbath any differently than other days of the week.[27] Admittedly, observing a day of rest is not easy. It requires more self-discipline to do our work in the other six days. Yet it is just one more way that God calls us to measure our lives by our faithfulness, and not our productivity.

---

[27] I do not believe that Sabbath observance will be the same for everyone. For the manual laborer, it may entail little physical exercise, and for the office worker it may entail much physical activity. The question that should guide our behavior should be how do we refrain from our "labors" and refresh our spirits. It is easy to become rule-bound or legalistic, as the Pharisees did, but I see few people today who fall into this trap, and many more who act as though Sabbath observance is moot for our age.

I have often heard it said that God calls us to excellence in all we do. Not so. We may be called to be a so-so employee for the sake of our children. We may be called to do the bare minimum on a graduate course. We cannot do it all. We must learn to prioritize some things over others. Too often, we prioritize our responsibilities outside the home first, and our families are left with the dregs.

I left a job I loved working in the Senate because my wife and I sensed that God wanted me to be home with my kids more. Family Life Today founder Dennis Rainey says that working intense hours for a season may be appropriate, but when a season turns into year upon year upon year, our families suffer. My work in politics became unhealthy for our family, so I left government service. As I was leaving the Senate, several highly accomplished older men confided in me they regretted having given too much to their careers at the expense of their families. Their success had not been worth the price they paid.

My own father, who is excellent, gave me much of his time and attention, limiting his work so he could coach my baseball team. I want to do no less for my children. The late French President Charles de Gaulle said, "The cemeteries of the world are full of indispensable men." In truth, we are indispensable to our families first.

These sacrifices may well mean that some vital tasks go unfinished, some good deeds unperformed. We are not God. We cannot do everything, nor should we try. Once we have done all we are called to do, we should walk away from our work with peace of mind. If it is God's business, then it is also God's problem. If we see something undone, and if it is not ours to do, we should pray God brings the right person to do it.

But what are we called to do? It is not always easy to discern how we should spend our time. Yet it is often less complicated than we suppose. Most of the time, we please God by working diligently, getting enough sleep, exercising regularly, eating right, going to church, spending time with our spouse and children, spending time with friends, serving others in a volunteer capacity, and observing a Sabbath rest. That should be the norm. At times we must deviate from this balance to work on a big project, help a sick relative, undertake a major home renovation, and so forth. But in general, our lives should be in a healthy balance, to the extent it depends on us. By necessity, that will mean that we are regularly walking away from big needs in the world.

Of course, we should not walk away from any need we are specifically called to do. The world is a fallen and broken place littered with human suffering. We cannot fix all of it, but only that which God has called us to do. Is it callous to walk away from such needs for the sake of balance? Sometimes, yes, but most of the time, no. It is more often wise. We are stewards of God's work, not owners.[28]

Acting as though we are indispensable may actually be an expression of pride. We may be finding an unhealthy sense of being needed by refusing to set boundaries on our work. Workaholics thrive on this sense of being integral to their jobs, but at the expense of other people and projects that deserve more time and attention.

Likewise, doing all we should, but nothing more, may require that we let our reputation be unjustly maligned. Explaining our actions may be required, but working to "clear my good name" may not be a task we should undertake. Paul undertook a vigorous defense of his actions and his message when he was unjustly arrested and imprisoned. In contrast, Jesus stood largely silent as unfounded accusations were hurled at him. When do we stand up for ourselves and when do we let the chips fall where they may? No iron-clad formula exists to figure this out. We should bear in mind that we belong to God to do his bidding, our reputations belong to God, and we stand or fall before him—quite apart from human judgment. We should examine our motivations to see whether we have an ungodly desire to protect our ego or a pure desire to do God's work in God's way.

---

[28] There are times of extraordinary challenges that require disproportionately intense work that may undermine our health. If this is God's call on us, then we must do it. The apostles were away on missionary journeys for months and years on end. If they had children at home, then those young children would have endured hardships for the sake of their fathers' ministry. However, such times are not the norm for most of us.

Some worthy and important projects fail for want of funding, volunteers, city permits, and so on. This may be due to human sinfulness, or it may be God's guidance, or some mysterious combination of the two. For many years, I was active with an after-school tutoring program for at-risk inner-city children in Washington, D.C. It eventually closed down due to lack of funding. Did Christians ignore God's instructions to give money to the program? Or was God redirecting his people to new projects? I do not know. But I am at peace knowing I did all I should have done, yet sad that the work did not continue.

Worry Is A Sin

If we are involved in God's business, then we should not worry. In Matt. 6:31-34, Jesus said,

> So do not worry, saying, "What shall we eat?" or "What shall we drink?" or "What shall we wear?" For the pagans run after all these things, and your heavenly Father knows that you need them. But seek first his kingdom and his righteousness, and all these things will be given to you as well. Therefore do not worry about tomorrow, for tomorrow will worry about itself. Each day has enough trouble of its own.

Our job is to do what God has put before us today. It is difficult to worry about what we are doing at the moment. Worrying is usually about what will happen in the future. Worry is also a sign that we are trying to own something that rightly belongs to God. We can always seek his kingdom and his righteousness today. We are never prevented from doing that much except through our own sin.

Likewise, Paul writes in Phil. 4:4-7, "Rejoice in the Lord always. I will say it again: Rejoice! Let your gentleness be evident to all. The Lord is near. Do not be anxious about anything, but in everything, by prayer and petition, with thanksgiving, present your requests to God. And the peace of God, which transcends all understanding, will guard your hearts and your minds in Christ Jesus."

We are not supposed to be anxious because God is with us and is eager to hear our requests. If we know that the all-powerful God of the universe has heard our prayer, then we can afford to leave the results to him and not be anxious. Our anxiety stems from our lack of trust in God and his providential care. This is not to say that what we hope for the future will come to pass. It may not. Our fears may be realized: the death of a loved one, illness, imprisonment, or bankruptcy, for example. The reason we can eschew anxiety lies in our confidence that God will walk with us through whatever trial lies ahead and will use suffering and hardship for our good if we submit to him and his ways. Of course, this peace is available to us only to the extent that we orient ourselves to God's view of the world. The first step begins with wanting what God wants for us. No easy task, that.

When I worked in the White House, I became the focus of a minor public brouhaha in the press. I knew that my job was potentially on the line, though I had not done anything wrong. Some more senior White House aides were seeking to insulate their own reputations by letting me be the "fall guy," and I was in a constant state of anxiety for weeks until the issue blew over. About fifty times a day I would begin to worry, then repent, then worry, then repent, over and over again. I was trying hard not to worry, but I kept thinking about the media stories about my possible firing. It was a relentless struggle, and I do not think I did very well. Yet in choosing to trust again and again, I was working to develop my "trust muscles," slowly getting stronger with each act of repentance and trust. It is a slow and difficult process, but it pays dividends.

"Cast all your anxiety on him, because he cares for you" (1 Pet. 5:7). When we choose to trust in a loving God, we can give up our anxiety and find peace. Choosing to trust is about where we will place our confidence, not about focusing on how we *feel* about the future. We may feel anxiety, but if we regard it as a temptation rather than a settled fact, we can override it by willing ourselves to be confident in God. We can consider our feelings of anxiety as temptations to disregard the goodness of God, and we can choose to reject those feelings as illegitimate. In time, the feelings will subside as our eyes are fixed on the horizon of our trust.

Jesus bids us to find rest in him. "Come to me, all you who are weary and burdened, and I will give you rest. Take my yoke upon you and learn from me, for I am gentle and humble in heart, and you will find rest for your souls. For my yoke is easy and my burden is light" (Matt. 11:28-30). Counter-intuitively, to rest we must put on a yoke and work. Our "yoke" is following God's commands. "This is love for God: to obey his commands. And his commands are not burdensome, for everyone born of God overcomes the world" (1 John 5:3-4). In other words, finding peace requires doing God's work in God's way.

Before I was married, I served as a missionary to Turks in West Berlin, Germany. I was given my food and lodging (both were very basic), plus $2.50 per week in spending money. Even in 1986 this was very little money. I learned to pray for everything I needed, even down to the batteries for my stereo. Time and again, I found God to be faithful to meet my needs in unexpected ways. Paradoxically, in having less, I grew more peaceful because of my closer connection to the Provider. So when I returned to the United States to seek a job in politics, I marveled at my own fearlessness. I had $200, one suit, a one-way bus ticket to Washington, DC, a place to stay for a few days, and a resume. More than all of this, I had confidence that God would give me a job if he wanted me to work in politics, or he would redirect me to another field. My trust muscles were strong from having lived in need.

The less we exercise our trust muscles, the weaker they become. That is why Paul warns, "Command those who are rich in this present world not to be arrogant nor to put their hope in wealth, which is so uncertain, but to put their hope in God, who richly provides us with everything for our enjoyment" (1 Tim. 6:17). "The deceitfulness of wealth" (Matt. 13:22) distorts our view of the world and feeds the illusion that we are in control, when in fact we are completely dependent on God. When we are comfortable, we have a propensity to fear losing our comfort, but when we are under pressure yet trusting God for his provision, we find it easier not to fear the future. In short, when our confidence is in our temporal circumstances, we have reason to worry, but when our confidence is in God, we have reason to be at peace about the future.

Faithfulness Often Leads To Success, But Not Always

When we do God's work in God's way, we will often experience success. God's ways—humble service, perseverance, focus on the unseen and eternal—often make us win races, like the tortoise beating the hare. God designed the world, and his ways best comport with the way the world is supposed to work.

U.S. Senator Rick Santorum of Pennsylvania served in Congress for sixteen years. He beat an entrenched incumbent member of the House of Representatives by doggedly knocking on doors. Against all odds, he won in a heavily Democratic district, though he was a Republican. He went on to win two six-year terms in the U.S. Senate. He consistently exhibited a humble spirit, caring for the poor, the unborn, and the persecuted in the legislation he authored and the votes he cast. He was courageous, seeking to do the right thing even when a majority of his constituents was pressing him to vote the other way. He led the fight to ban the heinous partial birth abortion procedure, enduring personal attacks as he took on the abortion lobby. He rose to the third-highest ranking position in the Senate and was one of the top political leaders in the nation. His faithful and humble service was a shining example of God's favor on a faithful servant.

Rick Santorum was the tortoise, steadily moving towards the finish line and repeatedly beating his opponents. His eyes were fixed on the eternal, and he did not worry about what might happen to him for his bold stands. Yet in 2006, Santorum was soundly rejected by Pennsylvania voters, losing by a whopping eighteen points to challenger Bob Casey. Although his faithfulness had been rewarded with success in four consecutive elections, he eventually lost.

Was God sleeping? No. Or did Rick Santorum fail God? I do not think so. Was it God's will that Santorum lost his election? Certainly he allowed it, but did he want it? God's purposes in such things are not always clear. What we do know is that a faithful and courageous man was rewarded with success, but only for a while. God's purposes in allowing him to lose are mysterious, but that is not our concern. Ours is the trying. The results belong to God.

Woody Allen said that eighty percent of life is just showing up.[29] Many people excel beyond their more talented and gifted peers because they come to work on time, promptly return phone calls and emails, meet their deadlines, and conscientiously follow their employer's instructions. Success often befalls the average and eludes the gifted for want of self-discipline. Faithful service often has a way of leading to success.

Still, sometimes faithful servants lose their businesses, declare bankruptcy, flunk out of school, get passed over for a promotion or are fired, lose their spouses, and are falsely maligned. The "when" and the "why" belong to God and his purposes. We can be confident that he will use our defeats as easily as our victories. Look at the cross. God took the ultimate tragedy in all of human history, the unjust and cruel torture and execution of his only Son, and turned it into the fulcrum of history and the very means of the world's salvation.

Heb. 11 teaches that faithful discipleship will sometimes lead to worldly success, and at other times faithfulness will lead to utter defeat:

> And what more shall I say? I do not have time to tell about Gideon, Barak, Samson, Jephthah, David, Samuel and the prophets, who through faith conquered kingdoms, administered justice, and gained what was promised; who shut the mouths of lions, quenched the fury of the flames, and escaped the edge of the sword; whose weakness was turned to strength; and who became powerful in battle and routed foreign armies. Women received back their dead, raised to life again. Others were tortured and refused to be released, so that they might gain a better resurrection. Some faced jeers and flogging, while still others were chained and put in

---

[29] I am reluctant to quote Woody Allen, given his well publicized perversion in marrying one step-daughter and victimization of another. In this, Allen failed to "show up" as a husband and father. But a good quote is a good quote.

prison. They were stoned; they were sawed in two; they were put to death by the sword. They went about in sheepskins and goatskins, destitute, persecuted and mistreated— the world was not worthy of them. They wandered in deserts and mountains, and in caves and holes in the ground.

These were all commended for their faith, yet none of them received what had been promised. God had planned something better for us so that only together with us would they be made perfect (vv. 32-40).

Notice that some of God's faithful servants "conquered kingdoms," "shut the mouths of lions," "became powerful in battle and routed foreign armies." They were heroes and champions and victors in their own time and in the eyes of men. Their faithful service resulted in worldly and temporal success. Yet other faithful servants were tortured, jeered, flogged, sawed in two, poor, and maligned. This set of servants was no less or more faithful than the successful ones, but God brought dramatically different results. Neither received their ultimate reward on earth, though some fared considerably better than others. Too many television preachers and health-and-wealth churches teach that godliness leads to success in the here-and-now. They ignore the many Scriptures that promise hardship and suffering. It is up to God who prospers and who suffers this side of heaven.

We do not know what lies in our future, but we know that our call is to obedience. Our real reward, the only one that will truly satisfy our deepest longings, lies beyond the grave. That is where we must fix our eyes, leaving to God the results of our service. And peace is the logical consequence of a heart attuned to eternity. When we are truly dead to ourselves, both our victories and our defeats are God's problems.

Olympic athlete Eric Liddell became famous for not competing on the Sabbath in 1924. He later became a missionary in China and died in a World War II prison camp. Before his death, he taught his fellow prisoners his favorite hymn, "Be

Still, My Soul," the lyrics of which so clearly marked his life,
as they should ours.

> Be Still, My Soul
> By Katharina von Schlegel

> Be still, my soul--
> The Lord is on thy side!
> Bear patiently the cross of grief or pain;
> Leave to thy God to order and provide.
> In ev'ry change He faithful will remain.
> Be still, my soul--
> Thy best, thy heav'nly Friend
> Thru thorny ways leads to a joyful end.

> Be still, my soul! thy God doth undertake
> To guide the future as he has the past.
> Thy hope, thy confidence let nothing shake;
> All now mysterious shall be bright at last.
> Be still, my soul! the waves and winds still know
> His voice who ruled them while He dwelt below.

> Be still, my soul! the hour is hastening on
> When we shall be forever with the Lord,
> When disappointment, grief, and fear are gone,
> Sorrow forgot, love's purest joys restored.
> Be still, my soul! when change and tears are past,
> All safe and blessed we shall meet at last.

5

Worship: Not Just Singing

*"It is a great delusion to think our times of prayer ought
to differ from other times. We are as strictly obliged to cleave
to God by action in the time of action as by prayer in the
season of prayer."*
Brother Lawrence, The Practice of the Presence of God

Worship is not just going to church, singing hymns and choruses, praying, and listening to a sermon. It should also include golfing, preparing tax returns, swimming, teaching your child to ride a bike, washing dishes, sleeping, and every other activity done to please God that is not specifically proscribed by Scripture.

The limited view of worship that exclusively confines it to private or corporate praise is deeply engrained in our culture. It is rooted in a flawed epistemology[30] that limits our understanding of the all-encompassing nature of the Kingdom of God, denigrates as "less important" the thoughts and activities that consume most of our lives, and prevents us from bringing all of our moments under the Lordship of Christ. Learning to worship God in all we do will revolutionize our lives and bring a sense of purpose and joy even to our most mundane tasks.

The Conventional Wisdom on Worship

Merriam-Webster's Dictionary defines worship this way: "**1:** to honor or reverence as a divine being or supernatural power **2:** to regard with great or extravagant respect, honor, or devotion

---

[30] Epistemology is "the study or a theory of the nature and grounds of knowledge especially with reference to its limits and validity" (Merriam-Webster's Dictionary). In plain terms, it refers to what we know and how we can know it.

(a celebrity worshiped by her fans)." The question is how do we honor or revere God?

Singing songs of praise is certainly part of worship. Church leaders are right to invite us to worship God in song on Sunday mornings. But is that enough? Does our reverence for God begin and end in the church sanctuary? Many of us have been wrongly taught that, while God is especially fond of corporate singing and prayer, he is indifferent to Sunday afternoon football games or Monday morning office meetings.

As a child, I felt guilty that I did not want to spend more time in church and less time playing with friends. I had learned in Sunday School that the church was "God's house," so surely a godly person would prefer to be in a worship service over anything else.

It is not without some scriptural foundation that we might think that worship primarily consists of singing. In Rev. 4:8-10, John writes,

> Day and night [the four living creatures] never stop saying: "Holy, holy, holy is the Lord God Almighty, who was, and is, and is to come." Whenever the living creatures give glory, honor and thanks to him who sits on the throne and who lives forever and ever, the twenty-four elders fall down before him who sits on the throne, and worship him who lives forever and ever.

From this and other passages, it is understandable to conclude that heaven is one continual time of singing songs and proclaiming God's praise. Plus, few people spend *too much* time proclaiming God's praise. Many people struggle to spend a daily time in Bible study and prayer, and we feel guilty for not doing more. We have this vague sense that we need to begin replicating our understanding of heaven in greater measure now. We recognize that we cannot spend every moment in church or devotions because we need to make a living. Still, we feel guilty that we often get more enjoyment from pursuing our favorite hobby than we do from attending church. We assume this is primarily due to our sinfulness and our selfishness.

If it is true that worship ends with the church service, then what is everything else? If we believe we honor God only in church or when we are doing explicitly Christian work, then we may suppose we neither honor nor dishonor him with our other times. We think that our non-church time is just neutral ground about which God is largely indifferent. There is the sacred and the secular. We think God is interested only in the sacred and he is indifferent to the secular, providing we are not disobeying him by breaking his explicit commands. God loves Sunday mornings more than other days of the week. He loves the part of our work week when we are sharing the Gospel with a colleague, humming a song of praise to ourselves, or refraining from office gossip or telling dirty jokes. But when we return to our computer or assembly line or customer service counter, we think God is uninterested in our explicit job responsibilities. But this is false.

The fragmentation of life into sacred and secular is deeply rooted in a flawed epistemology derived from the French Enlightenment.[31] When "man [as] the measure of all things" began to take root in the collective psyche of certain segments of seventeenth-century Western civilization, religious people feared their faith would be rejected as irrational. To provide a safe space for the faith in things unseen, many Christians and non-Christians alike bifurcated knowledge between facts and values. Facts came to be seen as "really true things" like 2+2=4, or gravity, or photosynthesis. Values like "God is good," "Jesus was God Incarnate," and "humans have eternal souls" were not subject to empirical verification. These religious ideas were in a different category from facts, thereby making them unassailable by Enlightenment rationality. The epistemological truce between facts and values relegated religious knowledge to what author Nancy Pearcey calls the "upper story," along with the belief in the tooth fairy and "unlucky numbers" and knocking on wood. The "lower story" became the realm of the factual and empirically true.

---

[31] In her brilliant book, *The Roads to Modernity,* Gertrude Himmelfarb convincingly makes the case that the French Enlightenment, as distinguished from those in Scotland and America, was anti-theistic. Not all Enlightenment thinkers rejected orthodox Christianity.

Many Christians prioritize the primacy of the "spiritual" by believing that the most important things—and perhaps the only important things—are evangelism, missions, Sunday School, and church business. They dismiss the secular as unimportant in eternity. In contrast, those outside the Church prioritize the primacy of the "secular," believing that the most important things—and perhaps the only important things—are health, wealth, reputation, leisure, and sexual gratification. Thus, many Christians and non-Christians alike agree there is a high wall of separation between the sacred and the secular, though they disagree about which side of the wall is most important.

Both sides err in denying the unity of knowledge. The loss of an integrated understanding of knowledge is spiritually lethal for non-Christians and spiritually stultifying for Christians. If we act as if God is indifferent to how we spend most of our waking hours, we fail to bring the Kingdom of God to all of his creation. We will fall into the trap of believing that God cares only about our tithe and not about the other ninety percent of our wealth, that he cares about our "spiritual" thoughts and actions and not about our "secular" life, that he cares about our Sunday mornings but not our Monday mornings.

Some Christians seek to please God in everything they do without formally understanding that their striving to produce an excellent and true legal brief or make an honest sale for customers or prepare a good history lesson for high schoolers should be as much acts of worship as their Sunday morning singing.

Other self-proclaiming Christians act as if God does not care about their behavior. Like the Pharisees, they "clean the outside of the cup and dish, but inside they are full of greed and self-indulgence" (Matt. 23:25). They praise God with their lips on Sundays, but are unfaithful to their spouse on Saturday. They cheat on their taxes, ignore their children, and take advantage of their customers, all while experiencing no cognitive dissonance. They are modern day Gnostics, obsessed with what they believe and indifferent to what they do. The parable of the sheep and the goats applies to them:

Then he will say to those on his left, "Depart from me, you who are cursed, into the eternal fire prepared for the devil and his angels. For I was hungry and you gave me nothing to eat, I was thirsty and you gave me nothing to drink, I was a stranger and you did not invite me in, I needed clothes and you did not clothe me, I was sick and in prison and you did not look after me." They also will answer, "Lord, when did we see you hungry or thirsty or a stranger or needing clothes or sick or in prison, and did not help you?" He will reply, "I tell you the truth, whatever you did not do for one of the least of these, you did not do for me." Then they will go away to eternal punishment, but the righteous to eternal life (Matt 25:41-46).

Between those who flout the grace of God and think it is a license to ignore the requirements of the law and those who give themselves fully to the work of the Lord with their every breath are many who are limited in their vision for what God intends for his creation. They miss the opportunity to see all of their moments as opportunities for worship.

Another flawed view of worship is the belief that worship must be emotionally ecstatic. Closed eyes, raised hands, and inward euphoria are misunderstood to be necessary components of genuine worship. Frequent repetition of worship choruses (what some derisively call 24/7 worship—twenty-four words repeated seven times, or sometimes just seven words repeated twenty-four times) are required until we enter "true worship." For those who do not experience this contrived sense of worship there may be feelings of inadequacy or guilt. In college, I frequently attended a Sunday afternoon worship service where it seemed everyone was having an ecstatic worship experience. I tried to emulate them, but I was not getting the same "buzz." This bothered me a lot, and I questioned my devotion to God. I wrongly assumed that my lack of exuberance in worship was a measure of my faith.

Others assume that a particular form of worship is the best form for all Christians. Some Christians accustomed to more traditional worship with organs, hymns, and outward formality can believe their form is superior for the reverence it pays to God. Those in more expressive worship services with drums, guitars, upraised hands, and loud singing might think their form is superior. And those in between believe they have hit the right balance. This emphasis on outward expressions neglects Jesus' words that true worshipers will worship "in spirit and in truth." Just as there is great diversity in God's people, there are myriad forms of worship.

The Biblical View Of Worship

A proper understanding of worship recognizes that God wants our every breath to be an act of praise and adoration. Worship certainly includes what takes place in church. Indeed, most of the 250 biblical mentions of "worship" refer to the private or public adoration of God in word. Singing hymns and choruses, kneeling, falling prostrate, raising hands, and gathering together in an assembly of praise are forms of worship. Yet Scripture is equally clear that such worship is legitimate only to the extent that it is accompanied by behavior that is fitting of true followers of God.

In Isa. 29:13, "The Lord says: 'These people come near to me with their mouth and honor me with their lips, but their hearts are far from me. Their worship of me is made up only of rules taught by men.'" The form of worship is inadequate if it is not accompanied by a genuine heart. First Sam. 15:22 is yet more explicit that outward expressions of worship are deficient if we do not seek to obey God in all our actions: "Does the LORD delight in burnt offerings and sacrifices as much as in obeying the voice of the LORD? To obey is better than sacrifice, and to heed is better than the fat of rams." To obey God is not just to refrain from certain activities, like adultery, murder, covetousness, and so forth. Obedience requires a life committed to loving the Lord with all our heart, soul, strength, and mind, and loving our neighbors as ourselves (Luke 10:27). These commands are all-consuming.

We have not begun to understand the extent of God's claim on our lives if we view the Sunday morning worship service as the primary means of worshiping God. We must see our

Sunday morning experience of one piece with our Saturday evening revelries and our Monday morning labors. Worship that is compartmentalized fails to reflect the worship God desires from us.

Again, in Jas. 2:14-17, we read:

> What good is it, my brothers, if a man claims to have faith but has no deeds? Can such faith save him? Suppose a brother or sister is without clothes and daily food. If one of you says to him, "Go, I wish you well; keep warm and well fed," but does nothing about his physical needs, what good is it? In the same way, faith by itself, if it is not accompanied by action, is dead.

Words without deeds are empty, but words *with* deeds are powerful. When our eating and drinking and love-making and playing and working and whatever we do are done for the glory of God (1 Cor. 10:31), we live the life of worship for which we have been created. Singer and songwriter Randy Stonehill captures the essence of true worship in his song, "Every Heartbeat is a Prayer":

> Won't you take me as your child of light
> Break me if you must, I won't despair
> Till every breath I breathe is a song of praise
> Every heartbeat is a prayer

Francis of Assisi is often quoted as having said, "Preach the gospel at all times. Use words if necessary."[32] The same could be said of worship: "Worship God in everything you do. Use words if necessary."

Principally An Act Of The Will

How we *feel* is not the measure of true worship. The core issue is our *will*, i.e., what we *choose to do*. Our emotions may often

---

[32] This quote captures the spirit of his writing, but there is no evidence the quote belongs to him.

be in sync with our will, but not always. Feelings are a faulty barometer of whether or not we are worshiping God.

Still, engaging God is not just a head game. In college, I remember chafing at the parts of church services that appealed to our emotions, thinking that such devices were illegitimate means of making us feel warm towards God when we should instead be led by our minds alone. But that is wrong. God has made us emotional beings. We should not fear expressing our feelings about God or to God. Positive emotions can be a tremendous encouragement to us as we seek to follow God. Feeling God's closeness can help us through difficult circumstances, embolden us to act courageously, and give us a deep sense of peace and contentment. Singing, meditation, Bible study, and prayer may well bestow upon us a "spiritual buzz." But not always, and for some people only rarely.

Mother Teresa was known for her constant smile in the face of desperate suffering and her affirming words about the presence of Christ in the darkest corners of our fallen world. On the outside, she seemed a paragon of radiant joy and spiritual exuberance. A book published after her death, *Mother Teresa: Come Be My Light,* reveals this saintly nun's inner life, which was marked by a persistent spiritual aridity and a sense that God was distant and detached from her. "[But] as for me, the silence and the emptiness is so great, that I look and do not see, — Listen and do not hear — the tongue moves [in prayer] but does not speak," she wrote in one letter to her confessor. In another she writes, "In my soul, I can't tell you how dark it is, how painful, how terrible. My feelings are so treacherous. I feel like refusing God. . . " (p. 245).

For Mother Teresa, as for other faithful followers of Christ, discipleship sprang not from a well-spring of emotional strength but from a fixed and steady act of the will. She persevered for decades with little sense of God's presence. Her commitment remained even without emotional highs. Her published confessions may be just the antidote that our emotion-driven culture needs. If even a godly woman like Mother Teresa could persevere in the absence of emotional sustenance, then perhaps many others will choose to press on with or without a Sunday morning shot of adrenaline.

Gnosticism

The modern emphasis on how we *feel* rather than what we *do* is not new. It is rooted in an ancient distortion that beset the early church and has continued to express itself in various manifestations through the ages. Gnostic heresies, which have many varieties, are as old as the Gospel itself. Gnosticism (*"gnosis"* is Greek for "knowledge") taught that the spiritual is good and matter is evil. We access knowledge through the spirit, not the body, making knowledge preeminent over actions. Getting access to knowledge is mystical and requires mental effort.

Within Christianity, these heresies expressed themselves in denigrating the role of the body, leading either to ascetic self-denial to beat the body into submission, or an utter disregard for what one did with one's body. For obvious reasons, the latter form was more popular since it led to the eschewal of self-restraint, especially sexually. Gnostic heresies maintained that having sex outside of marriage and with multiple partners was irrelevant to one's spiritual health, since the body was inherently and irredeemably evil. God, being a Spirit, cared only about one's spiritual state.

Some Gnostic heresies claimed that Jesus only seemed to have a body of flesh, when in fact he was ghostly, a pure spirit. *Docetism,* which is Greek for "to seem," maintained that Jesus' physical body only seemed real. His crucifixion was likewise illusory. The apostle John wrote his epistles to counter *Docetism.* He begins his letter by writing, "That which *we have heard,* which *we have seen* with our eyes, which we have *looked at and our hands have touched*—this we proclaim concerning the Word of life" (1 John 1:1, italics added). His epistle emphasizes Jesus' physical body, death, and resurrection, and he repeatedly makes the point that to follow God requires keeping his commands with soul and body. "This is love for God: to obey his commands" (1 John 5:3). Far from being irrelevant to spiritual growth, mastery of one's body is essential to a godly life.

In the present day, this notion that the spiritual is superior to the physical may express itself in an over-emphasis on emotional worship. "Going through the motions"—or worshiping

God without strong emotions—may be castigated as illegitimate. This distortion not only devalues the role of the will, but it leaves many Christians feeling inadequate about their own spiritual state if they do not experience emotional highs.

I enjoy raising my hands and closing my eyes in private and corporate worship, but I do not always experience an emotional buzz. It is just as often an act of my will, of symbolically offering to God my entire life. Sometimes I can feel quite flat or even low when I do this. But that in no way demeans my worship—providing my will is engaged.

A Willing Choice

When our emotional experience of worship is elevated above our will, we distort what genuine worship is. *Worship is first and foremost a conscious choice to glorify God.* It can encompass everything from changing a tire to opening the mail to sailing. Nothing, beyond that specifically proscribed in Scripture, is inherently unable to encompass worship. Whether our emotions follow our will is not important. Of course, we would prefer to have our emotions reflect our will, but in a fallen world that often does not happen. Our emotions are an unreliable gauge of our true inner state.

Our feelings may drive us to do what feels good, but our will, informed by Scripture, guides us to do the right thing.[33] No matter how many songs, movies, and commercials bid us to follow our cravings because "it feels so right," the measure of obedience is found in our will. The person who seeks to glorify God and the woman who seeks to glorify herself may take the exact same actions, but with opposite moral effect.

Contra to Gnostic thought, how we behave with our bodies is important to God. Paul warned the sexually libertine Corinthians to "flee from sexual immorality. All other sins a man commits are outside his body, but he who sins sexually sins

---

[33] Our will to do the right thing does not necessarily mean we actually do what God commands, since our understanding of God's law may be immature or corrupted. Yet, I suspect that if we believe we are doing right, even as we are doing something against God's law, he may still be pleased with us.

against his own body. Do you not know that your body is a temple of the Holy Spirit, who is in you, whom you have received from God? You are not your own; you were bought at a price. Therefore honor God with your body" (1 Cor. 6:18-20). Paul makes clear we can honor God by what we do with our body. Far from shunning the body, God chooses to make it a unique place for his presence, though he is omnipresent. Furthermore, our bodies, not just our spirits, have been purchased by God. We will rise from the dead with physical bodies, not just disembodied spirits. The Apostles Creed affirms "the resurrection of the body." Our bodies matter.

Hard, Cold Acts Of Obedience

Having established that God cares about our spirit and our body and that we are to do everything for his glory and honor, the question is, how we can actually worship him continually?

We need not be continually humming hymns to ourselves or ceasing our activity to pray every few minutes. We do not have to constantly meditate on Scripture to worship him. It is not only the adept multi-taskers who can worship God all the time. True, we are admonished to pray continually, to meditate on Scripture day and night, and to sing songs to God. Most of us would benefit by doing these things *more* than we do. However, that does not mean that they are required for worship. It would be distracting for me to hum songs while I am writing this book. I should concentrate on my thoughts, typing, grammar and syntax. If I am writing to bring honor to God rather than myself, then I am worshiping God as I write. And that is not just because I have written a "spiritual book." If I were writing a book on mechanical engineering or political philosophy, providing I were doing it to bring honor to God, I would be worshiping God no less.

To honor God in all we do requires clear thinking, even careful planning. Our minutes and our hours should revolve around seeking to worship God in our comings and goings. Once we understand that God has created us to steward his creation, to seek to straighten out that which is twisted, to do justice, to be merciful, to lead others to Christ, to care for the

poor and the oppressed, and to love our family and our enemies, we will seek to worship him in every moment of our day.

In Rom. 12:1, Paul writes that to die to ourselves is worship: "Therefore, I urge you, brothers, in view of God's mercy,
to offer your bodies as living sacrifices, holy and pleasing to
God—*this is your spiritual act of worship*" [emphasis added].
How was God's mercy exercised? In Christ's death on the
cross. He died for us, and now we must die to ourselves for
him, thereby worshiping him in gratitude.

Self-sacrifice for the sake of God is worship. We may
worship God by respecting other people's time and arriving on
time for meetings, by looking away from inappropriate advertisements, by cleaning up the office microwave, by carefully
listening to others, by smiling at parking attendants, by deciding against spending too much money, by going to bed on time
to be alert for morning devotions, by leaving the best slice of
meat for our dinner partners, by taking a bullet to protect
someone else. The list of ways to worship God is endless, and
all of it pleases him and helps mold us into the people he wants
us to be.

Practically, it is not always clear how we should best
spend our time. Asking God at the beginning of the day
whether he wants us to do any specific or out-of-the-ordinary
tasks is helpful. I have often heard God's still small voice
prompting me to reach out to a hurting friend or an intern who
would be grateful for my attention. More often, I am simply
reminded again to keep an attitude of service throughout my
day. Lately, I have been imagining that I am washing the feet
of the person with whom I am talking. While few people would
actually want me to wash their feet, if I am willing to do even
that, then I am more likely to love someone by looking him or
her in the eye with a smile or listening with kind attention.

Often, I have found that spending more time in prayer with
God helps me to be other-centered. Our natural, sinful impulse
is to seek independence from God and other people, so praying
more tempers that natural bent. Frankly, spending time with
God forces me to face up to my sins and selfishness. Far from
being a comforting crutch, life with God is strenuous, challenging, and sometimes even irritating.

The key is to remember that I am not my own, that I was bought at a price, and that I am made to worship God in all things. That is our calling—Christians and non-Christians alike. We were made to worship by serving God and others. Some people have the gift of service. They are ready and eager to serve others, and they do it with a cheerfulness that exudes the love of God. Others find service difficult and against their grain. Regardless of our special gifts, we are made to serve. Worship and service go hand-in-hand.

Interestingly, though, it is not always true that we should spend more time alone with God. Sometimes, the very thing God wants us to do is to act rather than to pray, i.e., feeding the hungry person, not just praying for him. In fact, when I was in college, the Lord led me to shorten my then-typical two-hour daily devotions so I would have more time to worship him by serving others. Only God can lead us to achieve the right balance between private meditation and public action, between words and deeds. Our job is to seek God's mind on the use of all of our time and to obey him.

Comfort And Consumerism

Our society encourages selfishness. Advertisements tell us to indulge in luxury, comfort, and consumption. It is easy to slip into the mode of seeking to scratch our every itch, to find our hopes centered on our next consumer purchase instead of how we can give ourselves away.

Recently, a Christian acquaintance told me breathlessly, "The most awesome thing just happened." Based on the ecstatic look on his face I expected him to tell me about someone whom he had just led to the Lord. Instead, he exclaimed, "When I was buying a plasma flat-screen TV, I found out that I could get an instant $100 rebate." Inside, I felt sick. Something seemed amiss. I am not saying that it was wrong for my acquaintance to purchase a TV or to be excited about the unexpected rebate. Yet his reaction reminded me of how we can be more enthusiastic about what we get than what we can give, the material than the spiritual, the temporal than the eternal.

The urge to endlessly consume in pursuit of satisfaction is natural, but naturally sinful. In the end, it does not satisfy us. At least about this, The Rolling Stones' Mick Jagger was right when he crooned, " I can't get no satisfaction!" The temporary thrill wears off. The new car that excited us last year is normal today. Photos of exotic vacation spots may prompt us to spend more than we should in pursuit of the next high. The pleasure will fade, the longed-for object will disappoint us, break down, and be discarded. The fruit, whether forbidden or permissible, gets old. In the lyrics of Switchfoot's "American Dream," "the ambition for excess wrecks us."

In contrast, we find fulfillment by being servants who give and give and give. Our mornings should bring thoughts about how we can give ourselves to God and our neighbor. Service brings meaning, purpose, joy, and fulfillment. It ennobles us, pulls us outside of our selfish ambitions, and satisfies our desires.

Summary

Worship entails honoring God in all we do. When we understand God's "jealousy" for our every moment, we begin to understand the extent of our obligation to him. He wants to own us, consume all we are, invading our space, crowding out our selfish aims. He does not need our attention (though he does delight in it), but we need to pay attention to him—for our own good.

We were created to bring God glory. As the *Westminster Shorter Catechism* says, "Man's chief end is to glorify God, and to enjoy him forever." By glorifying him we come to enjoy him and live life to the full. In worship, we find the path to joy.

6

Calling:
Not Just for Pastors
and Missionaries

*"For the secret of man's being is not only to live but to have
something to live for. Without a stable conception of the object
of life, man would not consent to go on living, and would
rather destroy himself than remain on earth, though he had
bread in abundance."*
"The Grand Inquisitor" in The Brothers Karamazov
by Fyodor Dostoyevsky

*"God ... hides himself in the ordinary social functions and
stations of life, even the most humble. God himself is milking
the cows through the vocation of the milkmaid."*
Martin Luther

Many Christians only see eternal purpose in their "spiritual work," wrongly believing that God is indifferent to the rest of their labors. They think he has a purpose in everything surrounding the church, but not in non-religious professional work.

I have heard many missionaries talk about their call to the mission field. They say, "God has called me to move overseas to share the Gospel with unreached people. I will be in full-time ministry." Rarely have I heard this testimony in reverse: "God has called me away from the mission field to do full-time ministry as a computer programmer at a high-tech firm."

Why not? Does God only have a purpose in salvation but no purpose in computers? And if he has a purpose in everything, then are we not potentially called to every arena of life? And if we are failing to recognize his call to do everything "for the glory of God" (1 Cor. 10:31), are we missing out on the exciting and fulfilling sense of purpose we should experience in all things?

Life Without Meaning

There is a story of men in a concentration camp who were forced to spend fourteen hours a day stacking bricks in a pile, then moving them back to the original pile in a pointless and repetitive cycle. This meaningless task, repeated many times a day, seven days a week, quickly broke the will of the prisoners, who went insane or committed suicide. In Greek mythology, Sisyphus was a proud king cursed to roll a huge boulder up a hill, only to watch it roll back down, eternally repeating this pointless task.

Prov. 29:18 says, "Where there is no vision, the people perish" (KJV). God made humans to live for a purpose. We find fulfillment in serving him and his purposes.

Philosophies that deny transcendent purpose grapple with how humans can go on living in the face of meaninglessness. Whether it is Darwinian evolution that reduces humans to random accidents or various post-modern philosophies[34] that reject any inherent meaning of life, the problem of meaninglessness besets their adherents. I, too, wrestled with the pointlessness of a world without God as I emerged from adolescence and, for a time, lost my faith in Christ.

I entered Houghton College, a Christian liberal arts college, as a vibrant and committed follower of Christ. I had given my life to the Lord at age sixteen and fervently sought to serve the Lord with my whole being. Yet as I read Jean-Paul Sartre and the French existentialists, I was gradually persuaded that my faith was just wishful thinking. I came to agree with Sartre that "existence precedes essence," that we are just meat puppets without a creator, an inherent purpose, or a destiny. As Sartre puts it in his *Existentialism is a Humanism*, "man first of all exists, encounters himself, surges up in the world—and defines himself afterwards." It is "very distressing that God does not exist, because all possibility of finding values in a

---

[34] These so-called philosophies are really anti-philosophies, since they deny the existence of meaning and truth.

heaven of ideas disappears along with Him; there can no longer be an *a priori* Good, since there is no infinite and perfect consciousness to think it." Despair is the logical result.

I took no joy in my growing atheism. In fact, I was loath to throw off my spiritual disciplines of Bible study and prayer, because I was still a doubting atheist. I still thought there was a chance God might exist. Therefore, I continued my daily devotions, which were often one to two hours of Bible study and prayer, beginning with this preface: "This is just in case you exist, God." Like another French philosopher, Blaise Pascal, I was reluctant to stop living for Christ until I was utterly convinced that he did not exist, given that the consequences of a mistaken atheism are infinitely greater than the consequences of a mistaken faith in God. My conviction that there was no God grew stronger as I debated my fellow students, whose arguments did not seem as compelling as Sartre's.[35] I knew that once I was sufficiently convinced that God did not exist, I would have to decide whether or not to kill myself.

My loss of faith was not derived from a desire to rebel against God. The life of lechery looked so empty. I loved God very much when I thought he existed, and I longed to be able to believe in him again. For me, as for Sartre, the loss of faith in God resulted in forlornness and despair. Unlike the secular existentialists, the notion of willing myself to live for a contrived purpose seemed hollow. If I concluded that living a heroic life of sacrifice and achievement was morally equivalent to a life of self-indulgence and violence, then existence seemed too heavy a burden. From secular existentialism, I descended into nihilism, seeing no purpose in living if there were no God and no transcendent purpose in life.

Gradually, my faith in Christ began to return as I considered the moral implications of atheism. I doubted the existence of God, but I could not believe that evil was an illusion. If evil exists, then it can only be defined in reference to an absolute reference point. In the words of singer and songwriter Jon Foreman of *Switchfoot*, "the shadow proves the

---

[35] Some of my friends were persuaded by my arguments and rejected their faith, to my chagrin, and they still have not returned to faith.

sunshine." I knew the shadows were real. I could never be persuaded that Nazi soldiers bayoneting Jewish babies in front of their mothers is anything but inherently, ontologically, transcendently, and absolutely Evil. If Evil exists, then God must exist since Evil needs an absolute reference point against which it can be defined. So I came back to faith through the backdoor of rejecting the alternatives.

The benefits I gained from having to grapple with my faith continue to this day. I came to own my faith in a special way, having examined the ghastly implications of a godless universe that was fundamentally unpersuasive to me. I am eager to discuss my faith with apostates and doubters and atheists, having gained a confidence in defending Christianity. I only wish I could find more people who are open to these discussions. Sadly, such conversation is usually considered out of bounds for polite society, and the silent walls of defense are erected as soon as I veer too close to such unseemly "God talk." These societal rules have been an effective tool of the Enemy.

My story of losing my faith is not unique. Life without ultimate meaning breeds despair. Eternity is in our hearts. When we deny what "we can't not know," to borrow the words of J. Budziszewski, our lives unravel. Fyodor Dostoyevsky illustrates this point in his seminal work, *Crime and Punishment*. The main character, Rodion Raskolnikov murders an innocent (though despicable) woman because he believes that right and wrong do not exist. After the murder, his vain attempts to deny the immorality of his crime lead him to go insane. We deny reality at our peril.

Another story, made famous by business management guru Peter Drucker, underscores the power of purpose in life. In the parable, a visitor to a medieval construction site asks three stonecutters the same question: "What are you doing?" The first stonecutter says, "I'm cutting stone. It's dull work, but it pays the bills." A second stonecutter says, "I'm the best stonecutter in the land. Look at how perfectly I've cut the edges." A third pointed to a nearby foundation and said, "I'm building a cathedral." This last man was the one who found fulfillment in his work.

Whether we recognize it or not, we all have a purpose. We are called by God to serve him and our fellow humans and care for his creation. Our calling is in our DNA and stitched in the very fabric of the universe. Denying it requires mental effort. Indeed, few people can live with the logical consequences of a meaningless world, lapsing back into a world of moral absolutes when evil touches them or those they love. Renowned ethicist and Princeton professor Peter Singer advocates mercy-killing for certain classes of disabled people. Yet when his own mother was in advanced stages of Alzheimer's, he spent his money to support her. He explained this contradiction by saying, "I think this has made me see how the issues of someone with these kinds of problems are really very difficult. Perhaps it is more difficult than I thought before, because it is different when it's your mother" (qtd. in Specter, 55) The reality that his mother was not just a piece of meat overrode his still extant but existentially unlivable philosophy.

What Is Calling?

Calling is simply another word for God's will for us—what he wants us to do. Christians often think of calling as something unusual and very special, just for certain people. Not so. In fact, all of us are called. God has a will for every human alive. The Christian faith stands in stark contrast to the emptiness of the secular existentialists' denial of transcendent purpose.

But does God have a purpose in everything? Does he care about what job we have? Is work a necessary evil or is it just a means of supporting the Church and missionaries? Are those in "full-time ministry" more pleasing to God than those who paint houses all day? Does God have a will for my work beyond making money so I can support my family? Is he interested in my tax planning strategies or in my bricklaying or my design of bus windshields?

Scripture is clear: all work (other than that which is specifically prohibited, like prostitution and theft) done for his glory pleases him. Gnostic thought elevates the spiritual work above earthly work, but that contradicts God's creation and redemption. Work was always part of God's plan for humanity, pre-existing the Fall. Now, work is done by the sweat of our brow, but God is still interested in what we are doing and how it is done. He is no more indifferent to his creation *before* the Fall than *after* it. We are called by God, Christian and non-Christian alike. God has a will for us in every moment: that we seek to glorify him in everything. This calling excludes nothing.

We sometimes think of calling as an angelic visitation that is special and unique for people being given a specific task, much like God calling Moses through the burning bush. Calling can be that, but it is usually much more prosaic. Our calling need not be emotional, dramatic, or miraculous. Simply looking at creation and reading the Bible provides us with all the "call" we need to fill a lifetime of service. God has already called every person. The question is whether we will listen and heed the call.

General Calling

Each of us has a general calling—a calling applicable to everyone made in his image—and a specific calling—something unique to us. In Dr. Os Guinness' book *The Call,* he defines calling as "the truth that God calls us to himself so decisively that everything we are, everything we do, and everything we have is invested with a special devotion and dynamism lived out as a response to his summons and service" (4).

Just as a car is made for transportation, God made us so we would glorify him. God does not *need* our praise, but we *need* to worship him to live a full and meaningful life. This general call is knitted into the fabric of our being. We can deny our general call, but we invite our eternal damnation if we do so, not to mention countless heartaches on this side of eternity. By affirming it and following our calling in all things, we grow and flourish into the life God purposed for us.

When I was in college, a guest preacher spoke in one of our school-wide chapel services. In his high-pitched and frenetic way of speaking, he nearly shouted at us, "Some of you are struggling to know God's will for your life. Well I know what it is! Love the Lord your God with all your heart, soul, mind, and strength, and love your neighbor as yourself!" His point was clear: we had a general calling which was clear enough, even absent more specific instructions.

Our general calling is all-encompassing, touching every moment of our lives. Nothing escapes its jealous reach. In a scene from Mel Gibson and Steve McEveety's movie *The Passion of the Christ*, Jesus is intensely laboring over the construction of a table. Once complete, he sits on it to make sure it does not wobble, clearly wanting to make an excellent table—as his expression of his general calling to bring glory to the Father. Though the scene is extra-biblical, it aptly captures God's concern for everything that takes place under the sun, from world wars to knitting. Martin Luther thoroughly understood the biblical notion of calling as inherent in all jobs, not just those of clerics and missionaries:

> The prince should think: Christ has served me and made everything to follow him; therefore, I should also serve my neighbor, protect him and everything that belongs to him. That is why God has given me this office, and I have it that I might serve him. That would be a good prince and ruler. When a prince sees his neighbor oppressed, he should think: That concerns me! I must protect and shield my neighbor. . . . The same is true for shoemaker, tailor, scribe, or reader. If he is a Christian tailor, he will say: I make these clothes because God has bidden me do so, so that I can earn a living, so that I can help and serve my neighbor. When a Christian does not serve the other, God is not present; that is not Christian living (qtd. in Gaiser, 361).

Our call is to serve God and man in all we do, as a tailor or tax collector or teacher. Jesus said the two great commands are to "Love the Lord your God with all your heart and with all your soul and with all your mind and with all your strength" and to "Love your neighbor as yourself" (Mark 12:29-31). Always remembering these twin admonitions should guide us moment to moment. The commands both constrain us from doing certain things and give us latitude to serve in a plethora of ways. The prohibitions are usually obvious: getting drunk, acting selfishly, boasting, lying, having sex outside of marriage, and so forth. We learned most of these things as children. Beyond these sins of commission, we are left with a broad range of options on how to serve God and man.

This wide expanse of freedom to serve is both exciting and challenging: exciting because we use our freedom and creativity to glorify him, and challenging because we must constantly keep in step with the Holy Spirit in discerning how and where to serve. Whether any particular activity not proscribed by Scripture is part of God's call is measured by our motivation. For example, I could actually disobey God by attending a Bible study if I am neglecting family responsibilities to do so. Likewise, someone feasibly could fulfill his calling by watching a football game instead of attending a Sunday night church service. The lodestar is whether our motivation is to serve the Lord and we are attuned to his guidance.

Specific Calling

Though God's general calling is the same for all of us, his specific calling is a unique requirement he has placed on each of us as individuals. His specific calling does not extend to every moment of our lives. God has not ordained how each of us should brush our teeth. However, he does sometimes guide us to one particular activity or set of activities over others. His specific calling is not always entirely clear and may require time and discernment to discover—and will likely change over time.

Moses was sent by God to return to Egypt, confront Pharaoh, and lead the Jews back to Palestine. Mary was visited by the Angel Gabriel and told she would bear the Son of God. Saul (later "Paul") was called to be a missionary on the Damascus Road. Each also had a general calling to love and serve God, which they lived out as they fulfilled their individual specific callings. Likewise, the prophet Jonah, in addition to his general calling to serve God, was given a specific calling to go to Nineveh to preach a message of repentance. When Jonah decided to sail in the opposite direction from Nineveh, he was denying his specific calling—and, therefore, his general calling to serve God in all things.

Not everyone experiences such dramatic calls with miraculous signs and angelic visitations. I know I have not. And not everyone is called to explicitly religious work. Yet God is intimately involved with our lives, and he often makes known his specific will for us. This specific calling may be in keeping with the gifts and abilities he has bestowed on us, or it may be a work he wants us to do in our weakness. Whereas Paul was gifted in the logical presentation of truth—perfect for a missionary to pagans—Moses apparently lacked the gift of public speaking, and asked that his brother Aaron help him. Sometimes our specific calling is pleasant, and sometimes unpleasant. Sometimes we are called to do the very thing we "thrill to," and sometimes we are called to do the last thing we want to do.

After college, I believe the Lord called me to be a missionary to Turkish guestworkers in West Germany.[36] I hated being a missionary. I believed in my work, but it went against my grain to sit in tea houses endlessly talking about day-to-day things—the very thing that was necessary to establish rapport with my Turkish friends. My A-type nature screamed in protest at the "wasted" time. Yet I believe that God called me there, at least in part to humble me, and also to use me to help lead one Turkish man to Christ. Mercifully, God led me away from Turkish missionary work and towards politics, a career much more in line with my strengths and desires. In the movie *Chariots of Fire*, the Scottish athlete Eric Liddell says, "I believe that God made me for a purpose, but He also made me fast. When I run, I feel his pleasure." When I

---

[36] Turks were invited to work in post-World War II Germany to compensate for the many German men killed in battle. They remain guestworkers, not fully integrating into Germany society and not becoming German citizens. Many will spend their working years doing menial jobs in Germany, only to retire in Turkey, comparatively wealthy thanks to the lower cost of living in their native land.

am working on public policy or drafting speeches for politicians, I feel his pleasure.

I believe that my missionary work with Turkish guestworkers in Germany and my work in public policy have both been expressions of God's specific calling to accomplish his purposes in me and in the world. One was unpleasant, one pleasant. It is possible that I misunderstood God's specific call, and I could have skipped my year working with Turks and gone directly to politics. Understanding God's specific calling is not always easy. Yet I believe that my missions work was in keeping with my general calling to glorify God. I moved to Germany out of a desire to please the Lord, not for selfish motives. Assuming that my work with Turks was God's specific call to me, he used it for his purposes. Missionary work was my "Nineveh."

I have experienced many more "mini-Ninevehs" in various arenas of my life where God has called me to follow him in doing something I would prefer not to do. Sometimes I am called to fast, to meet with a job seeker, to go on a prayer walk, to help a homeless man, to shovel a neighbor's walk. I sense God's leading and I know that to do otherwise would be to disobey him.

For most of us, life's moments are devoid of a specific calling, but we still have multiple ways to follow God's general call. During this "free time," we have liberty to seek to please him in a variety of ways. In this instance, instead of being a bull's eye, God's will is more often like a buffet at which we have multiple options. The options are acceptable, providing our motivation is always one of humility and service.

In this dizzying land of opportunity, it is easy to be confused about which path to take. I have sometimes made the mistake of projecting my indecision onto God, praying fervently for God to reveal his will to me and feeling very frustrated that I cannot discern which path is right. In retrospect, I believe that God would have been pleased with all of the options I was considering. His apparent silence was not from a desire to test me to see whether I could find the right way, like finding my way through a maze, but from his delight in freedom, permitting me to choose the path I thought best. He wants us to learn to "tune our hearts to his" so we can best discern the paths we should take.

It can be especially difficult to follow God when our specific calling is at variance with our gifts and skills. We may be gifted at leadership, but we, like Moses and Joseph, may spend years in obscurity tending sheep or locked in a dungeon. We may be gifted at writing but have little opportunity because of demanding jobs. We may be gifted at teaching but have no pupils.

I had never wanted to leave Capitol Hill. I love working inside government. I did so for almost twenty years in the Congress and the White House, but as of the time of this writing, I believe God has called me away from the long and intense hours of the political world so I can be more present for my family. Between the Fall and our eventual redemption, we are sometimes called to work against our grain.

Calling: More Than Our Occupation

We in the West are blessed with a plethora of career options. We will wrestle with what career to pursue, and most of us will change careers three times in our lifetimes. Yet for many people in the world, no such choices exist. Many people will do the same jobs their parents and their parents' parents did without questioning and without an option to do otherwise. Many unskilled manual laborers in India would be excellent college professors or accountants or attorneys—if only they had the opportunity.

Still, calling is not identical to occupation. Our paid work may not be consistent with our gifts, interests, or talents, and we may not enjoy it, but it is the work we are given by God. The North Korean Christian doing hard labor in a prison camp because of his faith in Christ is following his call by diligently doing the arduous work given to him. The laid-off scientist who is selling shoes at a retail outlet or the former pastor painting houses are both following God's call to provide for their families through honest work.

Some of us have the privilege of working in jobs that line up well with our gifts, and some of us do not. And yet we are all following God's call when we seek to glorify him in everything we do.

Evangelism And Calling

We have immortal souls, destined to live beyond the grave in heaven or hell. Our eternal destiny is shaped by the choices we make now. Therefore, whether we live in poverty or sickness or servitude in this world is less important than whether we are ready to face God in the final judgment. This recognition, which many people deny or ignore, leads us to have eternal vision, focusing on the unseen rather than the seen, always thinking about the eternal consequences of our temporal actions.

It is, therefore, understandable that we might then believe that the Great Commission—Jesus' final earthly admonition to his disciples to "go and make disciples of all nations, baptizing them in the name of the Father and of the Son and of the Holy Spirit, and teaching them to obey everything I have commanded you" (Matt. 28:19-20)—might trump everything else. If evangelism is more important than justice, then it would logically follow that missionaries are more important than politicians. In fact, they would be more important than all other professions combined, considering that the eternal infinitely outweighs the temporal. Evangelism would be more important than any other activity, and we would be right to see all other pursuits as handmaidens to evangelism. Computer programmers may be doing God's business, but not God's most important work of saving souls—except if they are sharing the gospel on the job or supporting the work of a missions agency.

Nevertheless, this view misunderstands the nature of the Gospel. The Lord is Lord of all creation, not just the human soul (as if we could reduce ourselves to just disembodied souls—something that has never been and never will be in heaven or in the New Earth). His will is that we make him Lord of our lives and Lord of all that is. We are called to be holy, set apart for him and his purposes. His will is that no one would go to hell but all would repent (2 Pet. 3:9). The question is, repent of what? Sinning, of course. But sin is more comprehensive than specific acts of omission or commission. It is a disposition that denies God's proper role as Lord of everything, and sets up someone or something in his place. The fundamental sin of the Garden was denying God's lordship, supplanting his authority with our own. Therefore, the Gospel requires that we recognize and submit to his lordship in all things—over money, matter, sex, the state—all of it.

The Great Commission was Jesus' final admonition to the disciples, but not his only admonition. All of Scripture still applies to us, including the creation mandate to steward his creation. Jesus said that the greatest commands are that we love God and our neighbor. The admonition to make disciples—which does not stop at just leading someone to Christ but includes nurturing those who are already followers—is part of the mosaic of commands we have been given. Reducing Christianity to evangelism is not biblical.

Jesus' lordship does not begin and end with our eternal destiny. It extends to how we live now. Jesus inaugurated the Kingdom of God, so it has already begun here on earth, though it will not be fully consummated until this world is made new after the final judgment. Reducing the Kingdom to just whether one is going to heaven effectively denies Jesus' lordship over everything. It leads to the mistaken and reductionist view of salvation as being simply between "me and Jesus." It drinks from the Gnostic well, denying that God has a will for all of creation. It reduces us to souls stranded in alien matter. It leads us to think of Christianity as principally fire insurance. It bifurcates Jesus as Savior and Jesus as Lord, as if it were possible to have one without the other.

I have known Christians working on Capitol Hill who believe God has called them solely to share the Gospel with their colleagues at the water cooler. They have little or no understanding of whether God cares about what laws they are helping to pass and what laws they are seeking to block. This stunted view renders them ineffective in the work in which they spend most of their waking hours. God is more than just the God of the water cooler. He is also the God of the desk.

The Kingdom of God is not only spiritual and individualistic, but material and corporate, too. It consists of a healthy and whole person in a healthy and whole society in which matter and all creation is no longer subject to the groaning of the Fall. Rom. 8:19-21 makes clear the Kingdom includes more than just our souls:

> The creation waits in eager expectation for the sons of God to be revealed. For the creation was subjected to frustration, not by its own choice, but by the will of the one who subjected it, in hope that the creation itself will be liberated from its bondage to decay and brought into the glorious freedom of the children of God.

God has plans for the world that are bigger than simply "personal salvation," though they include that. His lordship is meant to be transformative now, on this side of the final judgment. It is meant to up-end our personal lives, our corporate lives, our care for the environment, our treatment of the poor and oppressed, our care for the unborn and the infirm and the elderly. It is meant to overturn this world's twisted order of money-changers and idolaters and replace it with a just and merciful order. It has radical implications for everything. Dr. Jerry Herbert says it this way:

> Jesus came not only to save my soul but to announce the kingdom of God. That is, he came declaring in word and deed that the Covenant God was at last fulfilling, through Jesus' own ministry, his ancient covenant to restore his broken and sinful creation. In Jesus, the Creator God, our Father, is fulfilling his covenant promise to redeem the world. And we who are called by his name are caught up in his great rescue operation to restore and renew, by the work of the Holy Spirit, the whole of creation. This is the Gospel.[37]

---

[37] From private correspondence with the author. Dr. Herbert was professor of political science at the American Studies Program in Washington, D.C. He has served as an intellectual and spiritual mentor and role model to me for almost thirty years.

Therefore, reducing "calling" simply to a narrow view of the Great Commission minimizes, rather than recognizes, the comprehensive lordship of Christ and the nature of the Kingdom of God. This does not get us off the hook from boldly sharing the Gospel with our neighbors in word, but it includes boldly living out the Gospel *in deed*. The question is not whether evangelism is more important to God than gardening. The question is, what are we called to do at any given moment to advance the Kingdom of God? Being set apart for God's purposes includes evangelism and hemming trousers. "So whether you eat or drink or whatever you do, do it all for the glory of God" (2 Cor. 10:31). We would be wrong to neglect our responsibility to clean the bathrooms—if that is the work God has for us—in order to distribute tracts. Living under Christ's lordship, moment by moment, is our call.

If we are all called to make Christ Lord in everything we do, then accountants are as much engaged in obeying God as Bible translators. We should pray for homemakers, not just missionaries.[38] Unlike other vocations, missionaries need our financial support, so it is still understandable they would command a larger share of our attention, but this is a practical consideration, not a spiritual one.

We are all "Christ's ambassadors" (2 Cor. 5:20), and we are each called to share the gospel. As true today as when Jesus first said it, "The harvest is plentiful but the workers are few. Ask the Lord of the harvest, therefore, to send out workers into his harvest field" (Matt. 9:37-38). Too many people neglect evangelism from fear or laziness.[39]

Still, it is good to remember that it is the Holy Spirit who calls and saves. We do not close the deal—God does that. Therefore, it is not our job to save people, but God's. We bear

---

[38] The Falls Church Anglican, where I was a member, does this very thing. Each Sunday morning, we prayed for people in a variety of vocations, including missionaries and lobbyists and homemakers and architects.

[39] I have struggled with the temptation to neglect evangelism in my zeal to build up those inside the Church, yet this is neglecting an essential element of my call. Evangelism is not just for "professionals," but for all of us.

witness to the Gospel in all we do, using words when necessary.

What if we could know that no one would be saved by our service in a local rescue mission to the homeless? Would we be right to continue volunteering, or would we be wasting our time? Yes, continuing to serve would be the right choice if that is where we sense the Lord leading us to serve. God loves the poor and has commanded us to care for them. Not all worthwhile work is pre-evangelistic, but all worthwhile work is done for the glory of God.

Discerning Our Calling

How can we know God's will for us? God rarely speaks in a thunderclap. He bids us to seek him with all our heart, with the promise that we will find him. Seeking him requires effort, discernment, and practice. God wants to sanctify us through the process of seeking him. He wants us to learn wisdom so we will become wise. The struggle of the search helps us to internalize the lessons we need to learn. We often need to experience things in order to truly know them.

The Bible

To know God's will, we should begin with the Word of God. We should make a practice of immersing ourselves in the Bible. Through it, God speaks: "All Scripture is God-breathed and is useful for teaching, rebuking, correcting and training in righteousness, so that the man of God may be thoroughly equipped for every good work" (2 Tim. 3:16-17). It is not a dead letter. "For the word of God is living and active. Sharper than any double-edged sword, it penetrates even to dividing soul and spirit, joints and marrow; it judges the thoughts and attitudes of the heart. Nothing in all creation is hidden from God's sight. Everything is uncovered and laid bare before the eyes of him to whom we must give account" (Heb. 4:12-13).

When we long to know God's heart and be led by him, we must turn to the primary means through which he communicates with us. We should do it earnestly, not casually.

Scripture should be approached with at least as much attention as we rightly pay to serious literary works. Scripture is not always plainly understood on first reading. Exegesis, studying what the human author of the text intended for the recipients in its historical context, is the first step. If we skip this step, we risk misinterpreting the text. The second step is hermeneutics, interpreting the enduring principles for our situation today.

Meditating on Scripture is also an important way of drilling deep into God's heart. "Do not let this Book of the Law depart from your mouth; meditate on it day and night, so that you may be careful to do everything written in it. Then you will be prosperous and successful" (Josh. 1:8). Word studies can open up the Bible to deeper levels of understanding. Why did the author choose this word? What does this word mean? What is the derivation of the word in the original language? Meditation requires intense concentration. It may require thirty minutes to unpack just a few phrases of Scripture, but the long-term benefits are worth the time.

Memorize passages of the Bible so they can bounce around inside your head throughout your day. Spend your devotional time memorizing poignant and challenging verses. Find the verses that address the particular sins with which you struggle the most so you can use them as "the sword of the Spirit" (Eph. 6:17). Scripture should be constantly applied to our daily lives. Think of how many songs we know by heart. Why should we know any less Scripture, since it is the very Word of God to lead us through this confusing world?

When I went through a particularly fiery trial some years ago, I recited Col. 3:1-4 over and over again.[40] I did not do it as a talisman or magic incantation, but as a continual reminder of how God sees the world. Without having those verses memorized, they would have been less ready to guide me.

Godly and wise authors can help to illuminate the truths of Scripture. They bring to bear their superior knowledge of the

---

[40] "Since, then, you have been raised with Christ, set your hearts on things above, where Christ is, seated at the right hand of God. Set your minds on things above, not on earthly things. For you died, and your life is now hidden with Christ in God. When Christ, who is your life, appears, then you also will appear with him in glory."

Bible with years of holy living to unpack the Word. However, they should not serve as a substitute for study of the primary source. There is something special about reading God's Word directly and letting it saturate our minds that cannot be matched by secondary sources. Studying the Bible with other Christians is also valuable, because in community we can learn new insights from the Bible. There is also a joy in discovering together the depths of the Bible.

All of our thoughts and feelings should be measured against the plumb line of the Bible. Some Christians believe that God has spoken to them in ways that clearly contradict Scripture. But that would deny the authority of Scripture, ascribing to our own private experience an authority transcending the revealed Word of God. With the Psalmist, we need to affirm that "Your word is a lamp to my feet and a light for my path" (Ps.119:105).

The Church

Though flawed and corrupted, the Church is another important way through which God calls and leads us. Increasingly, Christians are quitting church, choosing to go it alone or in a permeable circle of friends. They ignore the admonition that we should "not give up meeting together, as some are in the habit of doing" (Heb. 10:25). Scripture teaches that we are to meet together and submit to the authority of church elders. Temptations to become untethered from church are dangerous. We need teaching, authority, and accountability to guide us how to lead godly lives. We are made for community. Being made in God's image, we were created to live in fellowship just as the Godhead lives in Trinitarian fellowship.

God often chooses to guide us through the counsel of godly men and women. Prov. 15:22 says, "Plans fail for lack of counsel, but with many advisers they succeed." When you are confused about God's general or specific call on your life, consult with people who walk closely with God. God will often use a chorus of voices to help us find the next step.

The Church is filled with sinners. We can be proud, idolatrous, lecherous, drunken, lustful and are beset by every sin common to our fallen race. It is not just that we previously sinned, but we continue to fall into sin. Even the godliest people sin regularly. We are not perfect—attaining perfection on this side of heaven is impossible.[41] As followers of Jesus, we must continually repent—turn away—from our sin, no longer embracing it but fighting against it. When we excuse our sin or embrace it, then we are in open rebellion against God and we are in danger of hell's fire.[42] First John 1:6 says, "If we claim to have fellowship with him yet walk in the darkness, we lie and do not live by the truth." Confession and repentance keep us anchored.

Many people act surprised and angry that church leaders and members sin. They hold others to a higher standard than they can attain. This "splinter-in-your-eye-while-ignoring-the-log-in-mine" approach breeds disillusionment with the Church Universal, driving people from church to church in search of perfection or to give up the search altogether. They will not find perfection. They will also miss out on the benefits of godly counsel from fellow sinners and pilgrims who can speak God's words into their lives.

One time, when I had been unjustly accused of betraying another's trust at work, I daily sought counsel from a small group of godly people who helped me respond righteously in a confusing situation. I was amazed at how God spoke so clearly through this chorus of men and women, leading me to quietly bear the injustice without fighting back or trying to justify myself. In time, their wise counsel was amply borne out by the fruits of their words. God preserved my reputation and

---

[41] Some Christian denominations believe that it is possible to completely stop sinning. I have yet to meet any of these perfected people.

[42] Calvinists and those who believe our salvation cannot be lost would say such people never were truly believers, but only appeared to be. Arminians believe salvation can be lost, and refusing to repent of conscious sin is potential grounds for losing one's salvation. Both Calvinists and Arminians agree that anyone who does not fight against sin is in danger of going to hell. We cannot know for sure who is going to hell, but we can have our suspicions. God is the ultimate judge who will judge fairly. And we dare not rely on what Dietrich Bonhoeffer called "cheap grace," expecting God to forgive us if we claim him as Savior but not Lord. There is no scriptural foundation to believe discipleship is optional for salvation.

provided me with a new job that I would not have gotten had I
followed my instinct to publicly defend myself. When God's
path is not clear in difficult circumstances, my wife and I
continue to rely on godly counselors. So often, they become the
voice of God in our lives.

Prayer

Prayer—talking with God—is an indispensable part of seeking
his call on our lives. Both pouring out our hearts to God and
listening carefully for his "still small voice" are ways that God
guides us. He often directs me to do one thing or not do another
thing by giving me a "sense." This "feeling" is fallible and
must be measured against Scripture. It is wise to bring it into
the light of community to "test the spirits" (1 John 4:1).
Hearing God's voice takes practice and patience.

Some people lament that they never sense that God is
speaking to them, and they think they are spiritually deficient
or that God is ignoring them. Yet God never ignores us, and the
perceived silence is not necessarily a measure of our walk with
Christ. Mother Teresa and St. John of the Cross both lamented
the "dark night of the soul," in which God seemed distant and
uninvolved. We know from Scripture that God is all-knowing
and ever-loving. Therefore, he is never distant, despite what we
feel. We must believe by faith that the Bible is true and that
God is near.

When God feels distant, I find it helpful to speak aloud the
words I think God might say to me, were I to hear his voice
audibly. In this exercise, we should humbly use our best
judgment as guided by Scripture, since we still "see through a
glass, darkly" (1 Cor. 13:12).

Fasting

Another way to discern God's will is to fast from good things.
The Bible does not prescribe the specifics of what and when
and how to fast, yet it seems to be an integral part of a mature
walk with Christ. Fasting has an impact on us and an impact on
the invisible, heavenly realms. Jesus indicated that his disciples

would fast after he returned to heaven (Matt. 9:15). Jesus fasted for forty days to inaugurate his ministry. If he who was sinless fasted, we should do no less.

I hate fasting. Some people get spiritual clarity when they fast; I get a headache and become grumpy. I dread it in prospect and am glad when it ends. Yet in the aggregate I see the valuable role it plays in helping me to discipline my body so that it is more fully at God's disposal. Paul writes against the pagans "whose God is their stomach" (Phil. 3:19). He wrote that "I beat my body and make it my slave so that after I have preached to others, I myself will not be disqualified for the prize" (1 Cor. 9:27). The Apostle Peter admonishes disciples to similar physical self-denial:

> Therefore, since Christ suffered in his body, arm yourselves also with the same attitude, because he who has suffered in his body is done with sin. As a result, he does not live the rest of his earthly life for evil human desires, but rather for the will of God (1 Pet. 4:1-2).

Taking a day to pray and fast in solitude is a helpful way to begin new stages of our lives. Whether it is before a job search, the birth of a child, taking a new job, and so on, withdrawing for a day to seek God's face can help us to better hear his voice. It provides us an opportunity to take stock of our lives to see whether our first desire is to serve him in all things, come what may.

Gifts

More often than not, our gifts and talents are good indicators of God's call on our lives. After all, it is God who planted them in us and gave us the opportunity to develop them.

God is not cruel, though the Evil One wants us to believe otherwise. We are called to suffering, but not all the time and in every way. The world is fallen and twisted, and yet God's grace manifests itself in the joy we find in the journey. God has called us to do his bidding in everything, and often the very thing he wants us to do is the thing we enjoy doing or in which we excel. He has made some of us skilled with our hands. Others are comfortable speaking before large crowds. Some are organizers, some are creative, some are resourceful. We do well to understand our gifts, because they may help us know how God wants to use us.

Many non-Christians are afraid to give their lives to Christ because they fear he will send them as missionaries to a remote African village. Maybe, maybe not, but we do not get to bargain with our jealous and all-consuming God. In response to the forgiveness of our sins, he gets all of us—our hopes and dreams, our fears, our time, our health, our wealth— everything. For those who give in and give it all over to God, the surprising thing is how God gives our life back to us in myriad ways. The joy in serving him comes in knowing we are pleasing him. It is also often a measure of doing the very thing for which we were created.

I suspect that had the rich young ruler (Mark 10:17-27) heeded Christ's call to sell everything he had and give it to the poor and follow Christ, he would have been exceedingly happy. The first step of self-denial would have been very difficult. But in the end—even on this side of heaven—he would have found a joy that comes from service. He may well have had a gift of stewardship, so he may have soon found himself making a lot of money again, but this time holding it loosely. Or perhaps he had a gift of service that he was betraying by seeking only to be served. The point is that God rarely deposits gifts in us and neglects to use them. [43]

I love public speaking. I used to feel badly when I spoke in public, because I naively assumed that most of my hearers would have preferred to be standing in my spot. I have since learned that many people are more afraid of public speaking than they are of death. I am exercising God's gift in me when I give a speech. Thankfully, I have been given many opportunities to do it.

---

[43] I say "rarely" because I do believe that I have some gifts that God is not presently using. I love management, though I do not have an opportunity to use those gifts right now.   Whether I can exercise them again on earth or whether that will wait for heaven, I do not know.

There is a caveat to the notion that God principally uses us in our gifting: Sometimes he does the opposite. As I mentioned before, our gifts do not necessarily define our calling. Sometimes we are called to work out of our weakness and against our grain. We must not use our lack of gifts in a given area to be a cop-out from following God wherever he calls us. God has his own purposes in calling us to do various things— sometimes to humble us, sometimes to remind us of our utter dependence on him, sometimes to make plain his greatness in the face of our weakness. Paul was given a "thorn in the flesh" to keep him from becoming conceited. We do not know what this "thorn" was, but we do know that it was a struggle for him. Despite his pleadings to have it removed, the Lord replied to Paul, "My grace is sufficient for you, for my power is made perfect in weakness" (1 Cor. 12:9).

Nonetheless, we can often get clues about God's specific calling for our lives by following the evidence. Learn where you are gifted, and explore how you can use those gifts to glorify God.

It's The Little Things That Count

God's call on our lives—both his general call to all humans and his specific calling—is both more and less expansive than many people think. It is more expansive since God cares about everything. As we have already seen, there is no part of creation about which God is indifferent. His original design before the Fall remains the same after the Fall: he wants us to bring him glory in everything we say, think, and do, barring nothing. He wants to be Lord of pottery-making, miniature golf course design, house-cleaning, commercial fishing, and everything else. All of our temporal aims should be means to please our Creator. He designed us for this not because he is a megalomaniac, but because we thrive when we give him glory. The Great I AM deserves our one hundred percent, because he is great and good and kind and gentle and just and redeeming.

His specific call on our lives is also *less* expansive in that he does not have just one single will for us in everything we do. He does not will that we eat our sandwich with just certain condiments. He made us in his image, which means that we, like him, are creative and resourceful. Most of the time, we can honor him in a wide variety of ways. He does not constantly whisper in our ears what to say at any given moment. He is ever present, but he gives us plenty of space to make choices.

We are sometimes called to do one specific thing, and we sin if we disobey him. He is a creative genius, to say the least, and he is often pleased to give us suggestions and inspire us with specific ideas. But more often he is pleased to let us use our imagination to decide how best to serve him and our neighbors. God gave us a brain to be used.

God loves freedom. The very reason we had the option to sin in the Garden was so that we would freely choose to obey him. This is the freedom that the evil Grand Inquisitor in Fyodor Dostoyevsky's short story found so intolerable. He believed it was cruel to give men freedom to choose to disobey: "for never was there anything more unbearable to the human race than personal freedom!" (*The Grand Inquisitor,* 20). The Inquisitor maintained that since God knew in advance that humans would choose poorly, he was wrong to give them the choice in the first place. Instead, he wants to replace human freedom with forced obedience.

Some Christians have mistakenly understood God's will as a bull's eye that we either hit or miss. This view of God's will quickly becomes domineering, narrow, and frustrating. It may result in the compilation of black-and-white rules for many areas of life. Fundamentalism's extra-biblical restrictions on movie-going or smoking or dancing or drinking are expressions of this misguided, albeit well-intentioned interpretation of God's will. Similarly, excessive focus on which of many good choices before us is the one God wants is another expression.

The freedom of choosing how best to serve God in each day's countless little decisions is intended to be a joyful burden to bear—like the burden of finding a good gift for a loved one. If God has not made clear that he has a specific will for us in a particular matter, and if he is principally interested in our motivation to please him in everything, and if our prudent judgment helps us to see multiple ways to bring him glory, then we can relax and enjoy choosing how best to bring him glory.

The practice of seeking to glorify God in the myriad little decisions we face daily is essential to the process of sanctification. By making good decisions in the small things, we grow up in the Lord, and we become equipped to tackle the big decisions rightly. Jesus said, "Whoever can be trusted with very little can also be trusted with much, and whoever is dishonest with very little will also be dishonest with much" (Luke 16:10). Like a boxer in training, we prepare for the big fight by sparring with lesser boxers.

I have often marveled at how martyrs have the grace to choose to die, and die well. Apart from a supernatural grace that equips them at the moment of crisis, I suspect it has flowed from their practice of dying to themselves daily to follow Christ. The final decision to lay down their lives is the culmination of countless lesser decisions to do the same. Their innate will to live has been subsumed by their practiced will to die to self and live for Christ.

Conclusion

We are not random accidents adrift in a meaningless universe. God has a call on each of our lives—the consultant, the student, the accountant, and the pastor. He wants to be Lord of everything we think, say, and do. His will is general and sometimes specific. The most important thing we should do at any given moment is seek to glorify him, in ways big and small. No area of our lives is beyond the reach of his concern. Not even a sparrow "will fall to the ground apart from the will of your Father" (Matt. 10:29). This understanding should imbue our moments with meaning and purpose.

In the words of Ps. 73:23-24: "Yet I am always with you; you hold me by my right hand. You guide me with your counsel, and afterward you will take me into glory." Or in the lyrics of *Switchfoot*,

> In this needle and haystack life
> I found miracles there in your eyes
> It's no accident we're here tonight
> We are once in a lifetime.

This gives us confidence to live each moment to God's glory.

7

Never Walk Alone:
The Importance of Fellowship

"It is not good for man to be alone."
God

God made us in his image. Just as the Triune God himself lives in fellowship—Father, Son, and Holy Spirit—we are made to live in fellowship. Those who by choice or by coercion live alone are rarely mentally healthy:

> "It's an awful thing, solitary," John McCain wrote of his five and a half years as a prisoner of war in Vietnam—more than two years of it spent in isolation in a fifteen-by-fifteen-foot cell, unable to communicate with other P.O.W.s except by tap code, secreted notes, or by speaking into an enamel cup pressed against the wall. "It crushes your spirit and weakens your resistance more effectively than any other form of mistreatment." And this comes from a man who was beaten regularly; denied adequate medical treatment for two broken arms, a broken leg, and chronic dysentery; and tortured to the point of having an arm broken again. A U.S. military study of almost a hundred and fifty naval aviators returned from imprisonment in Vietnam, many of whom were treated even worse than McCain, reported that they found social isolation to be as torturous and agonizing as any physical abuse they suffered (Gawande).

Solitary confinement is just one form of loneliness. We may feel alone in a crowd or a family. Loneliness is more than *being* alone. It entails emotional separation from others, cutting us off from the empathy we crave from being known. Some of us are introverts and others extroverts. But none of us was made to walk through life alone.

Some philosophers have denied this fact. Thomas Hobbes said that in the state of nature, humans' lives are "solitary, poor, nasty, brutish, and short." Hobbes, like many people today, believed atomistic individuals, rather than families, are the basis for civilization. These views are counter to what Aristotle recognized, namely that "man is by nature a political animal" (*Politics,* 59). Aristotle's views aligned with the Torah he had probably never read.

Of course, we all need some time alone, even extroverts. Periods of solitude can be healthy. Jesus told his followers, "But when you pray, go into your room, close the door and pray to your Father, who is unseen. Then your Father, who sees what is done in secret, will reward you" (Matt. 6:6). Jesus often "withdrew to lonely places and prayed" (Luke 5:16). But such solitude is meant to be temporary, intended to equip us to return to social interaction.

God made us to know and be known. Paul commanded us to "rejoice with those who rejoice; mourn with those who mourn" (Rom. 12:15)—both for our sake and for others' sake. Our natural propensity is to want to share our delights with other people. Sunsets, football games, concerts, cocktails, or sumptuous meals bid us to enjoy them with others. Doing any of those things alone reduces the pleasure we would otherwise feel. It is no wonder that heaven is described as a joyful feast with friends (Matt. 22:2).

As a result of the Fall, sin has divided us one from another. Though we crave community, our sinful inclinations push us away from others by destroying the very things necessary for healthy relationships. Adam blamed Eve for his sin, driving a wedge in their relationship. Though we need relationships, we often relegate them to secondary importance, behind looking out for number one. Like all sin, selfishness ultimately hurts us.

The question is, how we can follow God in community with others, as God designed us to do? Learning how to cultivate fellowship takes wisdom and practice.

Easily Neglected

It is sadly ironic that we often neglect the things that bring us the greatest happiness in life. Many people pay lip service to the importance of relationships but demean them in practice. Men, in particular, are prone to work too long to get the bonus or the promotion or even just a pat on the back, missing family dinners, baseball games, and school plays.

As I mentioned earlier, when I left my job in the United States Senate because the long hours were taking a toll on our family, I heard from many highly accomplished older men who regretted their decisions to excel professionally at the expense of time with their children. In their efforts to save the world, they had lost or damaged their families. The old adage is certainly true: "No one ever said on their deathbed, 'I wish I'd spent more time at the office.'"

Lavish family vacations and the latest technology for kids cannot compensate for parental neglect. So many important life lessons are taught by helping children with homework, raking leaves, and living in the prosaic moments of life, modeling what it means to do everything for God's glory.

Father-absence has become a pervasive problem in our society. According to the U.S. Census Bureau, one out of every three (34.5 percent) children in America lives apart from their biological father. Studies have shown that many fathers spend just a few minutes per day with their kids. Research has demonstrated strong links between how much time children spend with their fathers and crime, poverty, teen pregnancy, drug abuse, and educational success. Of juveniles or young adults serving in long-term correctional facilities, 70 percent did not live with both parents when they were growing up (McManus).

Neglect of spouses is also epidemic. Many married couples co-exist without truly connecting. Too often it is the husband neglecting his wife in favor of televised sports or other entertainment media. Wives often feel abandoned by their non-communicative husbands who are content to let last month's "I love you" fulfill their vows. It is no wonder that half of all marriages end in divorce.

Love is a Verb

My wife loves me so much. I know that not just because she tells me so every day, but because she acts so every day. She dreams with me and schemes with me (including in the writing of this book), and she cares about my desires big and small. She does so many things just for me, thereby loving me.

In *Fiddler on the Roof*, Reb Tevye asks his wife of many years whether she loves him. The thought had never occurred to her in that pre-romantic era of arranged marriage. She replies, "For 25 years I've washed your clothes, cooked your meals, cleaned your house, given you children, milked the cow," concluding that "if that's not love, what is?"

In Dostoyevsky's *The Brothers Karamazov*, one of the characters exclaims, "I love mankind . . . but I find to my amazement that the more I love mankind as a whole, the less I love man in particular." Of course, such love is no love at all.

Love is the foundation of every healthy relationship. Yet love is not always what it seems to be. Some people profess to deeply love a spouse, child, parent, neighbor or friend, but their putative love is just selfishness in disguise. Their attachment is parasitic, not self-giving. A friend of mine calls these people "suck people." They cling to others out of a desperate desire to fill their own God-shaped vacuum. They may appear to be concerned about the other's welfare, but in truth it is their own well-being they pursue. A mother in C. S. Lewis' *The Great Divorce* is unable to submit to God because she seeks to "love" her son, though she really desires to possess him when she says: "He is mine, do you understand? Mine, mine, mine, forever and ever." She would even prefer that her son return with her to hell rather than remaining in heaven without her. Such is the nature of self-love disguised as real love.

The prevailing thought in Western Civilization is that romantic love is a state of being which befalls a person, often randomly. Countless songs about falling in and out of love reinforce the false idea that love is principally a feeling. This notion of love contributes to the high divorce rate as couples break up when they are no longer "in love," as if no one were to blame. Supposedly harmless music like that of Frank Sinatra was highly destructive to our society inasmuch as it set up an impossibly high emotional standard for marital relationships. Once couples' emotional ecstasy subsides with the passage of time, as naturally happens, they think that love has left their relationship. This distorted understanding of love is self-love in disguise. How one *feels* dictates whether one will keep his or her vows of lifelong fidelity. Rick Warren captures it well:

> Today we've bought into this myth that love is uncontrollable, that it's something that just happens to us; it's not something we control. In fact, even the language we use implies the uncontrollability of love. We say, "I fell in love," as if love is some kind of a ditch. It's like I'm walking along one day and bam!—I fell in love. I couldn't help myself. But I have to tell you the truth—that's not love. Love doesn't just happen to you. Love is a choice and it represents a commitment. There's no doubt about it, attraction is uncontrollable and arousal is uncontrollable. But attraction and arousal are not love. They can lead to love, but they are not love (*Daily Hope*).

Real love is other-focused. It is self-giving, incarnational, and sacrificial. It requires effort, sometimes given with ease and sometimes in pain. It is never utilitarian—loving in order to be loved. It is not contractual—conditioning the love of others on reciprocation. Love sees others as ends in themselves, not means to an end. Much of what passes for "love" is anything but. It is self-love, and a poor self-love since it does not provide the nourishment we need to live whole lives. Learning to love requires a lifetime of effort.

Love is first and foremost an action. Loving feelings may be expressions of love, but only if they are accompanied by loving actions. The apostle John wrote, "Dear children, let us not love with words or tongue, but with actions and in truth" (I John 3:18). Or again, "This is love for God: to obey his commands" (1 John 5:3). The Christian rock group dcTalk captures the active nature of love in their lyrics: "I don't care what they say, I don't care what you heard, the word luv, luv is a verb."

Real love is an action motivated by a desire to care for someone. Some actions may be loving *in effect* though not *in intent*, as when a bully helps up the smaller boy he just knocked down so the playground monitor will not detect his offense. Conversely, some actions may be loving in intent, but not in effect, as when a young child uses a towel coated with gravel to "clean" the family car. Perfect love includes proper intent and effect. Feelings are optional, though they often follow our actions, but not always. We can genuinely love some people whom we do not like, choosing to love in action that person whose personality or actions annoy us.

The famous "love" passage by Paul underscores love as an action: "Love is patient, love is kind. It does not envy, it does not boast, it is not proud. It is not rude, it is not self-seeking, it is not easily angered, it keeps no record of wrongs. Love does not delight in evil but rejoices with the truth. It always protects, always trusts, always hopes, always perseveres. Love never fails" (1 Cor. 13:4-8). Notice the verbs littered throughout the passage—and the absence of any reference to feelings. Likewise, the golden rule says, "So in everything, *do* to others what you would have them *do* to you, for this sums up the Law and the Prophets" (Matt. 7:12, italics added).

Loving others well requires wisdom and practice. Aristotle explained that to develop good character requires doing good things over and over and over.

> Virtue, as we have seen, consists of two kinds, intellectual virtue and moral virtue. Intellectual virtue or excellence owes its origin and development chiefly to teaching, and for that reason requires experience and time. Moral virtue, on the other hand, is formed by habit, *ethos*, and its name, *ethike*, is therefore derived, by a slight variation, from *ethos*. This shows, too, that none of the moral virtues is implanted in us by nature, for nothing which exists by nature can be changed by habit. For example, it is impossible for a stone, which has a natural downward movement, to become

habituated to moving upward, even if one should try ten thousand times to inculcate the habit by throwing it in the air; nor can fire be made to move downward, nor can the direction of any nature-given tendency be changed by habituation. Thus, the virtues are implanted in us neither by nature nor contrary to nature: we are by nature equipped with the ability to receive them, and habit brings this ability to completion and fulfillment.

. . . The virtues, on the other hand, we acquire by first having put them into action, and the same is also true of the arts. For the things which we have to learn before we can do them we learn by doing: men become builders by building houses, and harpists by playing the harp. Similarly we become just by the practice of just actions, self-controlled by exercising self-control, and courageous by performing acts of courage.

. . . Moreover, the same causes and the same means that produce any excellent or virtue can also destroy it, and this is also true of every art. It is by playing the harp that men become both good and bad harpists, and correspondingly with builders and all the other craftsmen: a man who build well will be a good builder, one who builds badly a bad one. For if this were not so, there would be no need for an instructor, but everybody would be born as a good or a bad craftsman. The same holds true of the virtues: in our transactions with other men it is by action that some become just and others unjust, and it is by acting in the face of danger and by developing the habit of feeling fear or confidence that some become brave men and others cowards. The same applies to the appetites and feelings of anger: by reacting in one way or in another to given circumstances some people become self-controlled and gentle, and others self-indulgent and short-tempered. In a word, characteristics develop from corresponding activities. For that reason, we must see to it that our activities are of a certain kind, since any variations in them will be reflected in our characteristics. Hence it is no small matter whether one habit or another is inculcated in us from early childhood; on the contrary, it makes a considerable difference, or, rather, all the difference (33-35).

Notice how different is this notion of love from the world's emotive definition of love. To be loving requires repetition, repeatedly choosing wisely how to love our neighbors. Love and the other virtues are formed through our "transactions with our fellow-men." It is not enough to love in thought. Loving thoughts without loving deeds are not genuinely loving. James says much the same thing when he writes, "But someone will say, 'You have faith; I have deeds.' Show me your faith without deeds, and I will show you my faith by what I do" (2:18). Or in the words of the old saying, "Sow a thought and you reap an action; sow an act and you reap a habit; sow a habit and you reap a character; sow a character and you reap a destiny."

To cultivate a loving character requires that we shift our focus from ourselves to our neighbor. We need to become students of others, being "quick to listen, slow to speak" (Jas. 1:19). Loving others usually brings the added benefit of fulfilling our need to be loved. While there is such a thing as unrequited love, loving others typically motivates people to love us in return. Given that we need to be loved to lead healthy lives, our needs are met by meeting others' needs. Of course, true love is not transactional or utilitarian. We do not genuinely love others if our real aim is being loved ourselves. People often sense that such love is insincere at its core, whereas "love must be sincere" (Rom. 12:9).

When we set out to love others as God commanded us, we find ample benefits. In listening well, we grow to be heard; in valuing others, we are valued; in being patient with others, others are patient with us. There is not always one-to-one correlation in loving and being loved, but loving others makes us that much more lovable.

True Love is Easy and Hard

True love for others is both harder and easier than self-love. It is harder because it requires that we lay down our lives for others. Given our natural propensity to selfishness, sacrificial love for others is difficult. Such love requires a lifetime of effort to perfect. As we grow in wisdom, we come to see how imperfectly we love. We give our friends our favorite action films when they prefer comedies, or we send flowers when they prefer chocolate. It takes effort and study to learn how best to love others—both how they *want* to be loved and how they *need* to be loved. The drug-addicted homeless man *wants* to be loved with cash to buy more drugs, though the love he *needs* requires that he be given a hot meal and a ride to the rehabilitation clinic. Love requires that we turn our focus from ourselves to others. Whereas God knows perfectly how to love us, as finite beings we need to search out how best to love our neighbors. We should become students of one another.

On the other hand, love for others is easier than self-love in that we were created to love others. When we love our neighbor, we are doing more than fulfilling the law: we are doing what we were made to do. As we saw in Chapter 2, we were designed to serve. "The Lord Jesus himself said: 'It is more blessed to give than to receive'" (Acts 20:35). Sin has twisted us and made selfishness our most natural impulse. But our pre-sin state was loving, and our fully redeemed and exalted state in heaven will also be loving. In this in-between time, we must fight and claw our way past the monstrous self-love that cuts us off from others. Yet love for others is more satisfying than the insatiable demands from our tyrannical self. In loving we find joy and "*eudaimonia*"—Greek for "happiness."[44] It is not the same as popular notions of happiness, which are superficial and emotionally charged. *Eudaimonia* denotes something deeper and more fundamental, more like "human flourishing."

Plato said that the person who does evil and gets away with it suffers immeasurable spiritual harm, since doing

---

[44] Much classical Greek philosophy was dedicated to the pursuit of *eudaimonia*, including Plato.

injustice twists or shrinks one's soul, whereas reproof holds the potential to restrain evil. Without the correction that can be wrought by just punishment, the unjust tyrant descends into a spiritual hell *in this life*. To be sure, one can enjoy "sin for a season" (Heb. 11:25, KJV), but it does not last. "Do not be deceived: God cannot be mocked. A man reaps what he sows. The one who sows to please his flesh, from that nature will reap destruction; the one who sows to please the Spirit, from the Spirit will reap eternal life" (Gal. 6:7-8). Doing wrong results in misery, both in this world and in the world to come. Conversely, loving God and others is right and true and just and leads to joy on this side of death and eternal happiness on the other side. Mother Teresa said of her work with the poor and dying in Calcutta, "The miracle is not that we do this work, but that we are happy to do it."

Yet Paul also said, "If only for this life we have hope in Christ, we are to be pitied more than all men" (1 Cor. 15:19). He was arguing that the suffering and sacrifice were not worth the cost if we have no forgiveness of our sins and the hope of an eternity in heaven. However, the cause of Paul's suffering was that he was preaching the Gospel, i.e., that Christ died and rose again for our sins. Paul may well have agreed that a virtuous life was still worthwhile even if there is no resurrection of the dead. But the hope of the resurrection of Jesus Christ spawned so much antagonism that he would gladly give up *preaching* it if it were not true.

In my own life, I have been torn between thinking that the virtuous life has its own rewards and that it was not worth the suffering without an eternal benefit. I believe that the virtuous life without eternal life would still be more satisfying than the life of sin, but I doubt I would have the motivation to pursue this more satisfying way with carnal pleasures screaming for my affections.

Loving Ourselves vs. Self-Love

Focusing on loving others should not lead us to ignore our own needs. We are commanded to "love our neighbors *as ourselves.*" We know what it means to love others because we begin by loving ourselves. We are instructed to "look not only to your own interests, but also to the interests of others" (Phil. 2:4)—meaning that we are not wrong to pay attention to our own interests. The question is how to love ourselves without being filled with self-love. When should we deny our needs to satisfy others' needs? Should we give away our money without regard for our desire to vacation? Do others' needs always trump ours? What is the line between being self-seeking and self-exhausting? Are we cloaking our selfishness when we seek balance and margins in our lives? Must we *always* stop to care for the homeless man on the street, even when that makes us late for an important meeting?

There are no quick and easy answers to these questions. We are in no position to judge others' decisions in such prudential matters. Only God knows our hearts. He alone knows whether we are selfishly passing the homeless man or whether we are being responsible in continuing with the task we have been given for that moment. He alone knows whether we are being greedy in driving a Lexus and vacationing in the Bahamas. Our inability to justly judge others does not, however, mean that we are free to do whatever we want. Our job is to learn to listen to the Spirit throughout our day, obeying his instructions. Paul tells us to "walk in the Spirit, and you will not gratify the desires of the flesh" (Gal. 5:16). Developing an ear for that "still, small voice" in our minute-by-minute interactions and decisions will help us to learn how to love ourselves and others.

Friendship

I am encircled with friends. My closest friends love me for who I am. They love me the same in success or failure. They ground me and keep me on the straight and narrow and make me laugh uproariously. I love them back, I hope just as well as they love me.

Aristotle said, "The antidote for fifty enemies is one friend." Everyone needs a friend. Loving our friends is much easier than loving others. Just as we have special responsibilities to our families, so we have special responsibilities to our friends. We simply cannot love everyone equally. Jesus loved all of his disciples, but he had a special love for John—"the one Jesus loved." Unlike family, which is defined by kinship or adoption, friendship is voluntary and non-binding. We love our friends not because of a commitment or vow we have taken, but because we enjoy their presence and they ours. Jesus said, "Greater love has no one than this, that he lay down his life for his friends" (John 15:13). The love for our friends reflects the mutual love of the Godhead: Father, Son, and Holy Spirit.

Having good friends requires being a good friend. Friendship is initially kindled in conversation or common work, but it is nurtured and fertilized in the crucible of life's struggles. As we love our friends in action, we deepen our affection for them. Though this give-and-take is not contractual, it is mutual. To fan the flames of friendship, we must open ourselves to others in vulnerable self-disclosure. The greater the self-disclosure, the greater the possibility for deep friendship.

God ministers to us through friends. How many times have I felt the tangible love of God by the care of friends' listening ears, home-cooked food, or holiday parties? Friends are the "little platoons" that bind together communities, making them strong and durable. Soldiers regularly say that more than fighting for their nation, they fight for their "band of brothers" alongside them on the battlefield. Friendship is God's gift to us, a gift which we should nurture and cultivate through selfless love and genuine concern.

My best friend is my wife, Dana. I am blessed with many very good friends, some even from first grade, but Dana is far and away my closest and best friend. She loves me so deeply and so well, pouring out her life for me. Her love is all the more precious because of her chronic fibromyalgia. Dana gives and gives and gives, affirming my dreams and helping me reach them. We laugh together all the time (though our children do not think our humor is very good). We love being together, talking about everything from God and philosophy and vacation plans to what color to paint the house. Dana is my best earthly gift. She points me to God by her words and her life. I know that Jesus said there will be no marriage in heaven, but I plan to ask him for a special dispensation to stay married in heaven!

Friendship with God

As rich and meaningful as our best friendships may be, they do not measure up to the friendship we are intended to have with our Creator. Human friends inevitably disappoint us because they, like us, are fallen. Sin mars even the best friendships, breeding heartache and pain—more so than the pain wrought by strangers, since only a friend can betray us. Even our best friends will at least sometimes misread our needs, misjudge our motives, or fail to understand our deepest longings. We are deeply and profoundly flawed creatures, wounded by our own sin and others' sin. We need to be touched in places and ways known only by an omniscient and perfectly loving God.

Blaise Pascal said, "There is a God-shaped vacuum in the heart of every man which cannot be filled by any created thing, but only by God, the Creator, made known through Jesus." Because nature abhors a vacuum, it is often filled with things other than God. As Bob Dylan sings, "you're gonna have to serve somebody."[45] If we do not serve God, we will serve ourselves, money, false gods, addictions, leisure, sex, or any of the countless varieties of idols that compete for our affections.

Friendship with God began in the Garden but was damaged and made more difficult by sin. Whereas Adam and Eve's fellowship with God had been easy and natural, their sin has marred the perfect communion we once had. Because God is perfectly holy, he cannot abide sin. It is not that God is impatient or short-tempered. It is just that his nature, being completely good, cannot be united to sin. He cannot wink at it.

This is not to say that God cannot be around sinners. Indeed, Jesus was criticized by the religious class of his day precisely because he dined with the "wrong kind of people"— prostitutes, tax collectors (who were reputed to be dishonest

---

[45] From "Gotta Serve Somebody" on the 1979 album *Slow Train Coming.* I am still praying that Dylan will return to the Lord with his once full-throated allegiance. I do wonder what had gotten him off track.

and collaborators with the occupying Roman power), and all manner of sinners. But he cannot ultimately excuse sin, not even a small sin. James writes, "For whoever keeps the whole law and yet stumbles at just one point is guilty of breaking all of it" (2:10). It is not enough to say that I have not robbed 99.9 percent of all the banks in America. If I have robbed just one, I am a bank robber and fit for prison. So it is with sin. One sin is one too many to be reconciled to God. Apart from the perfect, propitiating sacrifice of his Son, no one could ever be justified.[46]

Walking with God is Hard but Essential

On this side of Eden, we struggle to be close to God. It is difficult, not because of God's impatience but because of our imperfection. Our sin drives us from the righteous life to which we have been called. Just when we find that we are in close fellowship with him, trusting him, hearing his voice throughout the day, eschewing pride and selfishness and embracing abject and joyful service, we fall off the wagon. The temptation comes to us stealthily, pulling us away from the God-centered life, and we must yet again confess and repent.

The struggle with sin is endless and wearying. Yet the struggle is essential to a holy life. When we cease struggling with sin, we are in deep trouble. C. S. Lewis wrote,

> No amount of falls will really undo us if we keep on picking ourselves up each time. We shall of course be very muddy and tattered children by the time we reach home, but the bathrooms are all ready, the towels put out, and the clean clothes in the airing cupboard. The only fatal thing is to lose one's temper and give it up. It is when we notice the dirt that God is most present in us: it is the very sign of His presence (*Letters, 365*).

---

[46] God can forgive us not because he is a nice guy, but because of the atoning death of Jesus. Without Jesus' sacrifice, God's holiness would make it impossible for him to forgive sin. The animal sacrifices of the Old Testament foreshadowed the once-for-all sacrifice of the perfect Lamb of God.

When we sin and genuinely repent, no matter how many times, God is quick to forgive us—"seventy times seven" (Matt. 18:22, KJV). We find such repetitious forgiveness difficult or even unwise to extend to others. The Evil One delights in coaxing us to sin and then accusing us of being beyond the reach of God's forgiveness. He tells us that we are too wicked to be forgiven, and we are too apt to listen to his lying voice. The truth is that God delights in forgiving us. The price has already been paid, and he is only too eager to see us repent. It is only when we grow weary of our cycle of sin and repentance and give up the struggle that he becomes angry with us. He knows that we are dust, weak and sinful. In embracing sin, we seek to deny our weakness and his lordship. Our relationship with God is difficult to sustain in the face of such recalcitrance.[47]

Friendship with God requires work. No good marriage or earthly friendship can thrive for long without effort. My parents enjoyed fifty-four years of an excellent marriage, and they always taught me that good relationships take work. The same is true for God. Our sinfulness gets in the way of our friendship with God. We must make strident efforts to die to ourselves. Now we look through a glass darkly, straining to hear God amidst the buzz of our sin and self-centeredness. We die to ourselves precisely so we can commune more fully with our Creator.

The adage "let go and let God" can be misapplied if we think that by fighting less against our sin, we can come closer to God. Striving to be close to God requires heavy lifting precisely because our soul and the world runs so strongly against intimacy with God. Jean Jacques Rousseau wrongly believed that humans were born perfect and only needed to do what comes naturally to lead a virtuous life. In contrast, the Bible teaches we are born in sin, and we must work to put down our sin.

---

[47] Whether ongoing unrepentant sin means we were never saved, that we have lost our salvation, or that we are forfeiting temporal and eternal rewards is unclear in Scripture. What is clear is that unrepentant sin is inconsistent with a right relationship with God.

My own experience in seeking God contradicts the notion that religion is comfortable and easy, shielding us from the harsh realities of life. For me, following God is a day-by-day struggle that is not easy, though the end effect is a deep and abiding peace. My faith can often be like a bed of nails to me, not a hammock. And yet paradoxically, my faith is tremendously comforting -- even when it is hard.

Friendship with God is our calling. James writes that, "'Abraham believed God, and it was credited to him as righteousness,' and he was called God's friend" (2:23). God wants the same thing for all of us. The cross acts as a bridge across the chasm of sin that naturally separates us from the Lover of our soul. Our friendship with God is a reflection of the friendship that exists *within* the Godhead. The Trinity is made of three distinct persons who commune with one another. God is never alone.

In *The Shack*, by William P. Young, the Trinity is fictionalized as three people in a mountain cabin who are spending a weekend with Mack, a father grieving the violent murder of his young daughter. God the Father is depicted as a large African American woman curiously named "Papa" (in order to challenge stereotypes about God being an old white-bearded man). Jesus plays himself, and the Holy Spirit is "Sarayu," a soft-spoken Asian woman. Young is not trying to ascribe to the Trinity these particular anthropomorphic personalities (except in the case of Jesus), but to illustrate the character of God and the loving relationship among the persons of the Trinity. In one scene, the joy of the interpersonal relationships is beautifully portrayed:

> Mack was shocked at the scene in front of him. It appeared that Jesus had dropped a large bowl of some sort of batter or sauce on the floor, and it was everywhere. It must have landed close to Papa because the lower portion of her skirt and bare feet were covered in the gooey mess. All three were laughing so hard that Mack didn't think they were breathing. Sarayu said something about humans being clumsy and all three started roaring again. Finally, Jesus brushed past

Mack and returned a minute later with a large basin of water and towels. Sarayu had already started wiping the goop from the floor and cupboards, but Jesus went straight to Papa and, kneeling at her feet, began to wipe off the front of her clothes. He worked down to her feet and gently lifted one foot at a time, which he directed into the basin where he cleaned and massaged it.

"Ooooh, that feels soooo good!" exclaimed Papa, as she continued her tasks at the counter.

As he leaned against the doorway watching, Mack's mind was full of thoughts. So this was God in relationship? It was beautiful and so appealing. He knew that it didn't matter whose fault it was—the mess from some bowl had been broken, that a dish that had been planned would not be shared. Obviously, what was truly important here was the love they had for one another and the fullness it brought them. He shook his head. How different this was from the way he treated the ones he loved! (104-105)

The Trinity laughing so hard together that they seemed not to be breathing! If God is love and the author of life, then there must be overflowing joy among the three-in-one persons of God. The Lord wants the same relationship with us.

Spending daily time alone with God often feels onerous to me. Many Christians struggle with the guilt of not spending more time in prayer and Bible study, as if we are neglecting a difficult and unpleasant chore—like cleaning the bathroom. Yet spending time communing with God is meant to feed our souls and build up friendship with him. Divine friendship is built by time, just as human friendships are. We need to walk alone with him, letting him hear our complaints, our hopes and dreams, our fears and pains, so we can hear him respond. Regardless of how it sometimes *feels*, seeking God's face is an essential part of pursuing God. "You will seek me and find me when you seek me with all your heart" (Jer. 29:13). Seeking

God is difficult and demanding, but it is the only way to build a friendship with the Almighty.

Listening for God's Voice

For many years I have made it a practice to quietly or audibly speak what I imagine God would say to me if I could hear his voice. My musings are fallible, because I do not perfectly know the mind of God, but my time spent immersed in Scripture has given me a good idea of what I think he may be saying to me. This exercise has helped me to hear him, speaking back to the world's lies. Sometimes I do speak out a sentence that contradicts Scripture, which I then must quickly admit is not God's word, but many more times I am able to better hear what I know he is saying because it mirrors scriptural admonitions. Sometimes I will simply recite the many Bible verses I have memorized, stringing them together, listening for God's word to me in every word.[48]

Why does God make it so hard to feel his presence and hear his voice? Even when he walked the earth he could have done more to make plain his divinity. His miracles, as spectacular as they were, could have been more grandiose still. Why did he not cast an actual mountain into the sea? Why did not the Father's voice boom from heaven, not just at Jesus' baptism, but every day? Because greater miracles would not necessarily translate into more faith.

To the hard-hearted, the problem is not a lack of evidence, but rebellion. Consider Lazarus' resurrection from the dead after four days in the tomb. Here was a fantastic and unmistakable miracle that even the most skeptical would have trouble denying. Amazingly, some of the witnesses reported the miracle to the High Priests as an indictment against Jesus, though they did not seem to question its authenticity. What Jesus did was beside the point. The miracle did not produce faith, but anger and hatred and jealousy. More remarkable miracles would not crack open hearts hardened by sin.

---

[48] This practice is not necessarily for everyone, and the possibility of ascribing to God thoughts and words that are not his is real and dangerous. On the other hand, I have found it a useful way to commune with God.

I once had a friend who gave up his faith in God, ostensibly because of philosophical problems. After countless conversations about apologetics and philosophy, he finally conceded that his loss of faith was rooted in his anger at his earthly father, an evangelist who played the righteous man in the pulpit but abused his wife at home. My friend was so angry at his father's hypocrisy that he wanted to punish his father by rejecting his God.

In the movie *Bruce Almighty*, actor Jim Carrey plays a man to whom God has lent his divine powers and authority for a while. Bruce can make the moon closer to the earth for romantic effect, let everyone win the lottery, and perform a host of other fantastic miracles. But when Bruce tries to make his former girlfriend love him again, he is completely powerless. "Love me, love me," pleads Bruce, but his girlfriend blithely walks away. Christian scriptwriter Tom Shadyac was accurately illustrating God's gift of human freedom that permits us to deny God. God yearns for our friendship, but whether his desire is fulfilled is incumbent on our choice.[49]

We were made to be friends with God. Human friendships can be rich and fulfilling, but they cannot replace friendship with our Creator and Savior. Human friendships will sometimes fall short, but friendship with God never fails us. Author Larry Crabb compares some relationships to that of a tick that cares only about what it can get from the dog, not what it can give the dog. And many selfish relationships are like two ticks each looking for a dog. Being fallible and incomplete, we need God. When we try to get from others what we can only get from God, we will be frustrated. Isa. 2:22 says, "Stop trusting in man, who has but a breath in his nostrils. Of what account is he?"

---

[49] Scripture also teaches that only those who are called can respond to God's love, but this is a mystery. Scripture shows both that we are free agents who can choose God and that God chooses those he saves. Neither truth can be denied without denying biblical teaching. See Rom. 9 and 2 Pet. 3:9.

Friendship with God will enable us to be the kind of friend we need to be and not seek from our friends what we can only get from God.

8

The Importance of Church

*"How good and pleasant it is
when brothers live together in unity!"
Psalm 133:1*

*"So between the death of Christ and the Last Day it is only
by a gracious anticipation of the last things that Christians are
privileged to live in visible fellowship with other Christians. It
is by the grace of God that a congregation is permitted to
gather visibly in this world to share God's Word and
sacrament."
German Martyr Dietrich Bonhoeffer,* Life Together

Following Christ is not meant to be done alone. We are called to walk together in fellowship. Repeatedly, the Bible counsels us to keep meeting together, praying together, singing together, reciting Scripture to one another, holding one another accountable, and exhorting one another. We are to live in community with fellow disciples.

In our post-modern, highly individualistic society, many people are dropping out of church. They have become frustrated with the Church for multiple reasons, including hypocrisy, shallow sermons, lack of close relationships, cultural backwardness, and stuffiness. And they are right: churches are filled with sinners—not just former sinners, but ongoing sinners. As for me, I sin and I sin and I sin and I sin. My will and my life as I actually live it just do not match up.

The problem is not new. Paul's letters address a raft of serious theological and behavioral problems among church members: petty fights, heresies, sexual sins, lawsuits among believers, self-aggrandizement, lack of concern for the poor, and much more. The bumper sticker has it right: "Christians aren't perfect, just forgiven." Justification begins our journey towards holiness, but sanctification's work will never be complete this side of the grave. Even the godliest people have blind spots and repetitious sins.

As frustrating as it is to be in community with people who hold up ideals that they regularly transgress, that is our calling. Dropping out of church is copping out and missing out. We were meant to follow God *together*. God wants to love us through his people; they become to us God's hands, feet, and voice in our lives, and we theirs. "Lone-ranger" Christianity is not viable. We are too weak. We need one another.

Community

One of the most important functions the Church plays in our lives is providing community. Merriam-Webster Dictionary defines community as "a unified body of individuals," or "a group of people with a common characteristic or interest living together within a larger society." As followers of Christ, we are unified in following the Lord, which is our "common interest."

Community is not the same as friendship, though there are friendships within community. Yet not everyone is a friend. We see many people in church with whom we are not friends, but the sense of belonging emanates from our common purpose. We cannot be intimate with most people in a church, regardless of its size. Even so, there is a joy in walking through the narthex or fellowship hall and knowing that we are bound together, and a joy in being recognized and accepted.

The familiarity that comes from spending time together enriches our lives, even when our idiosyncrasies show through. The man who talks too much about his model cars, the woman who chatters endlessly about her grandchildren, the businessman who furtively smokes in the parking lot—we have cast our lot together and belong to one another. As we age together, that sense of community often grows stronger, as children are born and then leave for college in a blink of an eye, at the death of an elderly man who has seemed old for as long as anyone can remember. The church softball teams, the youth groups, the singles groups, the seniors' outings—they all bind us together. In community, the whole is more than the sum of its parts.

As an aside, I believe church singles groups are excellent places to find a spouse. Though sometimes criticized as "meat markets" since many people are looking for a lifetime mate, the criticism is usually unwarranted. What better place to look for a spouse than in a church group! With the increasing anonymity and loneliness experienced by many people, we need to look for healthy venues in which to make connections. I met my wife "cruising for chicks" in adult Sunday School.

Sociologist Peter Berger coined the term "plausibility structure" to refer to social context that frames our beliefs about the world. Plausibility structures are not the same as creeds, but they make sense of them, providing them with meaning and making them believable. Where creeds are not fleshed out in living and breathing human beings, they become implausible and eventually wither. But when sermons about not fearing death are seen in the terminally ill parishioner who eagerly awaits seeing God face to face, the sermon comes to life. When the mentally retarded adult is accepted and loved at church picnics, caring for "the least of these" becomes plausible.

Biblical truths become real when they find expression in our community. To the extent that there is a core group of church members living out their faith in their daily lives, a church can thrive and grow, attracting more people to grow in Christ themselves. "By this everyone will know that you are my disciples, if you love one another" (John 13:35). Preaching is important, but without demonstrable love among church members, the preaching will ring false.

Small Groups

Large churches are fine, but they do not provide the safety and intimacy of a small group of committed fellow disciples walking together in pilgrimage. When we commit ourselves to a small group of fellow believers for regular Bible study, sharing, and prayer, our load is lightened. In small groups, we can better wrestle with ideas, with the sins that beset us, with the griefs weighing us down, and with the sense of camaraderie that can only be achieved in "little platoons."[50] The anonymity of modern life militates against the kind of fellowship we are meant to have with one another.

Some people bemoan committed small groups as being too cliquish and exclusionary, but we need the impermeable walls of a small group to feel safe enough to share our struggles. Many of our struggles would be inappropriate to share in a larger group, but masks fall off in intimate, regular, and committed fellowship with others. It is difficult to lead a double life in a small group. Christians who have fallen into habitual sin would benefit from the intimacy and accountability of a small group.

In my more than thirty-three years of walking with Christ, I have almost always been in a committed small group of fellow believers. The groups have sometimes been single-sex and sometimes co-ed.[51] They have consisted of Bible study, sharing, prayer, and sometimes singing. I have consistently been strengthened and encouraged through these relationships, both for what I received and from what I gave. They have been for me the very local manifestation of the Church Invisible, and they have so often been a means of receiving God's blessing. Whether it is experiencing the sense of relief from a burden shared with others in confession, the joy of experiencing new insights into God's Word, or the security in knowing that I could call up a fellow group member in the middle of the night if needed, these groups have strengthened me to live a healthier life in God.

The apostles were one such group. Although hundreds of disciples sometimes followed Jesus, his inner circle of twelve

---

[50] Edmund Burke wrote about "little platoons" that are the glue of society: "To be attached to the subdivision, to love the little platoon we belong to in society, is the first principle (the germ as it were) of public affections. It is the first link in the series by which we proceed towards a love to our country, and to mankind" (*Reflections,* 41).

[51] There are advantages and disadvantages to mixed-sex groups. Many of men's struggles with sexual purity in our sex-saturated society are inappropriate for mixed groups. On the other hand, there are advantages to having the benefit of the other sex's insights and sensitivities. Married couples are more apt to develop a tight-knit community when in a group together. Prudence dictates which is better at any given time in our lives.

men formed the nucleus of his fellowship. Jesus, being human, needed this fellowship, though he certainly gave much more than he received. He modeled for us the wisdom of having "a band of brothers" who walk together. While I do not see a biblical mandate to be in a small group, their utility is so great that not being in a group should be the exception rather than the rule.

Instruction

In church, we are taught about God, human nature, and how to live. Instruction is an essential part of our life together. We are constantly bombarded by teaching outside of church, much of it deceptive and wrong. Advertisements, talk radio, movies, songs, and TV tell us what is right and wrong, what to love and what to hate. Apart from the plumb line of Scripture, we can be readily deceived by the war of words and images fighting for our souls.

Sermons are one way we learn. "Let the word of Christ dwell in you richly as you teach and admonish one another with all wisdom" (Col. 3:16). Whether sermons are ten minutes or two hours, they can help us to concentrate our minds on who God is and what he requires of us. Ideally, sermons should not be self-help sessions, but expository, focusing on the Bible. They should be exegetical, explaining what the particular biblical author intended to say to his intended audience in its historical context, and hermeneutical, applying the principles to our current situation. Sermons should not be pastor-centric, since the pastor is a fellow pilgrim. Paul was alert to this danger, writing that "we do not preach ourselves, but Jesus Christ as Lord, and ourselves as your servants for Jesus' sake" (2 Cor. 4:5). A good sermon should point us to biblical truths without seeking to exalt the speaker.

We also learn from spiritual mentors. Men and women who have walked longer in a committed relationship to the Lord can impart practical wisdom. Hearing real-life personal stories and lessons from a peer can be more powerful than those delivered from a "professional" Christian in the pulpit.

The grittiness and authenticity of personal stories tend to capture our imagination more powerfully.

Sunday school and small group Bible studies are another excellent way to be schooled in the faith. The interaction that comes from wrestling with a passage of Scripture in a small group frees us up to ask the tough questions, together plumbing the depths of biblical wisdom. Private study is important, and sermons can be inspiring, but I have learned some of my most significant lessons in small group studies.[52] Adult Sunday School classes can similarly provide more granularity in scriptural study than sermons permit.

Accountability

Being fallen people, we need help to battle the sins that beset us. The first of twelve steps in Alcoholics Anonymous is admitting powerlessness in the face of alcohol (or any similar addiction). Most of us struggle with addictions to some sin, though not all of our sins bear the same social stigma. People can be addicted to over-eating, work, drugs, gossip, boasting, revenge—you name it. It is easy to look down on others' sins, marveling at the stupidity of the addiction. Our sins, however, carry a peculiar appeal to us. No one is immune to besetting sins. The question is what we do with them. We need to be held accountable by confessing our sins to one another, thereby robbing our habitual sins of some of their strength. Sin, like mushrooms, thrives in darkness. The light of confession strengthens us and weakens our sin.

Not every sin must be confessed to someone else, but only those that hold sway over us. We should find a brother or sister who can maturely handle being our confessor, reminding us that in our repentance we are forgiven, that our sin is not harmless but deadly and spiritually enervating, that we must take deliberate steps not to fall into it again, and that self-

---

[52] Small group Bible studies can also be about shared ignorance. I have witnessed people misunderstand the text and "share" their misunderstanding with others. Scripture is not like a Rorschach test in which everyone sees something different and everyone is right. It is important to be well-informed about the exegesis of the text to properly apply it to our lives.

flagellation only feeds Satan the accuser rather than freeing us to forget what is behind and strain towards what is ahead (Phil. 3:13-14). Our confessor can symbolically stand in God's place, saying the words that we need to hear and compassionately, yet firmly, helping us to move from bondage to freedom.

Besetting sins do not necessarily mean we must always fall prey to them. Just as alcoholics are always alcoholics even when they are sober, so we are sinners even when we do not sin. Sin crouches at our door, waiting to overtake us. We are most at risk when we are least aware of our frailty. "So if you think you are standing firm, be careful that you do not fall!" (1 Cor. 10:12). The battle with sin is incessant and often wearying. Not until we are fully redeemed will we be free from the burden of battling against sin.

Accountability has the added benefit of bringing shame on us. Shame is under-appreciated in our society.[53] It can play the role of helping us to "remain in our lane" even when our will is weak. In our efforts to throw off the putative hypocrisy of the Victorian Age, we are often loath to shame others, thinking it judgmental or impolite. It is better to aspire to be better than we are and to want to conceal our failings from the wider society than to pretend to be worse than we are and parade our sin for all to see, as is so often done on reality television shows. François de La Rochefoucauld wrote that "hypocrisy is the tribute that virtue pays to vice" (Maxims #218).

Today, shamelessness is the tribute vice pays to society. Consequently, that which should be frowned upon is accepted or even exalted. Divorce is treated the same as the flu: an unfortunate occurrence in which no one is at fault. The corresponding rise in the divorce rate is more than coincidental. No doubt, many more couples would work through their differences or remain in difficult marriages if society still

---

[53] Some societies rely on shame as the principal means of inhibiting bad behavior. This is also out of balance. Shame, absent an internal moral compass, may help to encourage good behavior in public, but not necessarily when no one is looking. Shame should not be the principal driver in our lives, but it can act as a guardrail when we are tempted to sin.

disapproved of divorce.[54] Premarital sex is widely accepted. Of course, shame is easily misused, for example, blaming people who are not at fault (like the use of the word "bastard" for children born to unmarried parents) or being merciless with people who are sorry for their failings. The biblical model is to extend forgiveness without condoning the behavior.

In the eighteenth century, British Member of Parliament William Wilberforce set out to elevate the morals of a then morally corrupt people. Wilberforce lamented that it was fashionable to appear less moral than one actually was.[55] Wilberforce wanted to reverse that perverted custom, and instead to make goodness fashionable. One of his tactics was to set up local societies dedicated to exalting virtue and shaming vice. In 1787, Wilberforce petitioned the King to reissue the "Proclamation for the Encouragement of Piety and Virtue and for the Preventing of Vice, Profaneness and Immorality" eighteen years after its original release—a release which had been deemed perfunctory and widely ignored. This time, the "Proclamation Societies," composed of leading men and women, convened meetings designed to develop positive peer pressures to adhere to moral standards. As I have written elsewhere,

> Inherent in the notion of "making goodness fashionable" is the belief that people pay attention to what others think. If some people followed the new and more upright norms of behavior solely out of concern for what their friends thought of them, that was for Wilberforce one step on the road to real virtue. He didn't want just superficial compliance with the

---

[54] There are times when couples should divorce for biblical reasons, but shame might inhibit them from doing so. However, there are many more times when couples should remain together and shame could keep them from divorcing. Many temporary marital problems often are resolved given time and effort. Quick, no-fault divorce is akin to abandoning a ship in stormy seas when it may, indeed, weather the storm.

[55] It is widely believed that morals have been on a steady and continuous decline for centuries. In fact, the dissolute morals of the late 1700s in Britain preceded the Victorian Age. Moral and cultural renewal can reverse what may seem to be inevitable decline.

Proclamation, but he recognized that norms and mores can lead to the embrace of the underlying virtue motivating the norm. And where the adherence was superficial, a sort of "positive hypocrisy," at least other people would be less likely to be tempted to wrong behavior by degraded mores (Rodgers and Wichterman, 206).

Today's equivalent might be small group Bible studies and accountability groups. We do not necessarily need to be quizzed about our sins to keep us on the straight and narrow. Just knowing that certain behavior would be met with strong disapproval by our community of friends and acquaintances can play an effective role in motivating us to avoid sin. As sinners, we are prone to sin, and our besetting sins can hold great sway over us. The "electric fence" provided by a community of virtuous people gives us added incentive to live upright lives.

Church accountability should also be more than informal. Serious and public sins may be subject to church discipline, especially where the person is unrepentant. Growing up in Westminster Presbyterian Church in Lancaster, Pennsylvania, I was struck by the seriousness with which our church leadership took unrepentant sin. One man left his wife for another woman. After seeking unsuccessfully to confront the man, the church elders convened a special meeting of the membership to describe the sin and formally put him out of fellowship, though he had already excluded himself. Similar church discipline was exercised several times over the years, and it sent a powerful signal to the rest of us that unrepentant sin is not to be excused (see 1 Cor. 5).

Unfortunately, many churches fail to exercise discipline, believing that such actions drive people away from church. Whether church attendance rises or falls is beside the point. Church membership requires adherence to the Lordship of Christ. When we engage in sin unrepentantly, then we show ourselves not to be followers of Christ. Discipline is a compassionate act, just as it is with children, because it is meant to restore the sinning brother or sister to repentance and full fellowship.[56]

Celebration and Collective Praise

Although worship is sometimes mistakenly equated solely with collective singing during a church service (see Chapter 4), that in no way undermines the importance of collective praise. We are instructed to sing "psalms, hymns and spiritual songs" to one another (Col. 3:16). Singing to the Lord alone is good, and singing together can also lift our spirits and encourage us.

Personally, my favorite part of Sunday services is the corporate singing and praise. Music that is well-led by competent musicians, with substantive lyrics and sung loudly by the congregation is more powerful for me than even a good sermon. It also portends the singing we will do together in heaven, where "a great multitude that no one could count, from every nation, tribe, people and language" will sing to the Lamb (Rev. 7:9). Whether our singing today is traditional or contemporary is unimportant, providing that we do it for God's glory.

Sacraments

Some of the most communal acts of the church are administering the sacraments.[57] Celebrating communion, i.e., the remembrance of Jesus' death and resurrection and its implications for our lives, is not intended to be solitary but in the fellowship of believers, just as the first communion was performed by Jesus in the company of his apostles. I find great

---

[56] The issue is a lack of repentance. All of us sin repeatedly. We are promised to be forgiven again and again, and so should we forgive others. However, when we embrace the sin and say it is okay, we are essentially saying that we know better than God. Church membership is only for those who promise to submit to God in their lives, and to repent when they fall into sin.

[57] Not all Christians agree on what the sacraments are. While all accept communion and baptism, Roman Catholics and some Protestants believe that marriage, confession, confirmation, anointing of the sick, and holy orders for clergy are also sacraments.

joy in walking forward to receive the elements at the altar or receiving them in the pew, passed from person to person, knowing that we are together in our discipleship.

Communion is more than a remembrance of what Christ did for us. It is also a reminder of what we must do: deny ourselves, take up our cross daily, and follow him to the cross. His death was substitutionary for us, but it was also exemplary. As we drink the wine symbolizing his blood, we also symbolically drink our own death. We died with Christ on the cross so that we might be raised with him. We must be willing to follow him to the cross in the thousand little decisions we make each day, choosing to die to our small aspirations, instead living for him and his grand design for us. That is one reason communion can be such a mournful event. Dying to ourselves is difficult, but it is a necessary prerequisite to knowing the joy of the resurrection.

Baptism is another communal sacrament, the outer sign of the inner change. We confess our faith in Christ *before* others, regardless of how the sacrament is administered (dunking, pouring, or sprinkling). The symbolism is again of death, especially in the dunking (hence the artwork on the cover of this book), of dying to self and becoming a new creation, born again in Christ. How and when the sacrament of baptism is performed has been divisive among Christians. Some baptize infants, believing that the Christian sacrament replaces circumcision, which was done to infant boys. Others believe that baptism is only for those who are able to confess Christ. Whatever one believes, the important thing is to be baptized.

I believe in dunking those who are cognitively able to understand the implications of following Christ, not infants. I was baptized as an infant, but chose to be baptized at age seventeen after I had committed my life to Christ. It was a powerful experience for me. I felt as though the Holy Spirit was filling me with his presence, as if I were an empty glass being filled to overflowing. Quite unexpectedly, I wept with joy during my baptism in a muddy Pennsylvania river in 1981. I will never forget it, and I am grateful for the experience, though I do not believe that my experience was normative.

Many people have not had the same experience as I, and I
know it is in no way necessary for salvation.

Collective Service

We are all called to serve God in all we do. Yet the Church
Universal expresses herself uniquely in collective acts of
service. Caring for the poor, the orphans and widows, the sick,
and prisoners are important church ministries. Whereas many
parachurch organizations exist for precisely these functions,
local churches also perform these roles and many other acts of
service. James writes "Religion that God our Father accepts as
pure and faultless is this: to look after orphans and widows in
their distress and to keep oneself from being polluted by the
world" (1:27).

Caring for others is not an activity just for those who have
the gift of service. It is for everyone. James further writes that
authentic faith necessarily expresses itself in acts of service:
"faith without deeds is dead" (1:26). Jas. 2:15-16 scorns those
who think that explicit evangelism precludes caring for
people's immediate physical and emotional needs. Caring for
physical needs is both a precursor to care for spiritual needs
and is an end in itself. God cares about the whole person, and
so must we. It is wrong to think that caring for practical needs
is only a predicate for sharing the Gospel.

Ron Sider's book, *Rich Christians in an Age of Hunger,*
while flawed in some of its prescriptions and its
overconfidence in statist policies to address poverty,
nevertheless serves an important function in reminding rich
North American churches that we are called to care for the
poor. Our service to the poor may be through financial gifts or
in-person service, but it is not optional for followers of Christ.
The Church has a long history of caring for the poor, and a sure
sign of infidelity to Christ is neglect of the poor, the lonely, the
addicted, and those who suffer. God has a special concern for
the downtrodden, and so should we.

Serving others, in addition to alleviating some of the
immense suffering in the world, changes us. Service can make
us grateful for what we have, putting our own problems into

perspective. We may feel oppressed when our car breaks down until we spend time with people who cannot afford to buy any vehicle. Getting a different vantage point—looking "down" on others (see Chapter 2)—helps us to be grateful for the blessings we have instead of focusing just on what we do not have. Our natural selfishness is thwarted when together we serve the needy.

Many churches have instituted annual mission trips to the needy, domestically and worldwide. Often whole families will travel to impoverished regions to help build or renovate a building, run camps for orphans, feed the hungry, dig wells, or provide agricultural advice. These "vacations" of service help those of us in North America realize how wealthy we are and remind us of our neighbors' needs.

At one time, I had considered such short-term trips a poor use of resources, wrongly believing that resources could be more efficiently spent by staying home and sending the money. However, the interpersonal relationships that are built on these trips are invaluable. Opening eyes and warming hearts toward others, these trips help knit together the rich and the poor and motivate us to give more in the future. Often a one-week summer mission trip will translate into many years of service to the needy, setting loose far more resources. They also give us more joy in giving and serving, since it is more gratifying to see needs being met with our own eyes instead of just reading about it in a newsletter.

Sacrificial service has the counter-intuitive effect of increasing our desire to serve. When we give a little, we are more likely to give more. In the 1960 presidential campaign, John Kennedy had a surplus of volunteers in many states. Rather than turn away volunteers, the campaign had extra volunteers write thank-you notes to other volunteers, making the letter-writers more connected to the campaign and the letter recipients feeling appreciated for their work. Direct mail experts know that small gifts beget larger gifts. Give $5 to a cause, and you are more likely to give $10 next time. By giving, we become invested in the cause.

When I attended Washington Community Fellowship Church in Washington, D.C., members were required to contribute a Saturday morning to clean the church a few times each year. The church could afford a sexton, but the founders believed that the commitment level of the members will be higher if the members do the work themselves. In fact, the Church had the most engaged and committed congregation as any to which I have belonged.

Tithing

One important way in which we serve others is by giving money to the local church and to the Church Universal (through parachurch organizations and ministries). We are to give a tithe—which means one-tenth of our gross income—to support the work of the church and to care for the poor.

Some Christians maintain that tithing is not required by Scripture, but is voluntary, based on what God directs each person to give. They further argue that the tithe in the Old Testament supported many works now undertaken by the modern state and supported by taxes. They are certainly correct that giving is supposed to be done freely and cheerfully: "Each man should give what he has decided in his heart to give, not reluctantly or under compulsion, for God loves a cheerful giver" (2 Cor. 9:7). They are also correct that government has taken on many functions once preserved for churches, including care for the poor, through the redistribution of wealth. Still, there is a biblical prescription to continue giving ten percent to the church. When Jesus condemned the Pharisees for tithing on everything, even down to their "mint, dill and cumin," he rebuked them for neglecting "the more important matters of the law—justice, mercy and faithfulness." However, he did not intend that they stop tithing: "You should have practiced the latter, *without neglecting the former*" (Matt. 23:23, italics added).

Even if we were to suppose that tithing is not biblically mandated, it is hard to imagine that Christians in the richest nation in the history of the world should give any less than ten percent. One could make a good argument that we should give more, remembering that while we vastly increase our standard of living—acquiring more clothes, larger houses, and more extravagant college educations—we must not neglect our brothers and sisters in the developing world who lack fundamental needs—clean water, basic health care, safe and affordable housing, and a stable food supply.

Evangelical Christians are the most generous demographic of givers in the United States, yet we give away just 4.3 percent of our income (Generous Giving).[58] Imagine if evangelicals began to tithe. Vast sums of money would become available for the poor, the lost, and the least. Our nation and our world would be transformed. Extend that to Roman Catholics, and the effect would be stunning.

Giving changes the world, and it also changes us. Giving helps us to fight selfishness, knits us to those in need, makes us grateful for all we have been given, and gives us joy. As a child, I remember being most excited about Christmas morning when I had purchased a special gift for someone else and I eagerly anticipated giving it to them. Gary Haugen, founder of International Justice Mission that frees men, women, and children from slavery worldwide, maintains that we find deep joy in using what God has given us to free others from bondage and deprivation. God gives to us precisely so we could share with others. God uses us as a "middle man" to do his bidding to increase the joy of the donor and the recipient.

When Christian philanthropist Foster Friess received an award from an organization for his years of generous giving, he joked, "If it were my money, you wouldn't get a dime of it!" He was using humor to communicate the serious truth that we are only stewards of God's wealth, and giving is one important means of that stewardship.

Evangelism

Integral to our life together in the church is evangelism, which means sharing the Good News about Jesus with other people. In Matt. 28, Jesus commissioned his disciples to "go and make

---

[58] I do not believe that all tithing must go to the local church. Many excellent ministries are parachurch and do the work of the Church Universal. My wife and I have chosen to give half of our tithe to our local church and half to Christian organizations.

disciples of all nations, baptizing them in the name of the Father and of the Son and of the Holy Spirit, and teaching them to obey everything I have commanded you" (v. 19).

Some Christians mistakenly believe that life in Christ is only about evangelism. They relegate all other aspects of discipleship to the second or third tier. Caring for the poor, working within one's profession, being a responsible citizen, and even Bible study, are considered less important than sharing the Gospel in word. Other Christians have so fallen in with the prevailing culture's antagonism to proselytism that they are afraid to share the Gospel lest they offend someone. Both approaches are unbiblical. As discussed in Chapter 5, the proper approach to evangelism is to understand it as an integral expression of following Christ, but not the only, or even the most important, expression. Jesus was as concerned about holy living as sharing the Good News.

Western civilization has become so relativistic that evangelism is bordering on the taboo. In some Western nations like Greece, it is illegal to proselytize, and Christian missionaries have been prosecuted for handing out the Gospel of Luke. Even where evangelism is not illegal, it is considered impolite, much like asking people about their salaries. Yet our culture continues to prize personal experiences. As such, we can tell people what Christ has done for us without necessarily raising people's defenses. This approach also has the merit of being more authentic and less preachy. Understanding and respecting cultural context is important in knowing how best to share the Good News, even in one's homeland.

Still, a deeply spiritual offense often accompanies the Gospel. As Paul wrote, "we are to God the aroma of Christ among those who are being saved and those who are perishing. To the one we are the smell of death; to the other, the fragrance of life" (2 Cor. 2:15-16). Some people so recoil at the notion of submitting to God that they react irrationally and angrily when they are reminded of God's call to repentance. Our witness may remind them of God, and they react to us as they do to God. Therefore, being culturally sensitive will minimize, but not necessarily eliminate, the offense of the Gospel.

Jesus warned his disciples that they would be hated because the world "hated me first" (John 15:18). Efforts at rebranding the Gospel, as the Emergent Movement has tried to do, cannot take the "sting" out of the Gospel without compromising it. We should seek to be Greek to the Greeks and Roman to the Romans, just as Paul was. But for many people, the offense of the Gospel remains, and we must patiently bear the unjust antipathy from our neighbors. Evangelism is not an optional activity for disciples. We all bear the call to witness to Jesus Christ.

The church should equip its people to share the Gospel, whether it is through programs like the Alpha course or visiting church newcomers in their homes, or in spontaneous conversations with schoolmates, work colleagues, and neighbors. Sharing the Good News can be a frightening prospect because we don't know how people will react to us or whether we will be ready to respond to difficult questions. It requires courage, wisdom, and boldness, which is not easy. Even Paul, bold as he was, asked the Ephesians to pray for him that he might declare the Gospel fearlessly (Eph. 6:20). One strategy that has helped me to overcome my internal resistance is to pray for at least five specific people, asking for the chance to share the Gospel with at least three of them, hoping that at least one might be saved. This strategy can help break down what seems a daunting task into manageable pieces. I suspect just praying this way alerts us to witnessing opportunities when they arise.[59]

It is important to remember that we cannot save anyone. Only God can do that. None of us controls the soul of another person—an important thing for parents to remember even about their own children. All we can do is faithfully testify, in word and deed, to the Gospel. Whether our witness moves a person to faith is up to the mysterious forces of human choice and God's election. Acknowledging that we cannot save others

---

[59] I am sad that I have had so few opportunities to be the one who harvests. I enjoy sharing the Gospel, but rarely do I get to "seal the deal." Yet Paul wrote in I Cor. 3:6-7 that "I planted the seed, Apollos watered it, but God has been making it grow. So neither the one who plants nor the one who waters is anything, but only God, who makes things grow."

is both frustrating and pacifying, since all we can do is our part and leave the rest to God. I yearn for some of my non-believing friends to come to faith. To my chagrin, I cannot make them believe. But neither am I responsible for their salvation, providing I have done my part to be a witness to Christ. All that is left to us is to live a holy life that makes following Christ more attractive, and to fast and pray for their salvation.

What Church Should I Attend?

Although Roman Catholics have traditionally been obliged to attend their local parish church, many American Christians tend to choose their churches much as they decide on their favorite restaurant or swimming club. What kind of music we prefer or the demographic of the congregation may steer us to one church over another. Other more substantial considerations include our theological beliefs, the maturity of the church leadership, and the commitment level of fellow congregants. Having the freedom to choose one's own church has many benefits, but some potential downsides, too. The question is, what factors should guide us in choosing what church to join?

The Primacy of Doctrine

The most important factor in choosing a church is its creed or doctrine. Do the church's doctrines square with Scripture? Feeling comfortable in a church is far less important than being in a place grounded in truth. Unfortunately, many Christians have come to denigrate the importance of doctrine, partly out of ignorance. They have not been theologically trained themselves, and so are dismissive of doctrine. This rootlessness is dangerous, making Christians susceptible to heresy and grave errors. Sound doctrine is rooted in Scripture, helping us to divine truth from falsehood. If we choose, instead, to live by the seat of our pants doctrinally, deciding what we believe as we go, we are liable to be overly influenced by the particular cultural and historical milieu in which we live instead of the whole counsel of God.[60]

Another reason many Christians undervalue doctrine is because their view of the nature of truth is flawed. Only about thirty-four percent of Americans—and slightly less than half of self-described "born-again" adults (forty-six percent)—believe in absolute moral truth, and most self-identified Christians believe the Bible teaches the same truths as other religions.[61] Augustine said of doctrine, "In essentials, unity. In non-essentials, liberty. In all things, love." For many Christians today, the essentials have shrunk considerably or are non-existent. Therefore, the warmth of a congregation, the pastor's charisma, the vitality of the youth programs, and the form of the worship service trumps what the church actually believes.

Believing that absolute moral truth exists is different than saying that we know the exact contours of that truth in all its fullness. We do not. We are finite and fallen. But there is a difference between absolute truth and absolutism. The former seeks moral truth because it exists, though it is not easily known. The latter pretends to know truth completely. Absolutism is dangerous and unattractive. Recoiling from that ugliness should not, however, lead us to hold the nonsensical view that all truth is relative. If truth is relative, then Jesus was wrong when he said, "I am the way, the truth, and the life. No man comes to the Father but by me" (John 14:6). Jesus did not have to die if forgiveness of sins could have been achieved without his incarnation, death, and resurrection. Ironically, relativism is itself absolutist: it sets up as an absolute that "all truth is relative." In its dismissal of all *other* absolute truths, it ignores its own pretentious claim to be True.

Although doctrine is vital, we do not worship it. Doctrine is but a symbolic expression of the transcendent reality in Christ. Soren Kierkegaard, the nineteenth-century Danish philosopher, rightly denigrated an over-emphasis on doctrine taught as dry formulae to the exclusion of a life lived in

---

[60] Ideally, churches should require potential members to attend a series of classes on theology and church history and be examined by the elders to ensure their faith is genuine.

[61] The Barna Group, 2009.

communion with the living God. Unfortunately, his writings, which were intended to be a corrective to the dry and passionless religion of his day, unwittingly led to a rejection of all creeds by many of his successors.[62]

Authenticity

While doctrine is critical to mature faith, it is not enough. A healthy church should consist of leaders and congregants who desire living out the creeds. The world abhors hypocrites. People who live double lives of outward religiosity but private sin earn the jeers hurled at them. When the head of the National Association of Evangelicals was discovered to be using drugs and homosexual prostitutes, the world mocked him. They used his failure to justify their unbelief.

In one sense, all Christians are hypocrites in that we aspire to a life that we are unable to perfectly live out. Even the godliest have ugly sins. We are all imprisoned in a "body of death" (Rom. 7:24). The question is, what we do with our sin: confess it and repent, or excuse or deny it? A mark of the truly godly is humble recognition of one's sins. A vulnerable and unpretentious acknowledgement is refreshing and attractive. It also points us to Christ, our Savior, rather than ourselves. Authentic Christians are willing to acknowledge their sinfulness to others, though they are rightly prudent about when and where they reveal their specific sins. Their candor and humility reveal us to be fellow travelers who are also beset by sin.

Christian leaders who fail to confess their failings, keeping their sins secret to maintain a righteous appearance, can actually discourage those they lead. No one is sinless, and when we pretend to be, we set up a false and unattainable

---

[62] Kierkegaard is known as the father of existentialism, the philosophical belief that existence precedes essence. Whereas Kierkegaard advanced existentialism precisely so people would have a relationship with God, succeeding existentialists, like Jean-Paul Sartre and Albert Camus, rejected the existence of God. They argued that there is no intrinsic meaning to life, but only that which we give it. Kierkegaard's work can be dangerous for twenty-first-century Christians who live in a post-modern culture that rejects all absolute truth.

facade that can discourage others who struggle with sin day in and day out. Worse yet is when we actually think we are righteous. Jesus said the Pharisee who proclaimed his own righteousness was condemned because he wrongly believed he was without sin.

Being Fed and Feeding

It is not wrong to seek a church that "feeds us." We are needy people who need to be fed. God wants to meet many of our needs through the church, which is an important reason why we are admonished to continue meeting together. It is good to find a church where we can fellowship with people in our age group, where we can appreciate the style of musical worship, where children can enjoy a vibrant youth program, where seniors can find companionship, and so on.

Yet church is not just about meeting our needs, but also meeting others' needs. Every church needs an engaged congregation. We should look for ways to use our gifts to help others, whether it is teaching Sunday School, ushering, visiting shut-ins, helping the unemployed, or countless other ways.

The Value of Staying Put

No church is perfect. Even the best have blind spots, limitations, and sins. It is not surprising that we sometimes get so disgusted by a church's failings that we want to move on to a healthier church.

Moving on may be the right thing to do, depending upon the circumstances. Or this response may be an unhealthy tendency, in which we are always longing for greener pastures—that turn out to be filled with manure! We are right to be on our guard against church-hopping, always searching for a better church, because it can short-circuit the benefits of sticking with a church, building intimacy and strength through perseverance. Developing a strong fellowship requires not just quality time but quantity time. In general, the longer we remain with a church, the more likely we are to build deep relationships forged through time and adversity.

Reading Groups

In the last couple of decades, I have found tremendous benefit being in reading groups with other Christians. The groups typically do not study the Bible, but consider biblical study and personal devotions to be a foundation in our lives—"reading the Word" —from which we spring forward to understand our times—"reading the world."

I have gained so much from reading fiction and non-fiction in a small group, helping me to better understand the implications of my faith for every corner of the world. Sometimes the readings have been by Christian authors analyzing bioethical challenges, philosophy, or entertainment culture. Other times the readings have been by non-Christians attacking Christian faith or biblical ideas of justice.

Some people believe that Christians should read only the Bible and Christian writers. Yet we benefit by understanding the *zeitgeist* and thinking together with other godly people about how to address today's problems. We do ourselves no favors by cutting ourselves off from serious or popular thinkers. If we do not understand what is shaping many of our neighbors, we will be unable to meaningfully address them. We also need to think together how to rebut some of the most difficult challenges to Christian faith and justice. This is best done in community with like-minded fellow believers from whom we can gain wisdom. We are called to be in the world but not of the world. This requires our "salty" engagement. John Stott explains the role of salt in a decaying world:

> Like salt in putrefying meat, Christians are to hinder social decay. Like light in the prevailing darkness, Christians are to illumine society and show it a better way. It's very important to grasp these two stages in the teaching of Jesus. Most Christians accept that there is a distinction between the Christian and the non-Christian, between the church and the world. God's new society, the church, is as different from the old society as salt from rotting meat and as light from darkness.

But there are too many people who stop there; too many people whose whole preoccupation is with survival—that is, maintaining the distinction. The salt must retain its saltiness, they say. It must not become contaminated. The light must retain its brightness. It must not be smothered by the darkness. That is true. But that is merely survival. Salt and light are not just a bit different from their environment. They are to have a powerful influence on their environment. The salt is to be rubbed into the meat in order to stop the rot. The light is to shine into the darkness. It is to be set upon a lamp stand, and it is to give light to the environment. (38)

If we fail to engage the world, we remain in the saltshaker. Engagement should not be with a bullhorn to an unheeding crowd, but with thoughtful, gentle, and respectful words that engage the deceptions of our day. That requires the full engagement of our minds. We should take seriously dominant ideas and thinkers, including those who lead our world astray. Reading groups can help equip us for winsome and effective engagement.

Conclusion

We are made to live in community, to have friends and to be a friend. Pursuing healthy relationships with Christians and non-Christians is an essential part of cultivating a faithful walk with God. In community, we will find God's direction, hear his voice, and feel his comfort. We will also be used as God's instrument in others' lives, even strengthening broader society simply through friendship.

In "Bowling Alone: America's Declining Social Capital," sociologist Robert Putnam traces the decline of civil society and its corresponding enervation of society as a whole. He notes that in a variety of ways, Americans are spending less time joining together in private, voluntary associations that strengthen the bonds of community:

The most whimsical yet discomfiting bit of evidence of social disengagement in contemporary America that I have discovered is this: more Americans are bowling today than ever before, but bowling in organized leagues has plummeted in the last decade or so. Between 1980 and 1993, the total number of bowlers in America increased by 10 percent, while league bowling decreased by 40 percent. (70)

Americans' withdrawal from communal engagement weakens the glue that holds us together as a people. Christians must resist this cultural current to ensure that we "bowl together," walking together as fellow pilgrims. We were made to be in community with one another. Only in community are we able to advance the Kingdom of God.

Conclusion

*"Of making many books there is no end, and much study
wearies the body. Now all has been heard; here is the
conclusion of the matter: fear God and keep his
commandments, for this is the whole duty of man."
Ecclesiastes 12:12-14*

I am afraid of myself. I know the sins I commit daily, and I
know the much greater sins of which I am capable. I have
no confidence that I will not someday be a headline for
some dramatic failure. I am at war with myself.

The lyrics by Switchfoot's Jon Foreman resonate with me:
"I am the war inside, I am the battle line, I am the rising tide, I
am the war I fight." This is part of the reason that I do not like
the thought of growing old; I worry that I will be unfaithful to
God. I see life as a constant battle. I also know that every
moment is a battle against the Evil One. War within and war
without. C. S. Lewis wrote, "There is no neutral ground in the
universe: every square inch, every split second, is claimed by
God and counterclaimed by Satan." (Lewis, *Christian
Reflections,* 33). This is life as I see it.

As a young Christian in high school, one of my heroes was
a popular entertainer who was a committed Christian. This man
exemplified my ideal: living fully in the world but not being
twisted by it. He produced art works that were broadly
understandable to a wide audience, but they had layers of

deeper meaning for those who knew the Bible. I wanted to emulate him in being the "unexpected Christian," living out faith in Christ in unlikely places (like politics). Unfortunately, this musician seemed to lose his way for several years, apparently succumbing to the temptations of fame and fortune. I was deeply disappointed in and angry with this fallen hero, so much so that I often had dreams in which I confronted him for his unfaithfulness.

Through an unlikely set of circumstances, I had the chance to meet this man. I was not excited about the opportunity because I was so disgusted by his turning away from God's ways, and all I had to say to him would be confrontational, not adulatory. At the urging of a friend, I went to a meeting with the man and a small group of congressional aides. As the meeting was winding down, my friend told the man that I had something to say to him. My years of dreams prepared me to say what I thought he needed to hear: I told him that he had lost his way and his work no longer lifted up the good, the true, and the beautiful. He responded by justifying his actions to me, but the Holy Spirit prompted me not to nod or in any way affirm what was obviously the man's rationalizing his sin. I am thankful that this man has since returned to a Christian walk, though I do not presume to say for sure whether my conversation had any impact on him.

That could be me, that man in his fallen state, but for the grace of God. I do not want to be unfaithful. I do not want to bring disgrace on Jesus (though I undoubtedly do so through my many un-Christ-like ways—my too frequent boasting comes to mind). And so I fight against myself and against the Evil One. I do not fight for my salvation—I am saved by grace and know that I can never be good enough to earn it. But I want God to be pleased with me when I see him face to face, and I do not want to shrink back in shame. I long to hear the words, "well done, my good and faithful servant." That is my deepest and most enduring longing.

Now I speak to my three children, for whom I have principally written this book, providing the short version of what I have been trying to say:

Dear Jenna, Justin, and Krista,

I love you guys so much. I am a blessed and happy man in large part because of your mom and you. I love our times together, and I love watching you grow up and see you express the gifts God has given you. I have so many things for which to be thankful, but our family (including my parents) is my greatest gift. My life is so good.

At the same time, life is hard. We are all sinful. Temptations are everywhere. But God is good and kind and gracious, and he loves you more than you will ever know. He promises to walk with you always, even through the valley of the shadow of death. But his grace is not cheap, and it will cost you everything—not to purchase it, because it cannot be bought—but because grace demands a response of complete surrender.

In one sentence, here is the central thesis of my book: if you want to really live, you must die. The world will sing its siren song that you will really live when you indulge yourself and "do it your way," but that is a lie straight from hell. It is The Lie. Satan re-tells that lie every day, and it remains as tempting today as it was in the Garden. Do not believe it.

The older I get, the more I see that dying to self is the only path to the life God intends for us—the full and joyful and exciting life. You must never take a vacation from dying to yourself—not on vacations or weekends or ever. Dying to yourself is a minute-by-minute struggle that leads to freedom. The god of your stomach will disappoint you, but the God of the Universe will never lead you astray. "Taste and see that the Lord is good; blessed is the man who takes refuge in him" (Ps. 34:8).

The surrender you undertook at the point of your salvation was only the first time of what should be a constant habit. I begin each day with this prayer: "You are worthy of all that I am and have. You made me and you saved me, and I belong to you. Use me as you wish this day. I am yours." And I end each day with this prayer: "I am completely dependent on you." Re-committing your life to Christ happens every day, every minute. Surrendering to Jesus remains a choice for as long as you live. Do it again and again and again.

And when you surrender, you will see that humble service in gratitude is your necessary response. Humility requires saying no to the world and yes to reality—the reality that your life is a gift from God and that you cannot "own" anything you purport to have or achieve. Pride is wrong, and it is at war with the way things really are. Face up to your sin, limitations, and failures and come to terms with your total dependence on God. You were made to serve God and your neighbor. In this way, you will bring glory to God.

You will be surprised by the joy that comes from serving. The worthy goal of self-fulfillment will be achieved only once you stop trying to fulfill yourself. Dying to yourself is terrifying at first, but once you experience the joy of living unto God, it gets easier. Once you know God's character, submission will become joyful. The more you lose yourself, the more you will find yourself—the self created by God and for God.

Think about your death every day. In Charles Dickens' novel *A Christmas Carol,* Ebenezer Scrooge is transformed by the realization that he will die and he will have an eternal destiny based on the choices he made while living. Death holds no terror for those who look forward to heaven. Routinely remembering that your earthly life is like a transitory vapor will not extinguish your joy of living. Instead, it will imbue every minute with meaning, purpose, and hope, and it will help you to remember to live for the Audience of One.

Do not forget that your success is measured by your faithfulness to God, not by your outward achievements. I would like to see you get good grades, a good job and raise a happy family, but far more important is doing what God calls you to do. The good news is that being faithful is far easier than being successful. Of course, obedience is not easy, but it is far less stressful than seeking success. Once you have obeyed, the results belong to God. You need not worry about what other people think of you or your achievements.

If you can act more like foreigners on earth, which is really what you are, and less like natives, you will be more focused on pleasing God and less worried about your rung on the ladder. The pressure is off. You belong to God, not to others, and what they think of you no longer matters. You do not need to be praised by others as long as you please our Father. In the end, I think you will be amazed at just how much you do achieve when your primary aim is not success but faithfulness.

Never stop worshiping God. Worship him when you are singing in church, hitting a golf ball, or changing the oil in your car. I am not saying that you have to continually think about God as you are doing these things or that you have to keep humming a song of praise. Rather, "whether you eat or drink or whatever you do, do it all for the glory of God" (1 Cor. 10:31). If it should be done at all, it should be done for him. Do not listen to lies that God only cares about the "spiritual things" and not the secular. The notion that there is a secular reality about which God is indifferent is wrong. It is God's world, and he wants you to live full lives for his glory. So anything done to his praise and glory— which should be everything—is worship.

And please reject the idea that only pastors and missionaries are in full-time Christian service. You should be serving God all the time, whatever your job is. This unbiblical idea that some jobs are holier than others is pernicious because it robs you of the understanding that everything you do is significant, leading you to think that much of your time is not valuable to God. Everything matters to God.

Some people today think they do not need fellowship with other Christians, trying to make it alone. They're wrong. You are made to live in community with others, reflecting the fellowship of the Trinity. Going it alone is unhealthy and burdensome. You need encouragement, accountability, counsel, and everything else that comes from knowing and being known—especially from fellow pilgrims.

However, fellowship should not be just at the pool hall or the tennis club, but with fellow believers in the local church. The tendency to eschew religious observance and embrace "spirituality" may be a hallmark of our age, but it is dangerous. The church was founded by God. So by neglecting the very institution established to battle against the gates of hell, you would expose yourself to danger. It is like wandering away from the campfire in bear-infested woods. Don't let the imperfection of sinners who make up the Bride of Christ keep you away from those who are your brothers and sisters.

You know me for who I am, sins and all. You know how often I fall short of the things I have written, but that does not make them wrong—it means I am wrong. I have written this book so that we might all share together in the Feast of the Lamb, now and in eternity. I long to see you join your mom and me in following Jesus, our Savior and Lord, as I see you doing even now.

"To him who is able to keep you from stumbling and to present you before his glorious presence without fault and with great joy—to the only God our Savior be glory, majesty, power and authority, through Jesus Christ our Lord, before all ages, now and forevermore! Amen" (Jude 1:24-25).

Love,

Dad

Appendix: Bible Verses to Memorize

I have found Scripture memorization to be an excellent way to daily battle with my sinful self-centered ways. I have memorized all of the following verses, though I need to continually work to "re-memorize" the ones I do not recite regularly. With me, it is "use it or lose it."

Some of these verses, especially the ones about dying to self, are so deeply engrained in me because I need to call upon them again and again. I reproduce them here to perhaps inspire you to begin memorizing the ones that address the challenges you face in your struggle to lay down your life for Christ.

Joshua 1:8-10

[8] Do not let this Book of the Law depart from your mouth; meditate on it day and night, so that you may be careful to do everything written in it. Then you will be prosperous and successful. [9] Have I not commanded you? Be strong and courageous. Do not be terrified; do not be discouraged, for the LORD your God will be with you wherever you go."

Job 1:21

[21]Naked I came from my mother's womb,
and naked I will depart.
The LORD gave and the LORD has taken away;
may the name of the LORD be praised.

Psalm 34

[1] I will extol the LORD at all times;
    his praise will always be on my lips.
[2] My soul will boast in the LORD;
    let the afflicted hear and rejoice.
[3] Glorify the LORD with me;
    let us exalt his name together.
[4] I sought the LORD, and he answered me;
    he delivered me from all my fears.

⁵ Those who look to him are radiant;
   their faces are never covered with shame.
⁶ This poor man called, and the LORD heard him;
   he saved him out of all his troubles.
⁷ The angel of the LORD encamps around those who fear him,
   and he delivers them.
⁸ Taste and see that the LORD is good;
   blessed is the man who takes refuge in him.
⁹ Fear the LORD, you his saints,
   for those who fear him lack nothing.
¹⁰ The lions may grow weak and hungry,
   but those who seek the LORD lack no good thing.
¹¹ Come, my children, listen to me;
   I will teach you the fear of the LORD.
¹² Whoever of you loves life
   and desires to see many good days,
¹³ keep your tongue from evil
   and your lips from speaking lies.
¹⁴ Turn from evil and do good;
   seek peace and pursue it.
¹⁵ The eyes of the LORD are on the righteous
   and his ears are attentive to their cry;
¹⁶ the face of the LORD is against those who do evil,
   to cut off the memory of them from the earth.
¹⁷ The righteous cry out, and the LORD hears them;
   he delivers them from all their troubles.
¹⁸ The LORD is close to the brokenhearted
   and saves those who are crushed in spirit.
¹⁹ A righteous man may have many troubles,
   but the LORD delivers him from them all;
²⁰ he protects all his bones,
   not one of them will be broken.
²¹ Evil will slay the wicked;
   the foes of the righteous will be condemned.
²² The LORD redeems his servants;
   no one will be condemned who takes refuge in him.

Psalm 39:4-7

[4] Show me, O LORD, my life's end
 and the number of my days;
 let me know how fleeting is my life.
[5] You have made my days a mere handbreadth;
 the span of my years is as nothing before you.
 Each man's life is but a breath.
 Selah
[6] Man is a mere phantom as he goes to and fro:
 He bustles about, but only in vain;
 he heaps up wealth, not knowing who will get it.
[7] But now, Lord, what do I look for?
 My hope is in you.

Psalm 42:5-6

[5] Why are you downcast, O my soul?
 Why so disturbed within me?
 Put your hope in God,
 for I will yet praise him,
 my Savior and [6] my God.

Psalm 56:10-11

[10] In God, whose word I praise,
 in the LORD, whose word I praise-
[11] in God I trust; I will not be afraid.
 What can man do to me?

Psalm 63:3

[3] Because your love is better than life,
 my lips will glorify you.

Psalm 66:8-12

[8] Praise our God, O peoples,
 let the sound of his praise be heard;

[9] he has preserved our lives
  and kept our feet from slipping.
[10] For you, O God, tested us;
  you refined us like silver.
[11] You brought us into prison
  and laid burdens on our backs.
[12] You let men ride over our heads;
  we went through fire and water,
  but you brought us to a place of abundance.

Psalm 73:23-26

[23] Yet I am always with you;
  you hold me by my right hand.
[24] You guide me with your counsel,
  and afterward you will take me into glory.
[25] Whom have I in heaven but you?
  And earth has nothing I desire besides you.
[26] My flesh and my heart may fail,
  but God is the strength of my heart
  and my portion forever.

Psalm 84:5

[5] Blessed are those whose strength is in you,
  who have set their hearts on pilgrimage.

Psalm 103

[1] Praise the LORD, O my soul;
  all my inmost being, praise his holy name.
[2] Praise the LORD, O my soul,
  and forget not all his benefits-
[3] who forgives all your sins
  and heals all your diseases,
[4] who redeems your life from the pit
  and crowns you with love and compassion,

[5] who satisfies your desires with good things
    so that your youth is renewed like the eagle's.
[6] The LORD works righteousness
    and justice for all the oppressed.
[7] He made known his ways to Moses,
    his deeds to the people of Israel:
[8] The LORD is compassionate and gracious,
    slow to anger, abounding in love.
[9] He will not always accuse,
    nor will he harbor his anger forever;
[10] he does not treat us as our sins deserve
    or repay us according to our iniquities.
[11] For as high as the heavens are above the earth,
    so great is his love for those who fear him;
[12] as far as the east is from the west,
    so far has he removed our transgressions from us.
[13] As a father has compassion on his children,
    so the LORD has compassion on those who fear him;
[14] for he knows how we are formed,
    he remembers that we are dust.
[15] As for man, his days are like grass,
    he flourishes like a flower of the field;
[16] the wind blows over it and it is gone,
    and its place remembers it no more.
[17] But from everlasting to everlasting
    the LORD's love is with those who fear him,
    and his righteousness with their children's children-
[18] with those who keep his covenant
    and remember to obey his precepts.
[19] The LORD has established his throne in heaven,
    and his kingdom rules over all.
[20] Praise the LORD, you his angels,
    you mighty ones who do his bidding,
    who obey his word.
[21] Praise the LORD, all his heavenly hosts,
    you his servants who do his will.
[22] Praise the LORD, all his works
    everywhere in his dominion.
    Praise the LORD, O my soul.

Psalm 139

[1] O LORD, you have searched me
   and you know me.
[2] You know when I sit and when I rise;
   you perceive my thoughts from afar.
[3] You discern my going out and my lying down;
   you are familiar with all my ways.
[4] Before a word is on my tongue
   you know it completely, O LORD.
[5] You hem me in—behind and before;
   you have laid your hand upon me.
[6] Such knowledge is too wonderful for me,
   too lofty for me to attain.
[7] Where can I go from your Spirit?
   Where can I flee from your presence?
[8] If I go up to the heavens, you are there;
   if I make my bed in the depths, you are there.
[9] If I rise on the wings of the dawn,
   if I settle on the far side of the sea,
[10] even there your hand will guide me,
   your right hand will hold me fast.
[11] If I say, "Surely the darkness will hide me
   and the light become night around me,"
[12] even the darkness will not be dark to you;
   the night will shine like the day,
   for darkness is as light to you.
[13] For you created my inmost being;
   you knit me together in my mother's womb.
[14] I praise you because I am fearfully and wonderfully made;
   your works are wonderful,
   I know that full well.
[15] My frame was not hidden from you
   when I was made in the secret place.
   When I was woven together in the depths of the earth,
[16] your eyes saw my unformed body.
   All the days ordained for me
   were written in your book
   before one of them came to be.

^{17} How precious to me are your thoughts, O God!
      How vast is the sum of them!
^{18} Were I to count them,
      they would outnumber the grains of sand.
      When I awake,
      I am still with you.
^{19} If only you would slay the wicked, O God!
      Away from me, you bloodthirsty men!
^{20} They speak of you with evil intent;
      your adversaries misuse your name.
^{21} Do I not hate those who hate you, O LORD,
      and abhor those who rise up against you?
^{22} I have nothing but hatred for them;
      I count them my enemies.
^{23} Search me, O God, and know my heart;
      test me and know my anxious thoughts.
^{24} See if there is any offensive way in me,
      and lead me in the way everlasting.

Proverbs 3:5-6

^{5} Trust in the LORD with all your heart
      and lean not on your own understanding;
^{6} in all your ways acknowledge him,
      and he will make your paths straight.

Proverbs 3:11-12

^{11} My son, do not despise the LORD's discipline
      and do not resent his rebuke,
^{12} because the LORD disciplines those he loves,
      as a father the son he delights in.

Proverbs 3:25-26

^{25} Have no fear of sudden disaster
      or of the ruin that overtakes the wicked,
^{26} for the LORD will be your confidence
      and will keep your foot from being snared.

Proverbs 14:12

[12] There is a way that seems right to a man,
    but in the end it leads to death.

Proverbs 14:32

[32] When calamity comes, the wicked are brought down,
    but even in death the righteous have a refuge.

Proverbs 18:17

[17] The first to present his case seems right,
    till another comes forward and questions him.

Ecclesiastes 12:12-14

[12b] Of making many books there is no end, and much study
wearies the body.
[13] Now all has been heard;
    here is the conclusion of the matter:
    Fear God and keep his commandments,
    for this is the whole duty of man.
[14] For God will bring every deed into judgment,
    including every hidden thing,
    whether it is good or evil.

Isaiah 2:22

[22] Stop trusting in man,
    who has but a breath in his nostrils.
    Of what account is he?

Jeremiah 10:23-24

[23] I know, O LORD, that a man's life is not his own;
    it is not for man to direct his steps.

[24] Correct me, LORD, but only with justice—
     not in your anger,
     lest you reduce me to nothing.

Matthew 5:3-12

[3]Blessed are the poor in spirit,
     for theirs is the kingdom of heaven.
[4]Blessed are those who mourn,
     for they will be comforted.
[5]Blessed are the meek,
     for they will inherit the earth.
[6]Blessed are those who hunger and thirst for righteousness,
     for they will be filled.
[7]Blessed are the merciful,
     for they will be shown mercy.
[8]Blessed are the pure in heart,
     for they will see God.
[9]Blessed are the peacemakers,
     for they will be called sons of God.
[10]Blessed are those who are persecuted because of
righteousness, for theirs is the kingdom of heaven.
[11]Blessed are you when people insult you, persecute you and
falsely say all kinds of evil against you because of me.
[12]Rejoice and be glad, because great is your reward in heaven,
for in the same way they persecuted the prophets who were
before you.

Matthew 6:19-21

[19]Do not store up for yourselves treasures on earth, where moth
and rust destroy, and where thieves break in and steal. [20]But
store up for yourselves treasures in heaven, where moth and
rust do not destroy, and where thieves do not break in and steal.
[21]For where your treasure is, there your heart will be also.

Matthew 6:33

[33]But seek first his kingdom and his righteousness, and all these things will be given to you as well.

Matthew 11:28-30

[28]Come to me, all you who are weary and burdened, and I will give you rest. [29]Take my yoke upon you and learn from me, for I am gentle and humble in heart, and you will find rest for your souls. [30]For my yoke is easy and my burden is light.

Matthew 28:19-20

[19]Therefore go and make disciples of all nations, baptizing them in the name of the Father and of the Son and of the Holy Spirit, [20]and teaching them to obey everything I have commanded you. And surely I am with you always, to the very end of the age.

Luke 9:23-25

[23]Then he said to them all: "If anyone would come after me, he must deny himself and take up his cross daily and follow me. [24]For whoever wants to save his life will lose it, but whoever loses his life for me will save it. [25]What good is it for a man to gain the whole world, and yet lose or forfeit his very self?"

John 3:16-21

[16]For God so loved the world that he gave his one and only Son, that whoever believes in him shall not perish but have eternal life. [17]For God did not send his Son into the world to condemn the world, but to save the world through him. [18]Whoever believes in him is not condemned, but whoever does not believe stands condemned already because he has not believed in the name of God's one and only Son. [19]This is the verdict: Light has come into the world, but men loved darkness instead of light because their deeds were evil. [20]Everyone who

does evil hates the light, and will not come into the light for fear that his deeds will be exposed. [21]But whoever lives by the truth comes into the light, so that it may be seen plainly that what he has done has been done through God.

John 4:34

[34]"My food," said Jesus, "is to do the will of him who sent me and to finish his work."

John 14:6

[6]Jesus answered, "I am the way and the truth and the life. No one comes to the Father except through me."

John 15:1-5

[1]I am the true vine, and my Father is the gardener. [2]He cuts off every branch in me that bears no fruit, while every branch that does bear fruit he prunes so that it will be even more fruitful. [3]You are already clean because of the word I have spoken to you. [4]Remain in me, and I will remain in you. No branch can bear fruit by itself; it must remain in the vine. Neither can you bear fruit unless you remain in me.

[5]I am the vine; you are the branches. If a man remains in me and I in him, he will bear much fruit; apart from me you can do nothing.

Romans 3:23

[23] . . . For all have sinned and fall short of the glory of God.

Romans 6:23

[23]For the wages of sin is death, but the gift of God is eternal life in Christ Jesus our Lord.

Romans 8:18

[18]I consider that our present sufferings are not worth comparing with the glory that will be revealed in us.

Romans 12:1-2

[1]Therefore, I urge you, brothers, in view of God's mercy, to offer your bodies as living sacrifices, holy and pleasing to God—this is your spiritual act of worship. [2]Do not conform any longer to the pattern of this world, but be transformed by the renewing of your mind. Then you will be able to test and approve what God's will is—his good, pleasing and perfect will.

Romans 12:9-16

[9]Love must be sincere. Hate what is evil; cling to what is good. [10]Be devoted to one another in brotherly love. Honor one another above yourselves. [11]Never be lacking in zeal, but keep your spiritual fervor, serving the Lord. [12]Be joyful in hope, patient in affliction, faithful in prayer. [13]Share with God's people who are in need. Practice hospitality.

[14]Bless those who persecute you; bless and do not curse. [15]Rejoice with those who rejoice; mourn with those who mourn. [16]Live in harmony with one another. Do not be proud, but be willing to associate with people of low position. Do not be conceited.

Romans 13:8-14

[8]Let no debt remain outstanding, except the continuing debt to love one another, for he who loves his fellowman has fulfilled the law. [9]The commandments, "Do not commit adultery," "Do not murder," "Do not steal," "Do not covet," and whatever other commandment there may be, are summed up in this one rule: "Love your neighbor as yourself." [10]Love does no harm to its neighbor. Therefore love is the fulfillment of the law.

¹¹And do this, understanding the present time. The hour has come for you to wake up from your slumber, because our salvation is nearer now than when we first believed. ¹²The night is nearly over; the day is almost here. So let us put aside the deeds of darkness and put on the armor of light. ¹³Let us behave decently, as in the daytime, not in orgies and drunkenness, not in sexual immorality and debauchery, not in dissension and jealousy. ¹⁴Rather, clothe yourselves with the Lord Jesus Christ, and do not think about how to gratify the desires of the sinful nature.

1 Corinthians 9:24-27

²⁴Do you not know that in a race all the runners run, but only one gets the prize? Run in such a way as to get the prize. ²⁵Everyone who competes in the games goes into strict training. They do it to get a crown that will not last; but we do it to get a crown that will last forever. ²⁶Therefore I do not run like a man running aimlessly; I do not fight like a man beating the air. ²⁷No, I beat my body and make it my slave so that after I have preached to others, I myself will not be disqualified for the prize.

1 Corinthians 10:12-13

¹²So, if you think you are standing firm, be careful that you don't fall! ¹³No temptation has seized you except what is common to man. And God is faithful; he will not let you be tempted beyond what you can bear. But when you are tempted, he will also provide a way out so that you can stand up under it.

1 Corinthians 10:23

²³"Everything is permissible"—but not everything is beneficial. "Everything is permissible"—but not everything is constructive.

1 Corinthians 10:31

[31]So whether you eat or drink or whatever you do, do it all for the glory of God.

1 Corinthians 13:4-8

[4]Love is patient, love is kind. It does not envy, it does not boast, it is not proud. [5]It is not rude, it is not self-seeking, it is not easily angered, it keeps no record of wrongs. [6]Love does not delight in evil but rejoices with the truth. [7]It always protects, always trusts, always hopes, always perseveres. [8]Love never fails.

1 Corinthians 15:54-58

[54]When the perishable has been clothed with the imperishable, and the mortal with immortality, then the saying that is written will come true: "Death has been swallowed up in victory." [55]"Where, O death, is your victory?
      Where, O death, is your sting?"
[56]The sting of death is sin, and the power of sin is the law. [57]But thanks be to God! He gives us the victory through our Lord Jesus Christ.
[58]Therefore, my dear brothers, stand firm. Let nothing move you. Always give yourselves fully to the work of the Lord, because you know that your labor in the Lord is not in vain.

II Corinthians 4:16-18

[16]Therefore we do not lose heart. Though outwardly we are wasting away, yet inwardly we are being renewed day by day. [17]For our light and momentary troubles are achieving for us an eternal glory that far outweighs them all. [18] So we fix our eyes not on what is seen, but on what is unseen, since what is seen is temporary, but what is unseen is eternal.

2 Corinthians 5:6-10

[6]Therefore we are always confident and know that as long as we are at home in the body we are away from the Lord. [7]We live by faith, not by sight. [8]We are confident, I say, and would prefer to be away from the body and at home with the Lord. [9]So we make it our goal to please him, whether we are at home in the body or away from it. [10]For we must all appear before the judgment seat of Christ, that each one may receive what is due him for the things done while in the body, whether good or bad.

2 Corinthians 5:16-21

[16]So from now on we regard no one from a worldly point of view. Though we once regarded Christ in this way, we do so no longer. [17]Therefore, if anyone is in Christ, he is a new creation; the old has gone, the new has come! [18]All this is from God, who reconciled us to himself through Christ and gave us the ministry of reconciliation: [19]that God was reconciling the world to himself in Christ, not counting men's sins against them. And he has committed to us the message of reconciliation. [20]We are therefore Christ's ambassadors, as though God were making his appeal through us. We implore you on Christ's behalf: Be reconciled to God. [21]God made him who had no sin to be sin for us, so that in him we might become the righteousness of God.

Galatians 1:10

[10]Am I now trying to win the approval of men, or of God? Or am I trying to please men? If I were still trying to please men, I would not be a servant of Christ.

Galatians 2:20-21

[20]I have been crucified with Christ and I no longer live, but Christ lives in me. The life I live in the body, I live by faith in the Son of God, who loved me and gave himself for me. [21]I do

not set aside the grace of God, for if righteousness could be
gained through the law, Christ died for nothing!

Galatians 5:16

[16]So I say, live by the Spirit, and you will not gratify the
desires of the sinful nature.

Galatians 5:22-23

[22]But the fruit of the Spirit is love, joy, peace, patience,
kindness, goodness, faithfulness, [23]gentleness and self-control.
Against such things there is no law.

Galatians 6:14

[14]May I never boast except in the cross of our Lord Jesus
Christ, through which the world has been crucified to me, and I
to the world.

Ephesians 2:8-10

[8]For it is by grace you have been saved, through faith—and this
not from yourselves, it is the gift of God— [9]not by works, so
that no one can boast. [10]For we are God's workmanship,
created in Christ Jesus to do good works, which God prepared
in advance for us to do.

Ephesians 4:29

[29]Do not let any unwholesome talk come out of your mouths,
but only what is helpful for building others up according to
their needs, that it may benefit those who listen.

Ephesians 6:10-20

[10]Finally, be strong in the Lord and in his mighty power. [11]Put
on the full armor of God so that you can take your stand
against the devil's schemes. [12]For our struggle is not against

flesh and blood, but against the rulers, against the authorities, against the powers of this dark world and against the spiritual forces of evil in the heavenly realms. [13]Therefore put on the full armor of God, so that when the day of evil comes, you may be able to stand your ground, and after you have done everything, to stand. [14]Stand firm then, with the belt of truth buckled around your waist, with the breastplate of righteousness in place, [15]and with your feet fitted with the readiness that comes from the gospel of peace. [16]In addition to all this, take up the shield of faith, with which you can extinguish all the flaming arrows of the evil one. [17]Take the helmet of salvation and the sword of the Spirit, which is the word of God. [18]And pray in the Spirit on all occasions with all kinds of prayers and requests. With this in mind, be alert and always keep on praying for all the saints.

[19]Pray also for me, that whenever I open my mouth, words may be given me so that I will fearlessly make known the mystery of the gospel, [20]for which I am an ambassador in chains. Pray that I may declare it fearlessly, as I should.

Philippians 1:21

[21]For to me, to live is Christ and to die is gain.

Philippians 2:3-11

[3]Do nothing out of selfish ambition or vain conceit, but in humility consider others better than yourselves. [4]Each of you should look not only to your own interests, but also to the interests of others.

[5]Your attitude should be the same as that of Christ Jesus: [6]Who, being in very nature God, did not consider equality with God something to be grasped, [7]but made himself nothing, taking the very nature of a servant, being made in human likeness. [8]And being found in appearance as a man, he humbled himself and became obedient to death—even death on a cross! [9]Therefore God exalted him to the highest place and

gave him the name that is above every name, [10]that at the name of Jesus every knee should bow, in heaven and on earth and under the earth, [11]and every tongue confess that Jesus Christ is Lord, to the glory of God the Father.

Philippians 2:14-16

[14]Do everything without complaining or arguing, [15]so that you may become blameless and pure, children of God without fault in a crooked and depraved generation, in which you shine like stars in the universe [16]as you hold out the word of life—in order that I may boast on the day of Christ that I did not run or labor for nothing.

Philippians 3:7-14

[7]But whatever was to my profit I now consider loss for the sake of Christ. [8]What is more, I consider everything a loss compared to the surpassing greatness of knowing Christ Jesus my Lord, for whose sake I have lost all things. I consider them rubbish, that I may gain Christ [9]and be found in him, not having a righteousness of my own that comes from the law, but that which is through faith in Christ—the righteousness that comes from God and is by faith. [10]I want to know Christ and the power of his resurrection and the fellowship of sharing in his sufferings, becoming like him in his death, [11]and so, somehow, to attain to the resurrection from the dead.

[12]Not that I have already obtained all this, or have already been made perfect, but I press on to take hold of that for which Christ Jesus took hold of me. [13]Brothers, I do not consider myself yet to have taken hold of it. But one thing I do: Forgetting what is behind and straining toward what is ahead, [14]I press on toward the goal to win the prize for which God has called me heavenward in Christ Jesus.

Philippians 4:4-8

⁴Rejoice in the Lord always. I will say it again: Rejoice! ⁵Let your gentleness be evident to all. The Lord is near. ⁶Do not be anxious about anything, but in everything, by prayer and petition, with thanksgiving, present your requests to God. ⁷And the peace of God, which transcends all understanding, will guard your hearts and your minds in Christ Jesus.

⁸ Finally, brothers and sisters, whatever is true, whatever is noble, whatever is right, whatever is pure, whatever is lovely, whatever is admirable—if anything is excellent or praiseworthy—think about such things.

Colossians 2:15

¹⁵And having disarmed the powers and authorities, he made a public spectacle of them, triumphing over them by the cross.

Colossians 3:1-4

¹Since, then, you have been raised with Christ, set your hearts on things above, where Christ is seated at the right hand of God. ²Set your minds on things above, not on earthly things. ³For you died, and your life is now hidden with Christ in God. ⁴When Christ, who is your life, appears, then you also will appear with him in glory.

Colossians 3:23-24

²³Whatever you do, work at it with all your heart, as working for the Lord, not for men, ²⁴since you know that you will receive an inheritance from the Lord as a reward. It is the Lord Christ you are serving.

Colossians 4:5-6

⁵Be wise in the way you act toward outsiders; make the most of every opportunity. ⁶Let your conversation be always full of

grace, seasoned with salt, so that you may know how to answer everyone.

1 Thessalonians 5:16-18

[16]Be joyful always; [17]pray continually; [18]give thanks in all circumstances, for this is God's will for you in Christ Jesus.

1 Timothy 6:6-11

[6]But godliness with contentment is great gain. [7]For we brought nothing into the world, and we can take nothing out of it. [8]But if we have food and clothing, we will be content with that. [9]People who want to get rich fall into temptation and a trap and into many foolish and harmful desires that plunge men into ruin and destruction. [10]For the love of money is a root of all kinds of evil. Some people, eager for money, have wandered from the faith and pierced themselves with many griefs. [11]But you, man of God, flee from all this, and pursue righteousness, godliness, faith, love, endurance and gentleness.

1 Timothy 6:17-19

[17]Command those who are rich in this present world not to be arrogant nor to put their hope in wealth, which is so uncertain, but to put their hope in God, who richly provides us with everything for our enjoyment. [18]Command them to do good, to be rich in good deeds, and to be generous and willing to share. [19]In this way they will lay up treasure for themselves as a firm foundation for the coming age, so that they may take hold of the life that is truly life.

2 Timothy 2:22

[22]Flee the evil desires of youth, and pursue righteousness, faith, love and peace, along with those who call on the Lord out of a pure heart.

2 Timothy 3:12

[12]In fact, everyone who wants to live a godly life in Christ Jesus will be persecuted,

2 Timothy 4:1-2

[1]In the presence of God and of Christ Jesus, who will judge the living and the dead, and in view of his appearing and his kingdom, I give you this charge: [2]Preach the Word; be prepared in season and out of season; correct, rebuke and encourage—with great patience and careful instruction.

Hebrews 4:12-13

[12]For the word of God is living and active. Sharper than any double-edged sword, it penetrates even to dividing soul and spirit, joints and marrow; it judges the thoughts and attitudes of the heart. [13]Nothing in all creation is hidden from God's sight. Everything is uncovered and laid bare before the eyes of him to whom we must give account.

Hebrews 12:1-3

[1]Therefore, since we are surrounded by such a great cloud of witnesses, let us throw off everything that hinders and the sin that so easily entangles, and let us run with perseverance the race marked out for us. [2]Let us fix our eyes on Jesus, the author and perfecter of our faith, who for the joy set before him endured the cross, scorning its shame, and sat down at the right hand of the throne of God. [3]Consider him who endured such opposition from sinful men, so that you will not grow weary and lose heart.

Hebrews 12:11

[11]No discipline seems pleasant at the time, but painful. Later on, however, it produces a harvest of righteousness and peace for those who have been trained by it.

Hebrews 13:5-6

[5]Keep your lives free from the love of money and be content
with what you have, because God has said,
   "Never will I leave you;
      never will I forsake you." [6]So we say with confidence,
   "The Lord is my helper; I will not be afraid.
      What can man do to me?"

James 1:2-8

[2]Consider it pure joy, my brothers, whenever you face trials of
many kinds, [3]because you know that the testing of your faith
develops perseverance. [4]Perseverance must finish its work so
that you may be mature and complete, not lacking anything. [5]If
any of you lacks wisdom, he should ask God, who gives
generously to all without finding fault, and it will be given to
him. [6]But when he asks, he must believe and not doubt,
because he who doubts is like a wave of the sea, blown and
tossed by the wind. [7]That man should not think he will receive
anything from the Lord; [8]he is a double-minded man, unstable
in all he does.

James 1:19-20

[19]Everyone should be quick to listen, slow to speak and slow to
become angry, [20]because human anger does not produce the
righteousness that God desires.

James 2:10

[10]For whoever keeps the whole law and yet stumbles at just one
point is guilty of breaking all of it.

James 4:7-8

[7]Submit yourselves, then, to God. Resist the devil, and he will
flee from you. [8]Come near to God and he will come near to

you. Wash your hands, you sinners, and purify your hearts, you double-minded.

James 5:16

[16]Therefore confess your sins to each other and pray for each other so that you may be healed. The prayer of a righteous man is powerful and effective.

1 Peter 2:11-12

[11]Dear friends, I urge you, as aliens and strangers in the world, to abstain from sinful desires, which war against your soul. [12]Live such good lives among the pagans that, though they accuse you of doing wrong, they may see your good deeds and glorify God on the day he visits us.

1 Peter 2:20

[20]But if you suffer for doing good and you endure it, this is commendable before God.

1 Peter 2:24

[24]He himself bore our sins in his body on the tree, so that we might die to sins and live for righteousness; by his wounds you have been healed.

1 Peter 3:13-15

[13]Who is going to harm you if you are eager to do good? [14]But even if you should suffer for what is right, you are blessed. "Do not fear what they fear; do not be frightened." [15]But in your hearts set apart Christ as Lord.

1 Peter 4:1-5

[1]Therefore, since Christ suffered in his body, arm yourselves also with the same attitude, because he who has suffered in his

body is done with sin. [2]As a result, he does not live the rest of his earthly life for evil human desires, but rather for the will of God. [3]For you have spent enough time in the past doing what pagans choose to do—living in debauchery, lust, drunkenness, orgies, carousing and detestable idolatry. [4]They think it strange that you do not plunge with them into the same flood of dissipation, and they heap abuse on you. [5]But they will have to give account to him who is ready to judge the living and the dead.

1 Peter 5:5-11

[5]All of you, clothe yourselves with humility toward one another, because,

"God opposes the proud
but gives grace to the humble."

[6]Humble yourselves, therefore, under God's mighty hand, that he may lift you up in due time. [7]Cast all your anxiety on him because he cares for you.

[8]Be self-controlled and alert. Your enemy the devil prowls around like a roaring lion looking for someone to devour. [9]Resist him, standing firm in the faith, because you know that your brothers throughout the world are undergoing the same kind of sufferings.

[10]And the God of all grace, who called you to his eternal glory in Christ, after you have suffered a little while, will himself restore you and make you strong, firm and steadfast. [11]To him be the power for ever and ever. Amen.

2 Peter 1:5-11

[5]For this very reason, make every effort to add to your faith goodness; and to goodness, knowledge; [6]and to knowledge, self-control; and to self-control, perseverance; and to perseverance, godliness; [7]and to godliness, brotherly kindness; and to brotherly kindness, love. [8]For if you possess these qualities in increasing measure, they will keep you from being ineffective and unproductive in your knowledge of our Lord Jesus Christ. [9]But if anyone does not have them, he is

nearsighted and blind, and has forgotten that he has been cleansed from his past sins.

[10]Therefore, my brothers, be all the more eager to make your calling and election sure. For if you do these things, you will never fall, [11]and you will receive a rich welcome into the eternal kingdom of our Lord and Savior Jesus Christ.

1 John 2:15-17

[15]Do not love the world or anything in the world. If anyone loves the world, the love of the Father is not in him. [16]For everything in the world—the cravings of sinful man, the lust of his eyes and the boasting of what he has and does—comes not from the Father but from the world. [17]The world and its desires pass away, but the man who does the will of God lives forever.

1 John 3:18

[18]Dear children, let us not love with words or tongue but with actions and in truth.

1 John 5:3-5

[3]This is love for God: to obey his commands. And his commands are not burdensome, [4]for everyone born of God overcomes the world. This is the victory that has overcome the world, even our faith. [5]Who is it that overcomes the world? Only he who believes that Jesus is the Son of God.

1 John 5:14-15

[14]This is the confidence we have in approaching God: that if we ask anything according to his will, he hears us. [15]And if we know that he hears us—whatever we ask—we know that we have what we asked of him.

Revelation 15:3-4

[3] Great and marvelous are your deeds,
  Lord God Almighty.
 Just and true are your ways,
  King of the ages.
[4]Who will not fear you, O Lord,
  and bring glory to your name?
 For you alone are holy.
 All nations will come
  and worship before you,
 for your righteous acts have been revealed.

Works Cited

Alcorn, Randy. *Heaven*. Chicago: Tyndale House Publishers, 2004.

Aristotle. *The Nicomachean Ethics*. Trans. Martin Ostwald. New York: Macmillan, 1962.

---. *The Politics*. Trans. T.A. Sinclair. London: The Penguin Group, 1981.

Bonhoeffer, Deitrich. *The Cost of Discipleship*. New York: MacMillan Publishing Co., Inc., 1937.

---. *Life Together*. San Francisco: Harper & Row, 1954.

Budziszewski, J. *What We Can't Not Know: A Guide*. Dallas: Spence Publishing, 2003.

Burke, Edmund. *Reflections on the Revolution in France*. Ed. J.G.A. Pocock. Indianapolis: Hackett Publishing Company, 1987.

Card, Michael. "Livin' We Die." *Legacy*. Benson Music Group, 1983.

"Charitable Giving." Generous Giving. Web. 6 April 2014.

Cicero, Marcus. *The Republic and the Laws*. Trans. by Niall Rudd. Oxford: Oxford University Press, 1998.

dcTalk. "Luv is a Verb." *Free At Last*. ForeFront, 1992.

Dostoyevsky, Fyodor. *The Brothers Karamazov*. Trans. Constance Garnett. New York: The New American Library, 1957.

---. *Crime and Punishment*. Trans. Richard Pevear and Larissa Volokhonsky. New York: Vintage Books, 1993.

---. *The Grand Inquisitor.* The Floating Press, 2009.

Dylan, Bob. "Gotta Serve Somebody." *Slow Train Coming.* Columbia, 1979.

Eliot, T. S. *Collected Poems 1909-1962.* London: Faber, 1974.

Elliot, Jim. October 28, 1949 journal entry (p. 174). *Journals of Jim Elliot.* Ed. by Elisabeth Elliot. Grand Rapids: Fleming H. Revell, 1978.

Foreman, Jonathan. "American Dream." Perf. by Switchfoot. *Nothing is Sound.* Sony, 2005.

---. "Dare You to Move." Perf. by Switchfoot. *The Beautiful Letdown.* Sony, 2004.

---. "Needle and Haystack Life." Perf. by Switchfoot. *Hello Hurricane.* Atlantic Records, 2009.

---. "The Shadow Proves the Sunshine." Perf. by Switchfoot. *Nothing is Sound.* Sony, 2005.

---. "War Inside." Perf. by Switchfoot. *Vice Verses.* Atlantic Records, 2011.

Gawande, Atul. "Hellhole." *The New Yorker*, 30 March 1990.

Gioia, Dana. "The Seven Deadly Sins." *Pity the Beautiful.* Minneapolis: Gray Wolf Press, 2012.

Guinness, Os. *The Call.* Nashville: W Publishing Group, 1998.

Himmelfarb, Gertrude. *The Roads to Modernity: The British, French, and American Enlightenments.* New York: Vintage Books, 2004.

Kuyper, Abraham. "Sphere Sovereignty." *Abraham Kuyper, A Centennial Reader*. Ed. by James D. Bratt. Grand Rapids: Eerdmans, 1998.

La Rochefoucauld, Francois Duc de. *Reflections; or Sentences and Moral Maxims*. Trans. J.W. Willis Bund and J. Hain Friswell. London: Simpson Low, Son, and Marston, 1871.

Lewis, C. S. *The Great Divorce*. New York: Collier Books, MacMillan Publishing Company, 1946.

---. *Christian Reflections*. Grand Rapids: Wm. B. Eerdmans, 1995.

---. *Mere Christianity*. New York: The Macmillan Company, 1960.

---. *The Screwtape Letters*. West Chicago: Lord and King Associates, 1976.

---. *The Voyage of the Dawn Treader*. C.S. Lewis Pte, Ltd., 1952.

---. *The Weight of Glory*. New York: Touchstone, 1996.

Lindsley, Art. *True Truth: Defending Absolute Truth in a Relativistic World*. Downers Grove, IL: InterVarsity Press, 2004.

Luther, Martin. "Sermon in the Castle Church at Weimar" (25 October 1522, Saturday after the Eighteenth Sunday after Trinity). Qtd. and trans. by Frederick J. Gaiser in "What Luther *Didn't* Say About Vocation." *Word & World* (2005): 359-361. Trans. of *D. Martin Luthers Werke: Kritische Gesamtausgabe*, 60 vols. (Weimar: Hermann Böhlaus Nachfolger, 1883–1980) 10/3:382.

MacDonald, George. *Unspoken Sermons, Series III*, 1867.

McManus, Mike. "Marriage Savers Answers 25 Tough Questions." *Marriage Savers*, March 2013. Web. 21 March 2014.

Nietzsche, Friedrich. *Twilight of the Idols*. Trans. by R.J. Hollingdale. London: Penguin Books, 1888 (printed 1990).

O'Connor, Flanner. *The Habit of Being: Letters of Flannery O'Connor*. Ed. by Sally Fitzgerald. New York: Farrar, Straus and Giroux, 1979.

Packer, J. I. *Rediscovering Holiness*. 2nd ed. Ventura, CA: Regal, 2009.

Pascal, Blaise. *The Mind on Fire*. Ed. by James Houston. Colorado Springs, CO: David C. Cook, 2006.

Pearcey, Nancy. *Total Truth: Liberating Christianity from its Cultural Captivity*. Wheaton, Ill.: Crossway, 2004.

Putnam, Robert. "Bowling Alone: America's Declining Social Capital," *Journal of Democracy,* Volume 6, Number 1, January 1995.

Rand, Ayn. *For the New Intellectual*. New York: Signet, 1961.

Rodgers, Mark and William Wichterman. "Making Goodness Fashionable." *Creating the Better Hour: Lessons from William Wilberforce*. Ed. by Chuck Stetson. Macon, GA: Stroud & Hall, 2007.

Sartre, Jean-Paul. *Existentialism is a Humanism.* Trans. by Bernard Frechtman. *Existentialism and Human Emotion*. New York: Kensington Publishing, 1957.

Michael Specter. "The Dangerous Philosopher." *The New Yorker* 6 September 1999.

Stonehill, Randy. "Every Heartbeat is a Prayer." *Thirst*. Brentwood Music, 1998.

Stott, John. "Four Ways Christians Can Influence the World." *Christianity Today,* October 20, 2011.

Taylor, Steve. "Harder to Believe Than Not To." *I Predict*. Myrrh Records, 1987.

Teresa, Mother. *Mother Teresa: Come Be My Light,* ed. Brian Kolodiejchuk. New York: Doubleday, 2007.

Townshend, Peter. "The Bargain." Perf. by The Who. *Who's Next*. Decca Records, 1971.

Warren, Rick. *The Purpose-Driven Life*. Grand Rapids: Zondervan, 2002.

---. "Love Is A Choice." *Daily Hope with Rick Warren*. Purpose Driven 2012, 30 April 2009. Web. 21 March 2014.

Westminster Assembly, "Westminster Shorter Catechism." London, 1646.

Young, William P., *The Shack*. Los Angeles: Windblown Media, 2007.

INDEX

About The Author

William B. Wichterman has been involved in national politics for more than 25 years, including as a Special Assistant to President George W. Bush in the White House and a senior congressional aide in the United States Senate and House of Representatives. He holds an M.A. in Political Theory from the Catholic University of America and a B.A. from Houghton College. Wichterman worked as a missionary to Turkish guestworkers in West Berlin, Germany before entering politics. He is the President of *Faith & Law*, a ministry to congressional staff seeking to integrate their faith with their policy work. He is married to Dana Wichterman and is the father of three red-heads. He is an avid sailor, a drummer, and he loves loud, hard, and fast rock-and-roll.